Women in Business Families

For centuries, almost all economic activity was family-based. The family business rested on the division of labour among family members. Therefore, the family was both socially and economically the foundation of the family business. Families were not only production units, but also education and consumption units that conveyed norm structures, values, and professional identity to next generation. Although female family members have always been active participants in family businesses over the centuries, their role has often been neglected in previous studies.

Women in Business Families: From Past to Present presents both conceptual and theoretically informed empirical papers addressing three related themes relevant for family business and gender in past and in present: challenging the heroic male image of entrepreneurs; notion of the visibility and invisibility of women; and women in business succession.

Women in Business Families: From Past to Present balances between both historical and contemporary analyses. The chapters integrate the notions of time and gender in focusing on family businesses or business families in past and in present. This volume will be of vital reading to researchers and academics in the fields of Gender Studies, Gender History, Family Business, Organisational Studies, Entrepreneurship, and the various related disciplines.

Jarna Heinonen is Professor of Entrepreneurship at the University of Turku, School of Economics, Finland.

Kirsi Vainio-Korhonen is Professor of Finnish History at the University of Turku, Faculty of Humanities, Finland.

Routledge Advances in Management and Business Studies

Turnaround Management and Bankruptcy
Edited by Jan Adriaanse and Jean-Pierre van der Rest

Strategies, Leadership and Complexity in Crisis and Emergency Operations
Stig O. Johannessen

Automotive Global Value Chain
The Rise of Mega Suppliers
Wilson Kia Onn Wong

Managing Social Purpose Driven Organizations
Looking at the Third Sector
Wee Beng Geok

Navigating Through Changing Times
Knowledge Work in Complex Environment
Edited by Anne Eskola

Transitions from Education to Work
Workforce Ready Challenges in the Asia Pacific
Edited by Roslyn Cameron, Subas Dhakal and John Burgess

Professions and Professional Service Firms
Private and Public Sector Enterprises in the Global Economy
Edited by Mike Saks and Daniel Muzio

Happiness, Wellbeing and Society
What Matters for Singaporeans
Siok Kuan Tambyah and Soo Jiuan Tan

Women in Business Families
From Past to Present
Jarna Heinonen and Kirsi Vainio-Korhonen

For more information about this series, please visit www.routledge.com/series/SE0305

Women in Business Families

From Past to Present

Edited by Jarna Heinonen
and Kirsi Vainio-Korhonen

Routledge
Taylor & Francis Group
LONDON AND NEW YORK

First published 2018 by Routledge

2 Park Square, Milton Park, Abingdon, Oxon, OX14 4RN
605 Third Avenue, New York, NY 10017

Routledge is an imprint of the Taylor & Francis Group, an informa business

First issued in paperback 2020

Library of Congress Cataloging-in-Publication Data
Names: Heinonen, Jarna, editor. | Vainio-Korhonen, Kirsi, editor.
Title: Women in business families : from past to present / edited by Jarna Heinonen and Kirsi Vainio-Korhonen.
Description: New York, NY : Routledge, 2018. | Series: Routledge advances in management and business studies
Identifiers: LCCN 2017059689 | ISBN 9781138635968 (hardback) | ISBN 9781351796583 (epub) | ISBN 9781351796590 (web pdf) | ISBN 9781351796576 (mobipocket)
Subjects: LCSH: Family-owned business enterprises—History. | Businesswomen—History. | Entrepreneurship—History.
Classification: LCC HD62.25 .W6636 2018 | DDC 338.0082—dc23
LC record available at https://lccn.loc.gov/2017059689

ISBN: 978-1-138-63596-8 (hbk)
ISBN: 978-1-315-20629-5 (ebk)

Typeset in Sabon
by Apex CoVantage, LLC

Contents

Notes on the Editors and Contributors vii
Acknowledgements xiii

Introduction 1

1 From Household Economy to Family Business 3
JARNA HEINONEN AND KIRSI VAINIO-KORHONEN

2 Gender, Economy, and Time 14
SEPPO POUTANEN

SECTION I
Challenging the Heroic Male Image of Entrepreneurs 33

3 Tough Times, Tough Measures: Widows as Heroic Entrepreneurs 35
ANU LAHTINEN

4 The Iron Lady, Elin Såger: Head of a Family Business 47
JARKKO KESKINEN, VELI PEKKA TOROPAINEN, AND MARI VÄLIMÄKI

5 Merchant Trade: A Family Affair 67
CATHRYN R. SPENCE

6 Marie Hackman—A Female Manager in the Family Firm Hackman & Co 82
ULLA IJÄS

SECTION II
Notions of the Visibility and Invisibility of Women 97

7 Moving Between Visibility and Invisibility: Understanding Social and Family Business Spheres 99
HENRIETTA NILSON AND ULLA HYTTI

8 'All the Days of Their Lives': Women, Business, and Family 111
DEBORAH SIMONTON

9 Statutory Invisibility: Urban Business Women's Legal and Political Rights 134
JARKKO KESKINEN AND KIRSI VAINIO-KORHONEN

10 A Lost Opportunity or a Lucky Escape? Non-Successor Daughters and the Family in Business 153
JANICE BYRNE AND SALMA FATTOUM

SECTION III
Women in Business Succession 177

11 The Leaders, the Outcasts, and the Others: Which Role for Daughters in Family Businesses? 179
FRANCESCA MARIA CESARONI AND ANNALISA SENTUTI

12 Enterprising Widows: Family, Business, and the Succession Process 199
CATRIONA M. MACLEOD

13 He Suddenly Died: Unplanned Succession in Family Firms 218
JARNA HEINONEN AND ELISABET LJUNGGREN

Index 239

Notes on the Editors and Contributors

The Editors

Jarna Heinonen is Professor in Entrepreneurship and Vice-Head of the Department of Management and Entrepreneurship at the University of Turku, School of Economics. In the field of entrepreneurship research her research interests include particularly family business, corporate entrepreneurship, entrepreneurship education, gender issues, and entrepreneurship policies. She has conducted research for the European Commission, the OECD, and different national ministries and other such bodies and is well connected to entrepreneurship stakeholders nationally and internationally. She is the Book Review Editor at the *International Small Business Journal* and has recently published in the *Journal of Small Business Management*, *International Small Business Journal*, *European Educational Journal*, and *Journal of Small Business and Enterprise Development*, for example. She has been a co-editor for the *SAGE Handbook of Small Business and Entrepreneurship*. She is also Visiting Professor at Kingston University in the UK and holds numerous positions of trust in the scientific community as well as in business and society.

Kirsi Vainio-Korhonen is Professor of Finnish History, at the University of Turku, Faculty of Humanities. In her own research she has gathered strong expertise on economic and gender history, female entrepreneurship, handicrafts relations, and household economy. Professor Vainio-Korhonen is a member of the National Committee for Research Data Management in Finland. Digital humanities issues are also part of her work as a member of the Advisory Council of the Finland's National Archives Service. Her most recent articles are Women and Professional Ambitions in Northern Europe, c. 1650–1850 (together with Johanna Ilmakunnas and Marjatta Rahikainen) and Midwives: Birthing Care Professionals in Eighteenth-Century Sweden and Finland in Early Professional Women in Northern Europe, c. 1650–1850 (Routledge 2017) and a monograph in Swedish on the eighteenth century midwifery De frimodiga. Barnmorskor, fodande och kroppslighet på 1700-talet (2016).

The Contributors

Janice Byrne (**PhD**) is an Assistant Professor of Organizational Behaviour and Human Resource Management at IESEG School of Management, Paris, France. Her research centres around three main content areas: gender, entrepreneurship, and education/training. Her current work addresses gender and family business succession, and gender and entrepreneurial role models, as well as gender streamed training and work-life balance issues for managers and entrepreneurs. Her work has been published in a number of leading journals, including *Academy of Management Learning and Education*, *Small Business Economics*, *Organizational Dynamics*, and *Industry and Higher Education*, as well as numerous media outlets. Byrne is a member of the editorial board of Academy of Management Learning & Education and is academic director of Led By Her, an entrepreneurship training program for women.

Francesca Maria Cesaroni is an Associate Professor in Business Administration at the University of Urbino Carlo Bo, Department of Economics, Society, Politics. She teaches entrepreneurship and small business at the School of Economics, University of Urbino. Her main research topics concern particularly small and medium-sized firms, entrepreneurship, women-owned firms, family firms, and generational transfer. She is the Director of the Research Centre on Entrepreneurship and Small-Medium-sized firms, University of Urbino, Italy. She is member of the Italian Association for the Study of Small and Medium-sized Businesses (ASPI). Since 2015 she is a member of the scientific board of IPAZIA, a scientific observatory on gender issues, at the Niccolò Cusano University, Rome. She is member of the Editorial Board of some scientific journals and reviewer of other international academic journals. Since 2017 she is the scientific director of UniurbLab at the University of Urbino, a didactic laboratory aimed at promoting students' entrepreneurial aptitude and encourage new business creation.

Salma Fattoum (**PhD**) is an Assistant Professor of Strategy and Entrepreneurship at INSEEC Business School, Lyon, France. Her work in entrepreneurship broadly focuses on family businesses and the issue of managerial succession, gender, and entrepreneurial growth. She defended her doctoral thesis on succession in French family businesses in 2010 at the University of Lyon 3 (EM LYON Research Center). She is continuing her research on family businesses with an interest in gender issues in the choice of successor. Her work has been published in a number of leading journals, including *European Management Review*, *Management International*, and *Journal of Enterprising Culture*.

Ulla Hytti is Research Director, Adjunct Professor in Entrepreneurship at the Department of Management and Entrepreneurship at the University of Turku, School of Economics. She is interested in researching entrepreneurship, entrepreneurial identities, entrepreneurship education, and gender in connection to family business, entrepreneurial careers, and innovation. Ulla has been a co-editor for the *Research Handbook on Gender and Innovation and Context, Process and Gender in Entrepreneurship, Frontiers in European Entrepreneurship Research*, and acted as a Guest Editor for a Special Issue on Gender and Innovation in the *International Journal of Gender and Entrepreneurship*. She has recently published in the *International Small Business Journal* and *Entrepreneurship and Regional Development*, for example. Ulla is Associate Editor at the *Journal of Small Business Management*.

Ulla Ijäs (PhD) is currently an acting university teacher in Finnish History at the University of Turku, Faculty of Humanities. Her research interests are merchant houses in the eighteenth and nineteenth centuries, merchant networks, migration, towns, gender, and consumption. Her latest publications are: British luxuries in the nineteenth century Vyborg. In Jon Stobart and Johanna Ilmakunnas (eds.), *A Taste for Luxury in Early Modern Europe. Display, Acquisition and Boundaries*. Bloomsbury, London 2017; The Mobile Urban Elite's Material Culture in Eighteenth and Nineteenth Century Northern Baltic Cities. In *Migration and Multi-ethnic Communities. Mobile People from the Late Middle-Ages to the Present*, Maija Ojala-Fulwood. De Gruyter, Oldenbourg (2018).

Jarkko Keskinen is Senior Lecturer, Adjunct Professor in Finnish History at the University of Turku, Faculty of Humanities. His research interests lie in eighteenth- and nineteenth-century social and economic history and family history. Keskinen has published widely on merchant communities and their social networking in urban communities. His most recent articles are Personal catastrophe, communal misfortune: Bankruptcy in a nineteenth-century merchant family, in Deborah Simonton and Hannu Salmi (eds.), *Catastrophe, Gender and Urban Experience, 1648–1920*, (Routledge 2017); The chosen ones: Godmotherhood as a networking strategy in the merchant community of Pori, 1765–1820, in Deborah Simonton and Anne Montenach (eds.), *Female Agency in the Urban Economy: Gender in European Towns, 1640–1920*, (Routledge 2013).

Anu Lahtinen (PhD) in Cultural History and European Doctorate in the Social History of Europe and the Mediterranean, is currently Professor of Finnish and Nordic History at the University of Helsinki. She holds the titles of Docent in Finnish History (University of Turku) and Finnish and Nordic History (University of Helsinki). Her focus is on social history and her special fields of interest include Nordic gender and family history, especially when it comes to the late medieval and early modern period. Lahtinen has published several monographs such as her thesis on female agency in late medieval Finland (2007). Her most recent articles include one on early modern childhood in *Nordic Childhoods, 1700–1870* (Routledge 2017) and another on Nordic stepfamilies in the late medieval period, in *Stepfamilies in Europe* (Routledge 2018). She has also published several edited volumes, most recently co-editing *Dying Prepared in Medieval and Early Modern Northern Europe* (Brill 2018). She is the editor-in-chief of *Historiallinen Aikakauskirja* (the leading historical journal in Finland) and the chair of the board of Tilaushistoriakeskus (Center for Commissioned History Projects)

Elisabet Ljunggren (**PhD**) works as Professor at Nord University, Faculty of Social Science, Norway, where she also is Vice Dean for Research and Development. She has been doing research with a gender perspective on entrepreneurship, innovation, and policies related to these issues for the last 25 years. Professor Ljunggren has published a number of articles and book chapters both in Norway and abroad. She has been a guest co-editor for *International Journal of Gender and Entrepreneurship* and *Journal of Enterprising Communities*, and co-editing several books. She has published in the journals *Entrepreneurship, Theory & Practice*, *Entrepreneurship and Regional Development*, *International Journal of Gender and Entrepreneurship* and *International Small Business Journal* and leading a number of research projects.

Catriona M. Macleod (**PhD**) is a postdoctoral researcher at the University of Glasgow and Network Facilitator for the Leverhulme Trust International Network on Producing Change: Gender and Work in Early Modern Europe. Her doctoral thesis *Women, Work and Enterprise in Glasgow, 1740–1830* focused on urban women's enterprise, financial management, and family business. Her research interests span early modern Scottish gender, economic, and social history, focusing on the history of work and the implications of women's agency for historian's assessment of economic performance.

Henrietta Nilson (**PhD**) is an Assistant Professor of International Business Studies at Dalarna University, Sweden. Earlier work has its focus on family businesses with the topic of Invisibility and Visibility as the main interest, which was the content of her thesis she defended in 2015 at Linnaeus University in Sweden. She has acted as Visiting Professor at a couple of universities (e.g. Gothenburg University, Halmstad Högskola). Her current research project focuses on family firms and Management Buy In, as well as collaboration between the different academic disciplines: entrepreneurship and the Wood technique. Nilson has published in several anthologies such as A critical pedagogy theory perspective on family business, in: (Eds.) Melin, L., Nordqvist, M., Waldkirch, M., and Kumetos, G., *Organizational theories and the family firm*. London: Edward

Elgar Publishing and Nilson, H., Johansson, W., A. 2012. Rådgivning i familjeföretag, in: (Eds.) Brundin, E., Johansson, A., W., Johannisson, B., Melin, L., Nordqvist, M., *Familjeföretagande: affärer och känslor*. Stockholm: SNS förlag.

Seppo Poutanen is Senior Research Fellow and Docent of Sociology at the Department of Management and Entrepreneurship, University of Turku, School of Economics. His areas of expertise include social epistemology, social theory, sociology of science, innovation studies, methodology of social sciences, and economic sociology. Seppo Poutanen has acted as Visiting Professor and Visiting Fellow at several universities (e.g. Stanford University, LSE, University of Essex, Goldsmiths College, UTS Business School). One of his current research projects focuses on the rise of entrepreneurial university. He has published his research in *Social Epistemology*, *Critical Public Health*, *Journal of Critical Realism*, *Sociological Research Online*, *International Journal of Gender and Entrepreneurship* and in several edited volumes. Seppo Poutanen's latest publication is a monograph with Anne Kovalainen: *Gender and Innovation in the New Economy—Women, Identity, and Creative Work*, New York: Palgrave Macmillan 2017.

Annalisa Sentuti (PhD) is Research Fellow in Business Administration, University of Urbino Carlo Bo, Department of Economics, Society, Politics. In the field of business management research, her research interests include particularly entrepreneurship, family business, women-owned firms, small and medium-sized firms, and gender studies. She is a member of the Research Center on Entreprenership and Small-Mid-sized enterprises (CRIMPI), the European Council for Small Business (ECSB), the Italian Society of Business Administration and Acccounting (SIDREA), and the Association for the Study of Small and Medium Sized Businesses (ASPI). Since 2016, she is a member of the scientific board of IPAZIA–Scientific Observatory on Gender Issues. She is author and co-author of several articles and books and is reviewer in many international scientific journals.

Deborah Simonton, FRHS, is Associate Professor of British History, emerita, University of Southern Denmark, Fellow of the Royal Historical Society, Visiting Professor, University of Turku. She studies the gendered and power relations articulated in the shifting economic structures of corporate towns in the context of commercial and polite culture. She published *A History of European Women's Work* (1998), *Women in European Culture and Society* (2010) and a companion sourcebook and edited *Routledge History of Women in Europe* (2006). She leads the Gender in the European Town Network, co-editing *Female Agency in the Urban Economy: 1640–1830* (2013), *Luxury and Gender in the Modern*

Urban Economy (2014) and *Catastrophe, Gender and Urban Experience* (2017). She is General Editor of *The Routledge History Handbook of Gender and the Urban Experience* (2017) and *The Cultural History of Work*, 6 vols. (2018).

Cathryn R. Spence is a Professor of History at Vancouver Island University, British Columbia, Canada. She is the author of *Women, Credit, and Debt in Early Modern Scottish Towns* (Gender and History series, Manchester University Press, 2016) and co-editor of the *Edinburgh Housemaills Taxation Book, 1634–6* (Boydell, 2014). She has written several chapters and articles that explore the intersecting topics of Scottish women, credit and debt, and work. Her research interests include urban and economic history, and the impact of gender and socio-economic status when navigating economic relationships in early modern Western Europe.

Veli Pekka Toropainen (PhD) is a Researcher in Finnish History at the University of Turku, Faculty of Humanities. His focus is on social history and his special interests include gender history in Finnish towns, especially in the early modern period. He has published several articles and book chapters of female entrepreneurship in seventeenth-century Turku. He is an editor of *Genos* (the leading genealogical journal in Finland).

Mari Välimäki, MA and Doctoral Candidate, works as an acting University Teacher in Finnish History at the University of Turku, Faculty of Humanities. Her doctoral thesis focuses on men, premarital relationships, and marriage in seventeenth-century Sweden. Her research interests include gender history and especially the history of men and masculinities and the history of sexuality, as well as history of emotions. Välimäki has published an article "Responsibility of a Seducer? Men, women and breach of promise in the early modern Swedish legislation" in Marianna Muravyeva and Raisa Maria Toivo (eds), *Gender in Late Medieval and Early Modern Europe*. Routledge, 2012, 191–204.

Acknowledgements

This volume is a joint venture by a number of individuals to whom we are most grateful. First, we would like to thank the team at Routledge and especially Brianna Ascher and Megan Smith for their encouragement and advice, as well as Mary Del Plato for her excellent help throughout the production process. Next, we would like to thank the Academy of Finland for its financial support which made it possible for us to invite many researchers interested in women in business families over time to an international workshop held in Turku, Finland in June 2015. The discussions we held there inspired us to begin this work and collaborate with the contributors to put this volume together. This volume draws mainly on the research ideas presented in the workshop and also on complimentary perspectives that we invited to take part. Furthermore, the authors of chapters 4, 6, 9, and 13, as well as the editors, particularly wish to acknowledge the financial support of the Academy of Finland (grant number 138148) and its contribution to their work. Finally, a huge thank you goes to all the authors of the chapters in this volume, each of who responded very positively to our critical reviews of their chapters and were willing to make the requested changes. We believe that this volume consists of excellent contributions by committed authors and contributes to existing knowledge on women in business families. We hope that this volume inspires researchers and readers across disciplines, as it has inspired us during the process bringing this volume together.

Jarna Heinonen
Professor of Entrepreneurship
University of Turku, School of Economics, Finland

Kirsi Vainio-Korhonen
Professor of Finnish History
University of Turku, Faculty of Humanities, Finland

Introduction

1 From Household Economy to Family Business

Jarna Heinonen and Kirsi Vainio-Korhonen

For centuries, almost all economic activity was family-based. The family business rested on the division of labour among family members. Therefore the family was, both socially and economically, the foundation of the family business. Families were not only production units, but also education and consumption units that conveyed norm structures, values, and professional identity to subsequent generations. Although female family members have always been active participants in family businesses over the centuries, their role has often been neglected in previous studies. The role of women in family businesses, or in business families, continues to be debatable in the twenty-first century.

This volume analyses and discusses the topical themes of family business and women in the past and present. The uniqueness of the volume lies in its attempts to focus on time and place in understanding gender in businesses and women's agency in firms by combining historical and contemporary perspectives and research. The volume integrates the notions of time and gender in focusing on family businesses or business families over time.

Through the contemporary focus on gender equality, a gender gap has been identified with regard to female entrepreneurship, and particularly to women´s involvement in businesses. We take three contemporary notions and topical phenomena of the current society as lenses and subject them to further analysis, both in the historical and contemporary perspectives, when analysing gendered practices and equality in business families over time. The three underlining themes are: 1) Challenging the heroic male image of entrepreneurs, 2) Notions of the visibility and invisibility of women, and 3) Women in business succession. We devote a section in the volume to each of the themes, which are highly relevant in the current (women's) entrepreneurship literature.

The volume balances between historical and contemporary analyses and the authors apply either historical or contemporary perspectives to the themes in exploring the applicability of the concepts in understanding the role of women in business families. The historians particularly explore whether the concepts have temporality, i.e. whether the concepts could already be found in early modern times, when capitalism emerged in the society, and whether they have any historical relevance. From the perspective of a piece of historical research this approach is novel, as historians usually focus on historical stories and occasions. The aim here is that historical analyses give deeper understanding and perspective on women´s business involvement in current times. The contemporary research on entrepreneurship demonstrates the stability of women´s roles in the economy and business and enlightens the reader in the ways in which female agency in business evolves over time. The chapters also focus on time and history when analysing the contemporary phenomena.

The chapter written by *Seppo Poutanen* sets the scene for the volume by putting forward the difficulty in crossing the disciplinary boundaries in understanding gender, economy, and time. To justify his approach, Poutanen suggests that it is not a question of the actual chronological time span which differentiates historians and business economists, but it is rather the conceptual gap and ways to circumvent or cross over the gap which create the challenge. By drawing from rereadings of previous studies in the light of new analyses, Poutanen addresses the challenge. His chapter emphasises the importance of understanding history as it is situated and the social history of cultural practices as an essential part of history. He demonstrates this further by giving some examples of previous research (e.g. the concept of housewifery) and how difficult it is to use historical concepts which had contemporary meanings when the concepts emerged but the contents of which have changed over time. Poutanen concludes his chapter by stating, "there is not one economy, nor gender or time, but many and they are multivocal". This volume, indeed, demonstrates how women have participated in business over time and how the women themselves have felt empowered for their agency and activities. The very analysis of women and business has then achieved its aims—the rewriting of business history and economic history—as suggested by Poutanen.

The first underlining theme of the volume touches upon the stereotypical, heroic image of an entrepreneur. The myth of the romantic and heroic individual as an entrepreneur still holds sway in current discussions on entrepreneurship and society in general. The populist image portrays the heroic entrepreneur as the warrior, superman, and pioneer, and often ignores the social setting in which the entrepreneurial process takes place. Even early academic entrepreneurship research, particularly in psychology and economics, focused on and gave priority to the individualistic level of analysis, although their explanatory power is not well accepted today. The myth and approach are, however, understandable as the individual entrepreneur is the most tangible element of entrepreneurship and, thus, remains at the centre of the entrepreneurial stage. Entrepreneurs are considered to be different from others and the difference must then explain what they do (Dodd and Anderson 2007). Furthermore, the heroic individual is typically presented as a male, if not otherwise defined, leading to the assumption that women as entrepreneurs are even more exceptional and abnormal. The chapters of the first section of the volume—*Challenging the heroic male image of entrepreneurs*—focus on entrepreneurial women who have possessed substantial responsibility, involvement, and power and have run successful businesses over the years. Interestingly, historians have been able to identify several such women, although officially only men were allowed to receive full business and political rights, both as entrepreneurs and as representatives of burgher estates.

The agency of an entrepreneur is formed in interaction with a special socio-economic context, and social learning is important in the process of becoming an entrepreneur (Chell 2008). *Anu Lahtinen* argues in her chapter likewise: in order to understand the historical concept of entrepreneurship, it is important to analyse both the role of individual agency and the significance of societal conditions. She points out that regardless of gender, any business in early modern Europe was heavily dependent on family relations, notions of cooperation, and reciprocity. Lahtinen analyses the entrepreneurship of two early modern merchant women, Valborg Innama in Finland and Kenau Hasselaer in the Netherlands. For both women, being a burgher widow was the crucial factor that paved the way for them in business. When the opportunity occurred, both seem to have had genuinely entrepreneurial personalities and been capable of seizing opportunities. At the same time, they maximised their legal status as widows and their unrestrained methods sometimes crossed the boundaries of what was considered acceptable for their gender.

Economic historians have often concentrated on the man's world, where male merchants and divergent institutions played a central role (Montenach and Simonton 2013). In their case study on Elin Såger, a merchant widow in Turku, Finland, *Jarkko Keskinen, Veli Pekka Toropainen, and Mari Välimäki* show a different and larger picture: the early modern legislation and the commercial milieu could also provide opportunities for women, decision-makers who took part with success in economic activities. On the other hand, the wide agency of widow entrepreneurs troubled the community, as these women behaved like men. It seems that in spite of her bold personality, Elin Såger could not, as a woman, fully take advantage of the opportunities that the legislation provided her. Instead, her business activities were constantly challenged by her male family members. The case study also shows how early modern business depended on the network of kin and family ties on many different levels. Elin Såger and her like were not only heads of family businesses, but also parents to their sons and parents-in-laws to their daughters' husbands, with whom they had divergent relationships and moral obligations, both as business managers and as mothers.

Cathryn Spence writes in her chapter about wives who were engaged in mercantile activity in early modern Scottish towns. She argues that cooperation between merchant husbands and wives was an integral part of earlier family businesses. Women were active as ship owners or as distributers. A small number of high-status women acted in the import-export trade, usually with their husbands or as widows, as wealthy and determined merchants trading in expensive goods like leather, cloth, and wine. Spence remarks though that probably even more often, a wife's successful involvement in the family business has left no written record at all. It is likely that the cases she describes in her article are, as she formulates it, "the tip of the iceberg" and several similar cases are lying unseen beneath the records. Like *Deborah Simonton* in her chapter, Spence concludes that husbands bore the legal responsibilities for family businesses and, thus, the names and economic actions of wives are largely absent from sources.

Beatrice Craig (2015) has demonstrated that the scholarship on business history is derived from early twentieth-century studies, such as Werner Sombart's and Joseph Schumpeter's theories, which make businesswomen "unthinkable" in history and focus only on "the ultimate alpha male" entrepreneurs. On this basis, *Ulla Ijäs* argues that the myth of a heroic and individualistic male entrepreneur does not in any way belong to the early modern world where cooperation and mutuality were necessities for both men and women at every level of business. Marie Hackman, the female manager of the family firm, Hackman & Co, in early modern Vyborg in Russia, represented family business in all aspects of her life and, since she was the only manager of the firm, acted according to this status, despite her sons or her biological sex. In all her actions, she put the family business first. The business was not based on individual profit seeking but on the common family good, enforced by communal values.

The masculinity of entrepreneurial myth is further opened up in the second section of the volume: *Notions of the Visibility and Invisibility of Women*. The research on entrepreneurship and family businesses indeed assumes the owner-manager and entrepreneur as a male and the wives/partners/daughters/sisters of the owner-manager rarely appear. This easily produces the dichotomous constructions of the "heroic male" entrepreneur or owner-manager and the often "invisible" woman, who is hidden in terms of founding or running the business, as assisting her spouse (Dodd and Anderson 2007; Hamilton 2006). Although several authors have recognised the various and even key roles women have in family businesses (e.g. Heinonen and Stenholm 2011) the notion of the invisibility of women reinforces the dominant and gender-biased "heroic male" discourse on entrepreneurship (Ogbor 2000). As such it also "prevents any understanding of entrepreneurial diversity by remaining uncritical of the social, cultural and institutional forces shaping the pattern and development of entrepreneurship in contemporary society" (Hamilton 2006, 254). The gender imbalance has partly been devoted to patriarchal structures in family businesses, which are generally perceived to be more conservative than other types of businesses. The chapters in this section enlighten the reader regarding the notion of the visibility and invisibility of women in business families, providing historical and contemporary cases demonstrating how women face and move between visibility and invisibility in their business, family, and social lives.

The concept and types of invisibility are addressed by *Henrietta Nilson and Ulla Hytti*. In their chapter they explore how moving between visibility and invisibility in different social and family business spheres is done to secure a self-rewarding and empowered role. Based on the single-case study of a Swedish woman with lifelong experience of one family firm, the authors challenge the overriding story underlining women's invisibility in terms of facing difficulties in gaining access to leadership positions or being paid for their work. The authors argue that research into family businesses should avoid equalling access to family business leadership as the sole measure of success for the individual family members or as the only avenue to having an important and meaningful role in the family and family business. Furthermore, Nilson and Hytti highlight the role of social spheres as an important arena for assuming agency and securing visibility.

In her chapter, *Deborah Simonton* opens up the discussion on early modern businesswomen's invisibility in public records, but not in the past itself. Women were often under-recorded or not recorded precisely because they were seen as subordinate to the male head of household, who was also the head of the business. Simonton points out that in history women's invisibility is often a "matter of record" in the sense that records usually named only male heads of household who represented family firms for tax collectors and clerical as well as civil registrars. Through her cases, Simonton demonstrates how the close reading of the indirect source evidence tells us that women exploited every tool at hand to be full partners in eighteenth-century urban family businesses in Aberdeen, Scotland. She argues that wives' activities, as well as their strategies as widows, shed light on how they had operated in family businesses during the period when their husbands were alive. Through the lifecycle of the Morice family, Simonton shows how women brought skills and connections into marriage that contributed to business. She also describes the dynamic of the business as a partnership of the couple.

Jarkko Keskinen and Kirsi Vainio-Korhonen argue in their chapter that the beginning of the nineteenth century seems to form a borderline between the medieval and early modern business communalism and a new ideology of individualism and capitalism that challenged the old social and gender order in urban business life. These new aims were visible as early as the eighteenth century, when the rights of burgher women to do business, and their political rights, began to be placed under scrutiny in a different way from before. New kinds of voices began to be raised in the social debate, claiming that women as individuals should be prohibited from doing business entirely because they were fundamentally gullible and simple due to being of the female sex. The case of merchant and burgher daughter Maria Augustin in Turku, Finland, describes how the letter of the law and, to an ever-increasing extent, the spirit of the time had started to see women as fundamentally unsuited for responsible business tasks. Exceptionally, the unmarried Augustin was declared fully and legally competent as a person to independently incur debts and enter into financial undertakings in her merchant business, but in spite of this full legal capacity she was denied the right to swear the burgher oath and thus, gain real burgher rights as a town merchant, due only to her sex.

In their chapter, *Janice Byrne and Salma Fattoum* focus on family in business and intra-family entrepreneurship rather than the continuity of one family business, as suggested by several researchers (e.g. Discua Cruz, Howorth, and Hamilton 2012; Moores 2009). They explore the gendered career outcomes of next generation family business members in terms of succession and business startup by focusing on two French business families through the career narratives of six family members. Their study demonstrates that, while daughters may not be considered (or may not consider themselves) as viable successors, the daughters may build independent entrepreneurial careers as a result of their family business background and even resources. As an outcome, women cannot be presented as disadvantaged victims of the male norm and patriarchal system, but rather as victors. Furthermore, their findings show how the daughters benefitted from a class privilege enabling them to access the necessary financial, social and human capital to start their own businesses, thus portraying a more positive picture for next generation women than the invisibility or marginalisation of women in business families.

In the third section of the volume the crucial process of family business succession is discussed. The transfer of the firm from one generation to another is one of the most important and widely studied topics in family business research, as it is crucial for family businesses to ensure that a smooth transition takes place and that the firm continues to be successful and effective after the succession (Sharma 2004). Furthermore, the process of business succession, and particularly women's and daughters' involvement in the succession process, has intrigued numerous researchers in the field. This again is easy to understand, given the heroic male image of the entrepreneur and family business owner as well as the notion of the invisibility of women discussed in the first and second sections of the volume. Primogeniture still seems to be the norm in many family businesses, implying that the eldest son is the most probable successor and women need to "fight for" and claim their position when wanting to take over the business. It is not only about convincing the family members and different stakeholders of the business about one's willingness and capability to take over the business. It also involves creating a suitable business identity for oneself and convincing oneself, as well as others, of one's required competences (Hytti et al. 2017). In the section, *Women in Business Succession*, based on their historical and contemporary analyses the authors have identified various paths for women to take over the business activities. There seem to be parallels between the women´s involvement in the succession process that are maintained through time and the enduring gendered responsibilities for family and business that form the basis for the changing roles and their divisions.

In their chapter, *Francesca Maria Cesaroni and Annalisa Sentuti* adopt an integrated perspective to daughters' involvement in family business succession. Based on their multiple case study of five daughters of family business owners in Italy, they explore possible profiles that daughters can assume nowadays in the succession process as well as their motivations, ambitions, roles, and satisfaction thereof. Based on their case studies, they demonstrate five distinct profiles for daughters: leader by choice, leader because "she has to", manager by choice, invisible co-leader, and outcast. Their study clearly illustrates the heterogeneous motivations and ambitions of daughters in relation to succession and highlights how strong normative commitment and feelings of obligation towards the family may "force" daughters to get involved with the family business. Furthermore, the study suggests that the marginal role of daughters is not necessarily a consequence of gender discrimination, but rather their own choice, indicating that they might be satisfied and totally happy with their secondary position.

In her chapter, *Catriona Macleod* investigates the fortunes of early modern urban businesswomen in Glasgow, Scotland, examining their roles in business succession, their networks, and their agency within the wider community. The results from the sample of widowed businesswomen she has examined suggest various strategies and succession models, including ceasing to trade; continuing the business until their own death; continuing the business and overseeing succession to the next generation; and continuing or establishing a separate enterprise. Some widows shared management roles with children or other business partners. Some restructured businesses to fit better with their own skills, capacities, or ambitions. According to Hamilton (2006) family business research would gain a more accurate picture of family business if the family, rather than the business, was prioritised and focused on. The results of Macleod's study show that her social exchange perspective reveals effectively the varied roles that women have long played in the family, local, and national economies.

Much of the family business literature focuses on successions which are planned and prepared in advance, in collaboration with the predecessor and the next generation to take over. Very often unexpected things happen, such as illness or sudden death, and the family business needs to be transferred to the next generation without planning or the presence of the predecessor. *Jarna Heinonen and Elisabet Ljunggren* have conducted case studies of three family businesses in Finland that experienced premature and unplanned succession due to the death of the owner, CEO, father, and husband. They explore how families and family businesses cope with such a situation, which is seldom studied due to its delicate nature. Their study contributes by bringing new insights about decision making during premature and unplanned succession and argues that even painful emotions such as grief can be a resource in the interconnectedness between family and the business, particularly when coinciding with pragmatic decisions. The study also suggests that daughters who are not considered as potential successors by their fathers may end up taking over the family business due to a lack of other options.

The selected themes of this volume clearly stem from contemporary business, but our research findings demonstrate that they are also identifiable in historical analyses. However, as anticipated, the content and meaning of the concepts may vary depending on the time and the context.

Several authors (e.g. *Simonton, Spence, and Macleod*) in this volume underline the fact that women's economic activity in the late medieval and early modern periods have been increasingly acknowledged by historians in recent years. Family-based economic activities, both in agriculture and industry as well as in urban milieus, relied on the acts and achievements of all household members: men, women, and children. During early modern times family businesses were managed within the walls of the owner's household and as a part of the household economy. Likewise, early professional women found their best career and work opportunities in the fields of female household tasks: in foodstuff and textile production as well as in care and service occupations. (Ilmakunnas, Rahikainen, and Vainio-Korhonen 2017).

The beginning of the nineteenth century seems to form a borderline between the medieval and early modern business communalism and a new ideology of individualism and capitalism that challenged the old social order in urban business life. Family and working life/businesses gradually became separate spheres of life and family firms transformed from being the milieus of both sexes to being merely male domains. Similarly, the breakthrough of the new individual business model was a long process and, especially in small business communities, individual merchants or business families could not afford to turn their backs immediately and permanently on the other members of the community, despite the tightening reciprocal competition, "selfish" profit seeking, and occasional conflicts. In the long-term businesses continued to be embedded in a wider community although work/business and family spheres were separated from each other in comparison to the household economy of early modern times.

Contemporary understanding of family business research considers family business as a system consisting of three sub-systems, namely the family, ownership, and business sub-systems (Tagiuri and Davis 1996). The uniqueness of family business stems from these overlapping sub-systems and particularly the notion of "familiness" which captures the resources and values generated via the interactions between the family, family members, and the business (Habbershon and Williams 1999; Habbershon, Williams, and MacMillan 2003). Through "familiness", family culture, and values characterise family business's behaviour (Kachaner, Stalk, and Bloch 2012). From this perspective family business is at its "purest" when the three sub-systems overlap each other, i.e. when it is at the core of the family business system. On such an occasion a member of a family works in a family business which she/he also owns. Family business researchers have identified and focused on other occasions where the roles of family members vary and have explored how the varied roles might shape family business behaviour. Interestingly, the core of family business at the intersection of the three sub-systems theoretically resembles the concept of the household economy of early modern times when the family functioned as a production unit. The historical analyses of the contemporary themes or notions, thus, make it possible to conceptualise family and business from past to present as depicted in Figure 1.1 Although family businesses *per se* did not exist in early modern times, the notion of heavily overlapping core elements—family, business, and ownership—has always existed in the form of the household economy.

As demonstrated by the chapters of this volume, women have played various crucial roles, both in business and families over time, although they are not necessarily written into historical business narratives. Interestingly, this seems to hold true also in contemporary entrepreneurship studies, which tend to present entrepreneurs as male, and female entrepreneurs as the exception. Even family business studies exploring the family business system as a whole rarely focus on women's agency in family businesses and, therefore, a more thorough understanding of it is called for (Smyrnios, Poutziouris, and Goel 2013). This volume does its best to address the gap from both the historical and contemporary perspectives.

Finally, during the past two centuries, Europe has developed from an agrarian economy into an industrial, and now post-industrial, society. During the twentieth century European women achieved personal sovereignty, freedom of trade, suffrage, and eligibility in national elections. The obstacles related to the education and work of women have also been dismantled. Surprisingly, these great social changes have not influenced the contemporary gender structure of European entrepreneurship and businesses, which originates at the beginning of the nineteenth century and separates family and work lives from each other (see Figure 1.1). The status quo is represented

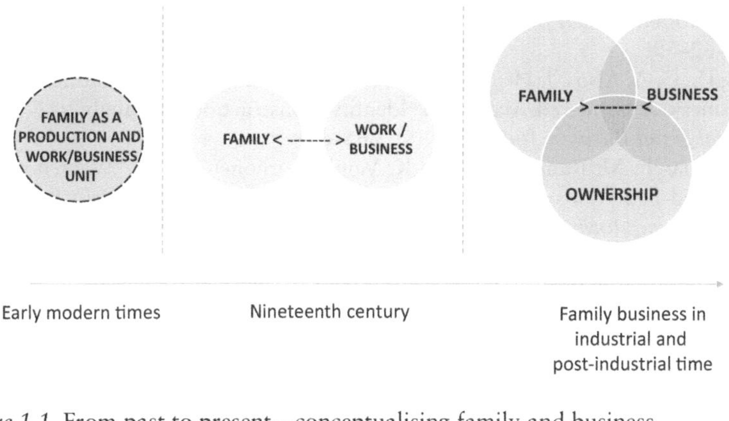

Figure 1.1 From past to present—conceptualising family and business

both by female and male professional business choices, as well as by the structures of entrepreneurship and family businesses. Female business activity is no longer hindered by any formal obstacles but the gender structures of entrepreneurship in a society, and particularly in family firms, have either not changed or they have changed much more slowly than in other spheres of society (e.g. politics or education). This volume demonstrates that women have indeed been strong agents in economic history, although they have not been equally visible in historical narratives. Furthermore, it seems evident that the role of women continues to increase, not only in historical texts left for future generations, but also in real life and businesses, although the pace of development is slow.

References

Chell, E. 2008. *The Entrepreneurial Personality: A Social Construction*. 2nd ed. London and New York: Routledge.

Craig, B. 2015. *Women and Business Since 1500: Invisible Presences in Europe and North America?* London: Palgrave Macmillan.

Discua Cruz, A., C. Howorth, and E. Hamilton. 2012. "Intrafamily Entrepreneurship: The Formation and Membership of Family Entrepreneurial Teams." *Entrepreneurship Theory and Practice* 37 (1): 17–46.

Dodd, S. D., and A. R. Anderson. 2007. "Mumpsimus and the Mything of the Individualistic Entrepreneur." *International Small Business Journal* 25 (4): 341–360.

Habbershon, T. G., and M. L. Williams. 1999. "A Resource-Based Framework for Assessing the Strategic Advantages of Family Firms." *Family Business Review* 12 (1): 1–25.

Habbershon, T. G., M. L. Williams, and I. C. MacMillan. 2003. "A Unified Systems Perspective of Family Firm Performance." *Journal of Business Venturing* 18 (4): 451–465.

Hamilton, E. 2006. "Whose Story Is It Anyway? Narrative Accounts of the Role of Women in Founding and Establishing Family Businesses." *International Small Business Journal* 24 (3): 253–271.

Heinonen, J., and P. Stenholm. 2011. "The Contribution of Women in Family Business." *International Journal of Entrepreneurship and Innovation Management* 13 (1): 62–79.

Hytti, U., G. A. Alsos, J. Heinonen, and E. Ljunggren. 2017. "Navigating the Family Business: A Gendered Analysis of Identity Construction of Daughters." *International Small Business Journal* 35 (6): 665–686.

Ilmakunnas J., M. Rahikainen, and K. Vainio-Korhonen. 2017. "Women and Professional Ambitions in Northern Europe, c. 1650–1850" In *Early Professional Women in Northern Europe, ca. 1650–1850*, edited by J. Ilmakunnas, M. Rahikainen, and K. Vainio-Korhonen. New York and London: Routledge.

Kachaner, N., G. Stalk, and A. Bloch. 2012. "What You Can Learn from Family Business." *Harvard Business Review* 90 (11): 103–106.

Montenach, A., and D. Simonton. 2013. "Gender, Agency and Economy: Shaping the Eighteenth-Century European Town." In *Female Agency in the Urban Economy: Gender in European Towns, 1640–1830*, edited by Deborah Simonton and Anne Montenach. New York and London: Routledge.

Moores, K. 2009. "Paradigms and Theory Building in the Domain of Business Families." *Family Business Review* 22 (2): 167–180.

Ogbor, J. O. 2000. "Mythicizing and Reification in Entrepreneurial Discourse: Ideology-Critique of Entrepreneurial Studies." *Journal of Management Studies* 37 (5): 605–635.

Sharma, P. 2004. "An Overview of the Field of Family Business Studies: Current Status and Directions for the Future." *Family Business Review* 17 (1): 1–36.

Smyrnios, K. X., P. Z. Poutziouris, and S. Goel. 2013. "Introduction: Trends and Developments in Family Business Research." In *Handbook of Research on Family Business*, edited by K. X. Smyrnios, P. Z. Poutziouris, and S. Goel, 1–13. 2nd ed. Cheltenham, UK and Northampton, MA: Edward Elgar.

Tagiuri, R., and J. Davis. 1996. "Bivalent Attributes of the Family Firm." *Family Business Review* 9 (2): 199–208.

2 Gender, Economy, and Time

Seppo Poutanen

Gender, Economy, and Time—An Introduction to Three Dimensions

For a long time women have been absent from the dominant analyses and narratives of the business histories, as noted over twenty years ago by Wendy Gamber (1997), Joan Scott (1998), and several other historians, mostly women. According to Robb (2016) this is no longer the case, given the explosion of studies on gender and economics. Within business history, the greater attention to gender, race, and ethnicity, as well as to intersectionality grew especially in the United States in the 1990s. Feminist research interests and the interest in women's historically inferior and invisible positions arose first in the analyses of national histories, missing women from labour history, and often in the analyses of local histories. Once historians started to study and explore women's history, the interest also grew towards business history, but this occurred much later than the study of gender and labour history, for example, as the debates in the Business History Review journal in the 1990s show (e.g. Popp 2004). Inherent and inbuilt in the research into women's history is the idea of challenging the existing knowledge, or expanding the reigning historical thinking and analyses of how history has unfolded and is now narrated.

Even though there has been a drastic rise in new historical studies about women and economics (e.g. Hartigan-O'Connor 2009; Rappoport 2012; de Jong and Higgins 2015; Robbins 2016), the topic of women and business history has not actualised as a large institutional field of its own. Rather, the question has been portrayed diffusely as a question of gender and economics, with a wide variety of approaches and topics, ranging from literary studies and historical analyses to economic studies of the topic (e.g. Acker 2004; Kerber 1980, 1988). Despite the growth of the field of gender and economics in the number of publications, the field also carries focuses on work, paid and unpaid labour, and analyses of intellectual cultural history and contemporary developments. Thus, the argument that women played a key role in the development of the current Western economic system, as posed by Robb (2016) is undoubtedly based on this wide variety of studies, ranging from literary studies to economics.

Despite the fact that women's actual presence in the economic history and current visibility in the light of the economic actions have gained foothold—twenty years later on from the first disciplinary debates—aspects are still missing in the ways business histories are being re-analyzed and rewritten (e.g. Decker 2013; Popp and Fellman 2017; Fellman and Popp 2013). Of such projects, e.g. in gender and history, the revisiting of gender and business history with the help of epistemologically informed narratives has recently gained popularity (Goodman 2010; Hansen 2012). The lack and scarcity of existing analyses in some fields of business and economy as a whole has not arisen from the absence of women from the real economic history and activities worldwide. Women were just not written into the reigning narratives of business and economic histories, and they are still to a large extent missing from those grand narratives of economic growth and development. This missing knowledge shapes our understanding of and ways of handling the economic growth and development.

The lack of women in the narratives has also meant that a gender analysis of business or economic history has been to a large extent missing. However, to a degree, gender can be found in the analyses of family firms, as the family was virtually synonymous with the firm, sometimes growing through marriage, but during the pre-industrial period large factories were rare (Dyer and Handler 1994). Tweedale (2013) shows in his analyses of the family firms in nineteenth-century England that businesses drew their strength from individual skills within families, and this was especially so in the craft-based industries. Whether the difference between "family firms" and "business families" is more a semantic one or whether it can differentiate the families earning their living through businesses (e.g. Kwolek-Folland 1998; Robbins 2016) is left for the other articles of this volume to analyse.

When analysing the division of labour, historians, economists, and sociologists have followed somewhat differing paths in explaining how the division of labour by sex appeared to be universal throughout human history. It is undisputed that the divisions of labour as well as being numerous, were also persistent and stubborn. However, the explanations of how the divisions came about have ranged from patriarchy to political rights, divisions between private and public sectors, to more culturally attuned explanations, and have even attributed these divisions to free choice (e.g. Hartmann 2010; Acker 2004; Walby 1988; Milkman 1986). Such variety was not strongly put forward in the case of women and business: There were few studies focusing on women's business ownership and self-employment over time, and very few of them used structural or theoretically attuned lenses in seeking theoretical explanations for the divisions, instead of descriptions (in sociology e.g. Allen and Truman 1992; Kovalainen 1993).

The existing analyses showing the presence of women in the activities and processes in economic history have both challenged and led to new interpretations of historical writing. Such documentation exists in humanities but to lesser degree in business economics. Similarly, these analyses have brought forward several new interpretations of economic development, which emphasise the intersectionality and the importance of addressing the multiple, previously unheard voices in the discussion on economic agency and activity. The hegemony of masculine economic agency has been long challenged, and with that challenge, economic and business histories are being rewritten with women's multiple voices and narratives (e.g. Hanawalt 1999; Robb 2016; Calhoun 1983).

What business is, who participates in it, and what it actually does, are historically defined very differently, and thus it makes little sense in talking about "women and business" or "gender and business" without a clear understanding of the time-related restrictions, chronological time, and historical time. This chapter for its part does not aim to build a chronological overview into the questions of history, economy, time, and gender, but aims to achieve the following two things.

First, the chapter aims to put forward the difficulty in crossing the disciplinary boundaries. In doing so, the second question is not the question of the actual chronological time span which differentiates historians and business economists, but rather, the conceptual gap and ways to circumvent or cross over the gap. Paul Ricoeur, in his "Time and Narrative", refers to Francois Simiand's well-known definition of "history as knowledge in terms of traces". Ricoeur talks about historical documents, and mentions that a historical document is at the same time both a "remain", and a "sign of what was but no longer is" (Ricoeur 1988, 16). This idea of time as a non-linear entity and the different shapes it takes when related to differing context brings forth the notion of how differently time has been constructed in history and how it looks now, as time-as-present. For this reason, time does not appear in this chapter merely as division between historical vs. present time, but also in relation to research and its subjectivity and changes in research paradigms and disciplinary fields over time. For these reasons, the chapter is not a systematic description and analysis of what is known about women's business history over time or its current forms. Rather, the article builds on a collection of discussions bound by and aligned through three concepts, "economy, time, and gender". The chapter emphasises the importance of understanding history as it is situated and the social history of cultural practices as an essential part of history, unfortunately often forgotten, and in interdisciplinary research, often also misunderstood (Castoriadis 1987; Cornell 1992; Scott and Tilly 2010; Sovic, Thane, and Viazzo 2016). This approach draws from new rereadings of previous studies in the light of new analyses.

The knowledge claims the author can make cover only the philosophy of science, gender theories, sociology, and certain meta-theoretical formulations. As the author has not been part of the research project where this edited collection stems from, and was invited to participate only in the last stages of the project, certain apologies are called for. The author apologises to scholarly historians for the rather shallow, layman approach to specific historic periods in business and economic history, and rather similarly to business economists for the lack of deep knowledge of current enterprising companies and their dynamics. Some decisions were made, due to space restrictions: for example, the Chandlerian paradigm (e.g. Chandler 1990; Jones and Zeitlin 2008), which is influential in business history, is left out of the discussion. A more detailed analysis of the Chandlerian paradigm in entrepreneurship theories and thinking would undoubtedly deserve a chapter of its own. Also, a wider discussion on historical time and its analysis (e.g. Lundmark 1993) had to be left out.

Equal Rights, Economy, and Gender

Many social and intellectual historians—both in the fields of history and the social sciences—have claimed with well-founded, detailed, and meticulously analysed evidence, that the division of labour by sex appears universal throughout human history (e.g. Scott 1998; Hartmann 2010). The ways the divisions of labour between the sexes has manifested, transformed, and changed through time and space, however, has varied, but the division seems to have been pervasive and persistent. This is not to claim that there is anything predetermined or biologically destined in the persistent sex divisions of labour. Rather, the question is how groups, families, communities, and societies have become built, and in that building process, how they have become related to and connected with other aspects such as individuality, egalitarianism, civility, and equal worth. This is also connected to the process of development of the economic system, and how individuals relate to this development and with what assets. This was first the historical development that removed marriage from its central role at the heart of the economy (Roberts 2005; Ågren and Erickson 2005).

The development of the economy took place with household production, for example, with men as weavers working at looms in their homes. The advantage of the cottage industry, or the domestic system, was that it was cheap and flexible, and not bound by guild regulations (Stott 2011). The economic advancements of Europe and also the United States were setting milestones for the rights of women.

A highly relevant question naturally is at what point in time and how did people become identifiable as individuals and have the sovereignty and personhood as understood in the Western world today? This last question refers to the history of men and histories of personhood, liberalism, and their tensions with other -isms, such as patriarchy and capitalism. It can be said that roughly from the seventeenth century on, individualism becomes more broadly to indicate separateness, individuality, and autonomy, as in liberalism.[1] The societal change brought in novel conceptualisations of how persons could and should operate in economy, too.

In general, it was first with the rise of the classical political liberalist ideas that emerged in the seventeenth and eighteenth centuries, and in the two—American and French—revolutions, that individual rights became an issue, and started to matter also for women. From the very beginning, much of what democratic liberalism calls for in terms of equal rights to opportunity and security also provided a solid return in economic productivity (Starr 2007). For women the idea that women should have equal rights to men rose first with the Enlightenment. Over time, women's rights have moved from initially gaining property rights to include individual non-material rights. The right to vote, the right to control fertility, and the right to work for equal pay were among the key rights in Europe. For example, in many parts of Europe women gained more rights in the family and over the family in dispute cases with husbands. In 1857 women in England were able to divorce their husbands, and similar laws were passed in France and Germany. The rights of black women followed with delays in the United States (Jones 2010).

Women had to wait longer for that person-related individualism and their citizenship rights throughout the Western world. At the time of the French Revolution, which ignited the modern era of individual rights, women's rights were brought into the political arena through the Enlightenment and its ideas, which set the tone and influenced on the subsequent revolution. Among those who argued for women's rights was John Stuart Mill (1984, 284), who in 1869 wrote: "Civilization and Christianity have restored to the woman her just rights. Meanwhile the wife is the actual bondservant of her husband; no less so, as far as the legal obligation goes, than slaves commonly so called". This "subjection of women" as detailed by J. S. Mill proved to be slow to disappear. It was first in the 1970s, for example, when Parliament in the United Kingdom accepted that laws which effectively retained the concept of "a woman as property" did not reflect demands for equality (Barnett 1996). In their article, Jarkko Keskinen and Kirsi Vainio-Korhonen especially discuss the business women's legal and political rights in eighteenth-century Finland (Keskinen and Vainio-Korhonen in this volume). As they discuss in their article, legal and political rights did not always develop in unison, or in any peaceful harmony in relation to men's widening legal and political rights. Many of J. S. Mill's ideas and views on women's societal status carry relevance even today.

It has been argued by many, citing historian Joan Scott's (1998) famous words that gender is a useful category, but using and analysing it in research is not at all a simple matter. Analysis using gender and analysis of gender does not conflate to the question of women vs. men, nor is it about visibility/invisibility alone. However, the presence and absence of women, the materiality of subject position and the rights of individuals are also at the core of gender analysis in history. Joan Scott noted this in her commentary article on American business history in 1998. At that time, twenty years ago, the discussion on gender and business history was growing rapidly in the United States. Since then, business history has claimed its own ground. In her analysis of social enterprise history and gender in seventeeth-century York, England, Perriton (2017) emphasises the parochial realms as the key to overcoming the focus on individual women per se, which so often was the main outcome in business histories.

The parochial realms refer to the positions individuals have in networks. In her study, Perriton shows how under English common law married women were not allowed to own real material or personal property (such as land or cash) nor were they allowed to make legal or binding contracts such as commercial transactions. Unmarried women and widows were allowed to own property and they were allowed to contract on the same terms as men (Perriton 2017). For those women who were economically active but married and thus not suitable to work in business, parochial networks helped them to create economic space and bypass some of the constraints by linking individuals and family groups. Through these wider connections, including friends, women were able to access roles or positions in voluntary associations, for example, in times when women were not allowed to have property and working for payment was not possible for some reason (Perriton 2017; Barker 2006; Mullin 2016). Networks may have even extended beyond families and relatives to acquaintances, but the general assumption is that they very seldom crossed social class boundaries. These resources were crucial in making ends meet and they gave some leeway for women without full citizenship rights and individual position.

In comparison to many central European countries and the development of rights for women and equal rights of ownership and subject position, Scandinavian women had to wait rather long for equal economic rights that allowed them to own, or trade their property and engage in economic transactions (e.g. Göransson 1988; Pylkkänen 1990). This did not stop them from being economically active and occupying a variety of agentic positions, as shown in many of the articles of this volume as well. The "marriage economy" refers mostly to the principal economic institution of marriage, and to inherited property. For example, the husband managed all property in Sweden-Finland and in Denmark-Norway up to the nineteenth century (Erickson 1993, 2005). Both the "marriage economy" and the land transfer system in the Nordic countries and in Germany included the care of the older generation (syting, Altenteil) (e.g. Moring 2016).

In her dissertation, *"Half the bed, locks and keys"*, Anu Pylkkänen showed how women's rights in the family economy of seventeenth- and eighteenth-century Finland were dependent also on whether the inheritance was rural or urban. Furthermore, the definition of marriage (and from that, the family) varied, as did the children's rights to inherit from their parents (Pylkkänen 2005). The right of primogeniture was never written in Scandinavian law, but it was followed most often in practice (Erickson 1993), as it was tied into the values of humans as men.

The rationale for the "delay" of formal economic rights for women has been connected by many to the late pre-industrialization in the Scandinavian countries. It has also been attributed to the relatively modest wealth accumulation, but other explanations also exist. The slow development from a kin-centered society to a more state-centered rule of law meant the slow recognition of individual (i.e. male) rights. As any historian would underline, contemporary sentiment inevitably colours our views of the past. The development of citizenship rights for women in Finland—having been part of Sweden and Russia's Grand Duchy—was closely related to the independence targets, nation building, and national identity building projects. The construction of the image of Finnish women as strong and capable took quite a while (Pylkkänen 2005), and it came mainly through the rural gender code. The gender code in rural areas was less differentiated and less dichotomous than in towns and in other European cultures (Pylkkänen 2005).

Even if at the general level agreeing on the agentic position—or lack of agentic position—for women, historians of labour, business historians, and family historians are not in unison on the details, processes, and outcomes of the division of labour and presence of gender in the economy and economic development—or indeed, on more detailed questions such as of the intersections of family and work (e.g. Coontz 2000). One of the arguments is that the idea and assumption of the "division of work" is simply based on modernist thinking and cannot capture the historical division of work or labour to the extent we wish for when analysing the economic agencies' activities and importance over time. Another often-presented argument is that history as a discipline has always been uneasy with universalism, which is one of the core assumptions of another key discipline here, of economics, or more broadly of sociology (e.g. Down 2001; Jacobs and Gerson 2005).

If we look at the current research literature on entrepreneurship, and the ways individuals are framed in contemporary entrepreneurship research, the emphasis on individuals' motivations and capabilities is strong in the given ecosystem (e.g. Autio et al. 2014). This frame assumes that often individuals may prefer self-employment and business ownership over salaried employment for various reasons other than income potential (e.g. Lomax 2017). Monetary rewards are thus not the only motivating factor. Additionally, to broaden the scope, some studies list motives such as the desire for independence and control over work and working conditions (e.g. Casson 1982). However, all choices are also affected by many constraints, many of them unknown. Analysing constraints in the contemporary economy cannot be compared to the analyses of constraints in historical times, as several of the articles of this volume also show.

Narratives of Time and Gender

How can we reach an understanding of the multitudes of narratives and stories of lived lives and of the businesses of women with the help of contemporary gender and historical theories? The aim is not to conflate the historical authenticity or experiences, "the traces of what has been but no longer is", into one explanatory model of gender, such as patriarchy. Instead, the aim here is to abstract the discussion by opening up ways to think about gender.

Gender is socially constructed (Lorber 2010), but that phrase does not tell us about the ways, boundaries, or habits of gendering economic activities at various times in history. We need to elaborate the phrase of "socially constructed gender" and ask what ways of explaining and analysing the phenomena the expression "socially constructed gender" becomes attached to?

Taking one example, Malinowski's detailed narratives about the Trobriander islanders' boat building and other activities all aim to understand how those activities make sense in the lives of the Trobrianders, and narrate their everyday lives (Abbott 2016). The aim was not to narrate how the individual persons lived their personal lives on the islands. The focus on individual narratives and individuals narrating their lives in contemporary business economics can also be seen as somewhat problematic, especially from the point of view where larger "ecosystems" of business activities are being explored.

The exploration of individual agency has been conducted mainly at the level of microanalysis. A problem with this work on the submerged practices (McNay 1992) of women is that it can slip into a celebration of the unknown, hitherto invisible experience and label it primary or authentic. History celebrating previously invisible women often remained with this kind of focus. Joan Scott has shown that in certain types of women's histories the reliance on experience as an original point of explanation very often hides other types of explanations (Scott 1996).

The crucial influence of time becomes visible in the histories of black women: the complexity of "agency" is not without relation to other types of positions and subjectivities (Wright 2002). Both postcolonialist feminism and postcolonialism have highlighted the grassroots and everyday lives of non-Western women and equally opposed to discrimination (Young 2003). McNay poses that there exists an instability of gender norms which arises from the historicity of social practices. The lived and transformed agency as a temporally embedded process of social engagement becomes important, and the idea of gender as a historical matrix, rather than a static structure, offers a much clearer agency for gender, as McNay (1992, 2000) brings up. This focus is linked to the discussion of the impossibility of talking about agency as a general category (e.g. Cornell 1992). Subject formation—or traces of it in history—refers to agency, and it has often been laced with oppositional and restricted positions.

Gender should perhaps not be thought of from rights, legislative or marriage economy perspectives only. Materialist feminism has focused on the centrality of macrostructural concepts of time and an analysis of change and diversity in gender relations, and viewed them as regime-types of changes (McNay 1992). Gender can also be thought of as a temporally regulated constellation of socio-symbolic norms and practices, operating through cultural processes and gendered practices. In addition, the language that seeps through both the materials and the analysis is crucial. Gamber's (1998) analysis takes up the question of language and the gendered nature of the language of business history. Narratives usually express both the objective structures and intentionality of an individual, and are constitutive of a "semantics of action" (Ricoeur 1991, 33).

Even if there is clear division of labour for women and men, gender does not produce this division, nor is the division clear cut, as we saw in the examples. Even historically, business does not merely reflect the stability or prevailing circumstances but actively produces gendered situations, boundary crossings, and oscillating circumstances that we then narrate as historical outcomes or facts based on the historical evidence, traces, and documents. We may ask the question, following partly the logic of Joan Scott, whether we are rereading and reinterpreting the historical traces, materials, and documents through our contemporary understanding, and whether this becomes especially highlighted in the case of business history. Joan Scott (1998) addresses the appropriateness of concepts, and she thought that if business history was devoted to a narrative about progressive development, by definition it must ignore the existence of those arrangements which were messy or unclear, or whether or not the entrepreneurs were women or not.

The epistemic differences between the disciplines do not stop there. History as a discipline has on the one hand been criticised as being a-theoretical, and economics and business economics as disciplines have on the other hand been seen as overly universal (e.g. Decker 2013). As disciplines, both history and economics and a large part of business economics are seen as domains of an objective reality (e.g. White 2005), but this assumption concerning the existence of an objective reality is critiqued also within these disciplines themselves. For example, feminist historians have wanted to establish a history for and of women, by revisiting the invisibility of women in formal history writings, by showing their subjects and emphasising their agentic positions (e.g. Scott 1996).

The concept of historical time has been given many interpretations. The importance of location in relation to gender in a specific time, place, and culture cannot be underlined enough. The understanding of science works here as a brilliant example: In the sixteenth century and even later, science and scientific experiments were carried out in domestic settings. In the domestic setting of the sixteenth century women partook in the science activities and—if not practising it—were close to science, as the history of one of the most renowned English sixteenth-century natural philosopher's, John Dee's, life shows. According to Harkness (1999), John Dee's wife, Jane Fromond Dee, had to ensure that the household was financially balanced for John Dee to practice scientific experiments at home. When science moved from the domestic sphere to universities, which women had no entry to throughout the seventeenth century, it became a male dominated domain. It was the change of location for science from the home to universities, which made women's positions in the scientific work invisible. Yet, as Londa Schiebinger (e.g. 1999), Rossiter (1999), Aldrich Kidwell (1999), and several others have later argued, women did not disappear from scientific work, but worked often on an equal footing, as the lives of the seventeenth-century astronomers describe: women were made responsible for observations and calculations which required great patience and skill (Stamhuis 2002).

Another example of the location, time, and context is the understanding of individual economic agency over time. Trying to define individual agency with a contemporary understanding of "agency" would not necessarily make sense. Here the concept of "husbandry" described below serves a brilliant example of the type of "agency" we can trace back in time. We can ask whether this type of agency is truly considered as an "agency" and whether that concept makes sense when used in historical analyses. An understanding of most concepts used, such as "business ownership" or "self-employment" can only be understood in the context of the position of women overall. This contextualisation of the concepts concerns both history and contemporary worlds.

The question of time extends to questions of gender, agency, and identity of the self—we need to ask the question when in historical time did identity become recognised? Paul Ricoeur offers one way of analysing this question: His conception of the narrative structure of the self refers to temporalised understanding of the self. For a non-historian, this becomes complex and requires some distance from the materials such as empirical traces and remains.

An example of how gender, identity, and agency fall together helps. By examining a widow's household economic activities in sixteenth- and seventeenth-century England and by comparing those activities to the economies of the marital household they shared with their husband, Whittle (2014) and for a later period for Scotland, Catriona MacLeod in this book, find widows as active economic agents, working with forms of work in agriculture, textiles, retailing, and inn- and tavern-keeping. In Whittle's study (2014) money lending was one sign of the position of economic agency, yet derivative of the marital position (also e.g. Laurence, Maltby, and Rutterford 2009). The marital position refers to the marriage economy, which was vital as it determined the opportunities for many women. Money lending was also the only activity that was more common in widows' inventories than the inventories of married men (Whittle 2014). In this economic agency in sixteenth- and seventeenth-century England and later, English Common Law governed the ownership and inheritance of property, defining the position of women in relation to men. In Norse societies women were allowed to conduct business (Göransson 1988). The tendency for separating work from living space did not separate women, or indeed children, from the work was part of the pre-industrialist economic order. This concerns essential elements of women's work, which remained located within the house (Whittle 2011).

Economy, Time, and Gender—Some Closing Remarks

The rewriting and narrating of women into formal history is a process which has developed for a very long time, and establishing women's history in new ways, such as through transforming the way history was written, has brought up new knowledge. The new knowledge has concerned both knowledge of the histories and knowledge of the disciplinary field itself. One aspiration in this rewriting has been the strive to answer the question raised by many historians whether research—be it historical or economic—has finally overcome the idea of history as the story of man's heroism, the affirmation of an exclusive male agency. For its part, this edited volume tries to answer this question.

As a result, many of the "craft-based" skills, such as the methods and materials used within the disciplinary field of history, remain unacknowledged outside the discipline (e.g. Decker, Kipping, and Wadhwhani 2015). Partially resulting from the disciplinary tensions, this chapter seeks to outline some of the important aspects of economic positionality, agency, and time. How to take into account and at the same time overcome these barriers in research (that deals with specific topics, such as gender and business) are crucial questions to address. How can we talk about and conduct research into the phenomenon of "women and business" by expanding the theme over centuries? What is—or could be—the common denominator that expands the mere description of the phenomenon bound to its time and avoids the conflation of the topic of this publication "women and business" into mere "sex" and business into "monetary based exchange relations"?

In her analysis of "housewifery" Ruth Schwartz Cowan (2010) indirectly addresses the difficulty of using historical concepts which have contemporary meanings, when the concepts first emerge, and prior to this did not exist in the first place, and secondly because their contents were not the same in history as they are today. We may ask what actually becomes socially constructed and transformed in the materiality of the history when the concept is not understandable outside and beyond its historicity. For this question, the concept of "housewifery" offers a good example. Schwartz Cowan analyses the etymology of the word "housewifery", which can be traced back to its emergence in the English language in the thirteenth century.

"Housewifery" has a long history as conceptual category in family history. The sexual division of household work such as cooking, sewing, laundry work, and house maintenance, and reproduction rested on women who were wives, daughters, relatives, and slaves, and as persons were not subject to rights and were all inferior to men in the households. It was not until the thirteenth century when the home took on a specific meaning that differed from earlier in relation to work and privacy. Historians have shown us how in the thirteenth century "husbands" worked on the house (hus) which they were bonded to through rent or ownership. In households, usually the wife and husband together took care of the "husbandry" (Schwartz

Cowan relates fourteenth-century "husbandry" closely to what could be called farming today). A husband was thus not the partner of a wife but the governor of the house and land, however small or large it was. As Schwarz Cowan describes, any economic security the wife and husband had, they had achieved by working together, that is, by "husbanding" their resources, be it then land, animals, or other resources (Schwartz Cowan 2010, 84). As concepts, husbandry and housewifery were evolving with the transformation taking place in contents and meanings.

The articulated separation of the two spaces, "home" and "work" over time with the development of the economy and proto- and pre-capitalism led to the differentiation of household husbandry tasks as well: men's work differentiated from household work, and housewifery became rooted in the land and in person, and later to be replaced with the term "housework". As Schwartz Cowan describes, the labour that was called "housewifery" from the thirteenth to the eighteenth century in England was rephrased as "housework" in the nineteenth century.

In a parallel fashion to the development of the market system, gendered property rights and the gendered division of labour developed over time (e.g. Popp 2004). The complexity of intersecting factors, ranging from ideologies and changing relations to state-formation and individual rights and obligations vis á vis the public all have their effects on the understanding of gender and business. Gender and business was and is most often embedded in families and social relations. To what extent, however, do these relations shape the ways of organizing gender and business today? The assumption here is not based on any kind of continuum of changing gender order and changing family business, but on myriads of layers consisting of developing cultures, social relations, processes, and changing institutions. Attempting to reimagine a future (Scott 2011, 33) means that we use critical thinking towards the concepts we use and reinstate their relations. For a long time, women's history served a dual goal: for one, to restore women in history and second to restore our history to women (Kelly-Gadol 1976). The attempt to add women to the prevailing historical knowledge has not been without its tensions, especially when business history is being discussed (e.g. Decker 2013).

Through the etymology of "housewifery" Schwartz Cowan extends her analysis to the changing position of "a woman" in the transition of the economic system towards industrial manufacturing conditions in England. This transition and how women's agency became an asset in the pre-industrial conditions has been described in a detailed manner in the social and intellectual history of economic systems. Using today's concepts to explain past history may disturb the understanding of hierarchies, gendered jobs and work, not to mention the positions and relations of women and men (Schwartz Cowan 2010). The limits of time and limits of narratives refer to the ways in which the ultimate unknowability of time pushes narrative to its limit, as argued by Ricoeur (1991).

Economic history, business history, family history, and gender history are destined to have common ground. Still, it is rather difficult to come up with one common frame of reference when analysing the topic of women and business families over time. This article has not emphasised a single perspective or theoretical lens in the analyses of gender and family businesses either. Rather, the fragmentation of historical time, the uneven development of an economic and market based economy and the pace of development of liberalism, state, citizenship, and individual rights set the frame for the analyses of processes that relate to individual women and "business families". Gendered property rights in Europe were first and foremost social relations based on the household (e.g. Göransson 1993). Households were the basis of economic activity and in Europe especially households and their relationships created the space for the market economy, especially in relation to the early formation of the bourgeoisie. Here the historical development took differing routes in England, France, and Scandinavian countries. During the period when the Swedish bourgeoisie emerged, property rights and control of economic wealth were exclusively for men.

Anita Göransson (1993) has brought up that the idea of the firm was originally modelled on the idea of the household and its social relations. Katrina Honeyman (2000) argues that industrialisation was, in part, a gendering process and gender-made process. These processes were not detached from the structural constraints which in part rendered women an invisible work-force and labour reserve. For women, the development of the market economy was intertwined with the development of citizenship rights. These developments were not smooth processes from the gender perspective. The intersectionalities of social class, uneven wealth accumulation, and the male dependencies of women of different types, whether a daughter, wife, or in other family positions, led to a variety of outcomes where several societal and cultural processes met the development of the market economy.

Joan Scott notes that the history of women in business supplements an existing business history, but she also asks whether it substantially changes it. Scott notes that an effort is incomplete as long as the analysis rests exclusively on the emancipatory impulses of women's history (Scott 1998, 242). What is needed is a re-analysis of history by enlarging our understanding of the scope of women's activities. This is done in the articles of this volume. Joan Scott argues further that one of the key aspects in the analysis of women's business histories is the ability to show the inaccuracy of the notion of women's passivity and of their incapacity for economic activity.

Winding up this chapter on the economy, gender, and time: of these three concepts, the question of time remains the most elusive and prone to reinterpretation, rereading, and even misunderstanding. Historical time—which for the layperson at a glance appears unproblematic—has proved to be most difficult to define even by historians. For example Browne (2014) suggests that historical time should be understood as lived and polytemporal. She is not alone in her thinking but follows Ricoeur's, Koselleck's, and

Butler's thinking of time, just to mention a few influences from philosophy. These all seek to develop non-linear conceptions of historical time. Multiple configurations of time: narrated time, calendar time, and generational time (Browne 2014, 4), all for their part aim to reconceptualize historical time. The different layers of time become one in many of the studies. Yet, time, according to Browne, is experienced and constructed through social practices and temporalities. This idea also underlines the outcome of this article: there is not one economy, nor gender or time, but many and they are multivocal. By showing that women participated in business and that the activity was empowering for most of these women, the analysis of women and business has achieved its aims: the rewriting of business history and economic history.

Note

1 Some rather ahistorical assumptions of liberalism in relation to individuality and gender would require critical analysis but due to lack of space are not elaborated here in any greater detail.

References

Abbott, A. 2016. *Processual sociology*. Chicago: University of Chicago Press.

Acker, J. 2004. "Gender, Capitalism and Globalization." *Critical Sociology* 30 (7): 19–37.

Ågren, M., and A. L. Erickson. 2005. "Introduction." In *The Marital Economy in Scandinavia and Britain, 1400–1900*, edited by M. Ågren and A. L. Erickson. Aldershot: Ashgate.

Aldrich Kidwell, P. 1999. "Women Astronomers in Britain, 1780–1930." In *History of Women in the Sciences*, edited by S. G. Kohlstedt. Chicago: University of Chicago Press.

Allen, S., and C. Truman. 1992. "Women, Business and Self-Employment: A Conceptual Minefield." In *Women and Working Lives*, edited by S. Arber and N. Gilbert. London: Palgrave Macmillan.

Autio, E., M. Kenney, P. Mustard, D. Siegele, and M. Wright. 2014. "Entrepreneurial Innovation: The Importance of Context." *Research Policy*, no. 43, 1097–1108.

Barker, H. 2006. *The Business of Women*. Oxford: Oxford University Press.

Barnett, H. 1996. *Sourcebook on Feminist Jurisprudence*. London: Routledge Cavendish.

Browne, V. 2014. *Feminism, Time and Non-Linear History*. New York: Palgrave Macmillan.

Calhoun, C. 1983. "Habitus, Field and Capital: The Question of Historical Specificity." In *Bourdieu: Critical Perspectives*, edited by C. Calhoun, E. LiPuma, and M. Postone. Cambridge: Polity Press.

Casson, M. 1982. *The Entrepreneur: An Economic Theory*. New York: Rowman & Littlefield.

Castoriadis, C. 1987. *The Imaginary Institution of Society*. Cambridge: Polity Press.

Chandler, A. D. 1990. *Scale and Scope*. Cambridge, MA: Harvard University Press.

Coontz, S. 2000. “Historical Perspectives on Family Studies.” *Journal of Marriage and Family* 62 (2): 283–297.

Cornell, D. 1992. *The Philosophy of the Limit*. London: Routledge.

Decker, S. 2013. “The Silence of the Archives: Business History, Post-Colonialism and Archival Ethnography.” *Management & Organizational History* 8 (2): 155–173.

Decker, S., M. Kipping, and R. D. Wadhwani. 2015. “New Business Histories! Plurality in Business History Research Methods.” *Business History* 57 (1): 30–40.

Down, S. 2001. “Knowledge Sharing Review: The Use of History in Business and Management, and Some Implications for Management Learning.” *Management Learning* 32 (3): 393–410.

Dyer, W. Gibb, Jr., and W. Handler. 1994. “Entrepreneurship and Family Business: Exploring the Connections.” *Entrepreneurship, Theory and Practice* 19:71–83.

Erickson, A. L. 1993. *Women and Property in Early Modern England*. London: Routledge.

Erickson, A. L. 2005. “The Marital Economy in Comparative Perspective.” In *The Marital economy in Scandinavia and Britain, 1400–1900*, edited by M. Ågren and A. L. Erickson. Aldershot: Ashgate.

Fellman, S., and A. Popp. 2013. “Lost in the Archive: The Business Historian in Distress.” In *Coping with Excess: How Organizations, Communities and Individuals Manage Overflows*, edited by B. Czarniawska and O. Löfgren, 216–243. Cheltenham: Edward Elgar.

Gamber, W. 1997. *The Female Economy: The Millinery and Dressmaking Trades 1860–1930*. Urbana: University of Illinois Press.

Gamber, W. 1998. “A Gendered Enterprise: Placing Nineteenth-Century Businesswomen in History.” *The Business History Review* 72 (2): 188–217.

Goodman, J. 2010. "Editorial: History as Creative Writing.” *Rethinking History* 14 (1): 1–3.

Göransson, A. 1988. *Från familj till fabrik: Teknik, arbetsdelning och skiktning i svenska fabriker 1830–77*. Lund: Lunds universitet.

Göransson, A. 1993. “Gender and Property Rights: Capital, Kin, and Owner Influences in Nineteenth- and Twentieth-Century Sweden.” *Business History* 35 (2): 11–32.

Hanawalt, B. 1999. “Women and the Household Economy in the Preindustrial Period: An Assessment of Women, Work, and Family.” *Journal of Women's History* 11 (3): 10–16.

Hansen, P. 2012. “Business History: A Cultural and Narrative Approach.” *Business History Review* 86 (4): 693–717.

Harkness, D. E. 1999. “Managing an Experimental Household: The Dees of Mortlake and the Practice of Natural Philosophy.” In *History of Women in the Sciences*, edited by S. G. Kohlstedt. Chicago: University of Chicago Press.

Hartigan-O'Connor, E. 2009. *The Ties That Buy: Women and Commerce in Revolutionary America*. Philadelphia: University of Pennsylvania Press.

Hartmann, H. 2010. “Capitalism, Patriarchy, and Job Segregation by Sex.” In *Global Perspectives on Gender & Work: Readings and Interpretations*, edited by J. Goodman, 54–66. Lanham and Boulder: Rowman & Littlefield Publishers Ltd.

Honeyman, K. 2000. *Women, Gender and Industrialization in England, 1700–1870*. Basingstoke: Palgrave Macmillan.

Jacobs, J. A., and K. Gerson. 2005. *The Time Divide: Work, Family, and Gender Inequality*. Cambridge, MA: Harvard University Press.

Jones, G., and J. Zeitlin. 2008. "Introduction." In *The Oxford Handbook of Business History*, edited by G. Jones and J. Zeitlin, 1–8. Oxford: Oxford University Press.

Jones, J. 2010. "Black Women, Work, and the Family under Slavery." In *Global Perspectives on Gender & Work: Readings and Interpretations*, edited by J. Goodman, 92–105. Lanham and Boulder: Rowman & Littlefield Publishers Ltd.

Jong, A. de, and D. Higgins. 2015. "New Business History?" *Business History* 57 (1): 1–4.

Kelly-Gadol, J. 1976. "The Social Relations of the Sexes: Methodological Implications of Women's History." *Signs* 1 (4): 809–823.

Kerber, L. K. 1980. *Women of the Republic: Intellect and Ideology in Revolutionary America*. Chapel Hill: University of North Carolina Press.

Kerber, L. K. 1988. "Separate Spheres, Female Worlds, Woman's Place: The Rhetoric of Women's History." *Journal of American History* 75 (June): 9–39.

Kovalainen, A. 1993. *At the Margins of the Economy: Women's Self-Employment in Finland, 1960–1990*. Ashgate: Avebury.

Kwolek-Folland, A. 1998. *Incorporating Women: A History of Women and Business in the United States*. New York: Twayne.

Laurence, A., J. Maltby, and J. Rutterford. 2009. "Introduction." In *Women and Their Money 1700–1950: Essays on Women and Finance*, edited by A. Laurence, J. Maltby, and J. Rutterford. London and New York: Routledge.

Lomax, R. 2017. "Self-Employment: A View from the Inside." *Transfer* 23 (3): 367–369.

Lorber, J. 2010. "Night to His Day: The Social Construction of Gender." In *Global Perspectives on Gender & Work: Readings and Interpretations*, edited by J. Goodman, 15–32. Lanham and Boulder: Rowman & Littlefield Publishers Inc.

Lundmark, L. 1993. "The Historian's Time." *Time & Society* 2 (1): 61–74.

McNay, L. 1992. *Foucault and Feminism: Power, Gender and the Self*. Cambridge: Polity Press.

McNay, L. 2000. *Gender and Agency: Reconfiguring the Subject in Feminist and Social Theory*. Cambridge: Polity Press.

Milkman, R. 1986. "Women's History and the Sears Case." *Feminist Studies* 12 (2): 375–400.

Mill, J. S. 1984. "The Subjection of Women." In *The Collected Works of John Stuart Mill, vol. 21: Essays on Equality, Law and Education*, edited by J. M. Robson. Toronto: University of Toronto Press.

Moring, B. 2016. "North European Families in the Past: Family Ties Revisited." In *The History of Families and Households: Comparative European Dimensions*, edited by S. Sovic, P. Thane, and P. Viazzo, 23–46. Leiden: Brill.

Mullin, K. 2016. "Feminism and Women's Work, 1776–1928." In *Routledge Historical Resources: History of Feminism*. www.routledgehistoricalresources.com/feminism/essays/feminism-and-womens-work-1776-1928.

Perriton, L. 2017. "The Parochial Realm, Social Enterprise and Gender: The Work of Catharine Cappe and Faith Gray and Others in York, 1780–1820." *Business History* 59 (2): 202–230.

Popp, A. 2004. "British Business History: A Review of the Periodical Literature for 2002." *Business History* 46 (2): 155–170.

Popp, A., and S. Fellman. 2017. "Writing Business History: Creating Narratives." *Business History* 59 (8): 1242–1260.

Pylkkänen, A. 1990. *Puoli vuodetta, lukot ja avaimet. Nainen ja maalaistalous oikeuskäytännön valossa 1660–1710* [*Half the bed, locks and keys: Woman and household economy in the light of legal practice 1660–1710*]. Helsinki: Lakimiesliiton kustannus.

Pylkkänen, A. 2005. "Forming the Marital Economy in the Early Modern Finnish Countryside." In *The Marital Economy in Scandinavia and Britain, 1400–1900*, edited by M. Ågren and A. L. Erickson. Aldershot: Ashgate.

Rappoport, J. 2012. *Giving Women: Alliance and Exchange in Victorian Culture*. Oxford: Oxford University Press.

Ricoeur, P. 1988. *Time and Narrative*. Chicago, IL: University of Chicago Press.

Ricoeur, P. 1991. *From Text to Action: Essays in Hermeneutics, II*. London: Northwestern University Press.

Robb, G. 2016. "Enterprising Women." *Journal of Women's History* 28 (1): 166–171.

Robbins, R. 2016. "A Woman's Work Is Never Done? Women and Leisure in the Nineteenth Century and Beyond." In *Routledge Historical Resources: History of Feminism*. www.routledgehistoricalresources.com/feminism/

Roberts, M. 2005. "Recovering a Lost Inheritance: The Marital Economy and Its Absence from the Prehistory of Economics in Britain." In *The Marital Economy in Scandinavia and Britain, 1400–1900*, edited by M. Ågren and A. L. Erickson. Aldershot: Ashgate.

Rossiter, M. 1999. "Women's Work in Science, 1880–1910." In *History of Women in the Sciences*, edited by S. G. Kohlstedt. Chicago: University of Chicago Press.

Schiebinger, L. 1999. "Maria Winkelmann at the Berlin Academy: A Turning Point for Women in Science." In *History of Women in the Sciences*, edited by S. G. Kohlstedt. Chicago: University of Chicago Press.

Schwartz Cowan, R. 2010. "Housewifery: Household Work and Household Tools Under Pre-Industrial Conditions." In *Global Perspectives on Gender & Work: Readings and Interpretations*, edited by J. Goodman, 84–92. Lanham and Boulder: Rowman & Littlefield Publishers Ltd.

Scott, J. W. 1996. *Feminism and History. Oxford Readings in Feminism*. New York: Oxford University Press.

Scott, J. W. 1998. "Comment: Conceptualizing Gender in American Business History." *Business History Review* 72 (2): 242–249.

Scott, J. W. 2011. *The Fantasy of Feminist History*. Durham, NC: Duke University.

Scott, J. W., and L. A. Tilly. 2010. "Women's Work and the Family in Nineteenth-Century Europe." In *Global Perspectives on Gender & Work: Readings and Interpretations*, edited by J. Goodman. Lanham and Boulder: Rowman & Littlefield Publishers Ltd.

Sovic, S., P. Thane, and P. Viazzo. 2016. "The History of European Families: Old and New Directions." In *The History of Families and Households: Comparative European Dimensions*, edited by S. Sovic, P. Thane, and P. Viazzo, 1–22. Leiden: Brill.

Stamhuis, I. 2002. "Sally Gregory Kohlstedt: History of Women in the Sciences." *Minerva* 40: 211–213.

Starr, P. 2007. "Why Liberalism Works." *American Prospect* (April): 34–40.

Stott, A. 2011. *Europe 1700–1944: A Continent transformed* (weblog). http://europetransformed.blogspot.fi/
Tweedale, G. 2013. "Backstreet Capitalism: An Analysis of the Family Firm in the Nineteenth-Century Sheffield Cutlery Industry." *Business History* 55 (6): 875–891.
Walby, S. 1988. *Patriarchy at Work*. London: Wiley-Blackwell.
White, H. 2005. "Introduction: Historical Fiction, Fictional History and Historical Reality." *Rethinking History* 9 (2–3): 147–157.
Whittle, J. 2011. "The House as a Place of Work in Early Modern Rural England." *Home Cultures* 8 (2): 133–150.
Whittle, J. 2014. "Enterprising Widows and Active Wives: Women's Unpaid Work in the Household Economy of Early Modern England." *The History of the Family* 19 (3): 283–300.
Wright, W. D. 2002. *Black History and Black Identity: A Call for a New Historiography*. Westport, CT: Praeger.
Young, R. J. C. 2003. *Postcolonialism*. Oxford: Oxford University Press.

Section I

Challenging the Heroic Male Image of Entrepreneurs

3 Tough Times, Tough Measures

Widows as Heroic Entrepreneurs

Anu Lahtinen

Introduction

The classic image of an entrepreneur is essentially that of a modern Western man. There has been talk about entrepreneurial personality, someone who is ready to embrace risks, change, and constant growth (Chell 2008, 96–97, 107–109; Bijedic et al. 2007, 61; Sardeshmukh and Smith 2016, 130). The entrepreneur is defined as a person who recognises an opportunity and seizes it successfully. A heroic modern individual, unchained by any human relations or class divides, has been set as a model for entrepreneurs and pioneers of innovation (see e.g. Weightman 2008, 383–393). As Elizabeth Chell (2008, 260) puts it, for example: "A small business owner who does not engage in the process of opportunity recognition, formation and exploitation is not an entrepreneur". However, Chell goes further to point out that an entrepreneur cannot thrive with personal talents only. The socio-economic conditions should also be taken into account.

The idea of a heroic individual risks leading to assumptions that the "entrepreneurial personality" is an inborn ability, and thus, given the imbedded assumption of a male entrepreneur, something that most women are not born with. This approach ignores the social influence that plays a part in the making of an entrepreneur (Chell 2008, 205). For many time periods, women have been allowed a rather limited access to resources, education, and financial support that ultimately help a person to become a successful entrepreneur (Sardeshmukh and Smith 2016, 130). However, as Chell has pointed out in her comprehensive research on the making of the entrepreneurial personality, the agency of an entrepreneur is formed in interaction with a special socio-economic context, and social learning is important in the process of becoming an entrepreneur (Chell 2008, 244–267). In order to understand entrepreneurship, it is important though challenging to try to analyse both the role of individual agency and the significance of societal conditions.

When we take a look at the past societies, the significance of socio-economic conditions may become more visible. As many researchers have pointed out, social contacts and family relations were recognised as part and parcel of early modern business. Any business was heavily dependent on social relations, family relations, notions of cooperation, and reciprocity (Kooijmans 1997). Looking at successful female entrepreneurs in an early modern setting may help to understand the origins of the Western business world and the continuities in gender relations there.

In this chapter, I analyse the entrepreneurship of two early modern women, Valborg Innama (Finland, then part of the Swedish realm, b. before 1540, d. ca. 1602) and Kenau Hasselaer (the Netherlands, 1526–1588) as entrepreneurs.[1] I have chosen two merchant women who were active in separate countries in order to make visible some striking similarities in their lives. My starting point is that despite the geographical distance, the lives and businesses of these two women come quite close to each other and can be used to reflect the patterns of early modern (female) entrepreneurship. I have consciously chosen two women who can be considered to have been entrepreneurs in the same sense that Elizabeth Chell gives the term, two widows seizing opportunities that came their way. At the same time, I want to put emphasis on the special conditions that made their careers possible and the obstacles that they met.

In the latter part of the sixteenth century, the Finnish town of Turku (Sw. *Åbo*), then part of the Swedish Realm like most of the present day Finland, saw the rise of the Innama trading house, in the hands of Henrik Innama and later his widow Valborg Innama (b. before 1540, d. ca. 1602).[2] At approximately the same period, in Haarlem and Arnemuiden, the Netherlands, a merchant's widow Kenau Hasselaer made a special career, too, as a shipbuilder, merchant, and a Weighing House Master and Collector of Peat (Dutch *waagmeester en collecteur van de impost op turf*).[3] Both of these women, Valborg and Kenau, have made their way into history as economic survivors of the deaths of their husbands and also of the warfare and political unrest of their time. They both had a posthumous reputation that has partly overshadowed what they actually did or did not achieve during their lifetime (see e.g. Kurtz 1956, 5–6, 13–41; Kloek 2001, 77–85).

First, I will briefly present the context and lives of these two women. Second, I will discuss the business approach of Valborg Innama and Kenau Hasselaer, their entrepreneurial space of action, and the socio-economic situation in which they pursued their careers. Using the above-mentioned analysis by Elizabeth Chell, I am going to discuss what kind of opportunities these women needed to perceive and seize in order to be successful. In this context, I will pay attention to whether Valborg and Kenau were playing down their gender or whether they chose to follow patterns that were considered female. I will discuss the conditions of entrepreneurship in early modern Northern Europe in general and in the context of gender, and how these women and their businesses were reacted to by their contemporaries or interpreted by later observers.

Life Courses of Valborg and Kenau

Valborg and the Innama Trading House

It is a long-term phenomenon that women's success in business often, though not always, tends to depend on her family relations. Thus, it is unlikely that anything would have been heard of Valborg Innama had she not married the merchant Henrik Innama (d. 1563). It seems to have been Henrik who started the Innama trading house, and at some point, in the late 1550s, a woman probably in her late teens, Valborg Eriksdotter, was married to him. It is very likely that Valborg's family was in business; however, information about her parents and grandparents is lost to the present-day world (Oja 1937, 94–95).

The 1560s was a lively period in the town of Turku. With a couple of thousand inhabitants, Turku was a relatively small town on the European scale; however, it was a big town and port of import on the Swedish scale. Turku was the capital of a large bishopric as well as the center of the Duchy of Duke John (Johan, later King John III, 1537–1592), second son of the then ruling King Gustavus I. From the year 1556 to the year 1563, Duke John's presence boosted economic activity and trade both in the town and in the Turku Castle, situated near the town (for the general development, see e.g. Lavery 2006, 38–41). The Innama trading house enjoyed the benefits of this situation; moreover, in 1562, Henrik Innama was the ship master of the vessel *Ursus Finlandicus* that took Duke John from Turku to the Polish-Lithuanian state when he went to arrange his marriage to the Princess Catharina Jagellonica (Oja 1937, 94–95).

Soon, however, the whole kingdom, and Turku especially, got involved in the turbulent power struggle between the sons of King Gustavus I, who had died in 1560. The eldest son and heir to the throne, Erik XIV (1533–1577), got into a political conflict with his brother, Duke John. Very soon the conflict escalated into warfare. In 1563, the town and castle of Turku were conquered by the troops of King Erik, the properties of his supporters were confiscated, and Duke John and his wife were taken away as prisoners. Many supporters of Duke John were beheaded, and it seems that Henrik Innama was among them (Lavery 2006, 41–42).

After the death of her husband, Valborg Innama was considered a widow of a traitor to the King, and she and her property were treated accordingly. Supporters of King Erik XIV confiscated valuables from the storehouses, from jewelry to saddles and food, and they even took over the residence and trade house. Even after the first shock was over and the troops of Erik had left, times were difficult for trade. Erik XIV had launched wars against Denmark, Lübeck, and the Polish-Lithuanian state, and this meant that the Southern Baltic Sea was not very safe for trade ships. Because of the last-mentioned war, Innama's ship and its cargo were confiscated by the Council of Danzig, which left Valborg with many troubles.[4]

Nevertheless, Valborg managed go on with trade, and she also continued doing business with the Crown. It appears that she received help from some noble persons, and because of warfare and growing state administration, services of shippers and merchants like Valborg were needed. Also, there is no doubt that she saw an opportunity and seized it with verocity. Already in the 1560s, Valborg was mentioned as providing spirits to Russian diplomats staying in Turku. In 1567, she was shipping bread, vinegar, and iron to Stockholm in the service of the Crown.[5]

Business opportunities brightened up in 1568, when King Erik XIV was dethroned and the old acquaintance of Valborg Innama, Duke John, was crowned as King John III. Now Valborg got a real chance to get back the property that had been confiscated from her, and she now had a direct connection to the ruler who remembered Valborg and her husband well from his time in Turku. Valborg now could trust that the King would personally send orders to protect her property and reimburse to her what she had lost. From the 1570s onwards, the Innama Trading House grew above all others, and—which is very exceptional—Valborg kept the reins of the business despite remarrying three times: first with merchant Peder Ingevadsson (1567–1571), then with merchant Olof Karlsson (1572–1578 . . . 1583), and finally, a ship master, Lukas Larsson (1592–1604). With Henrik Innama, Valborg had two daughters and possibly a son. After her death, the Innama trading house was inherited by her nephew, merchant Bertil Tomasson Innama (Oja 1937, 96–101).

It was not unheard of for a woman to take care of a trading house as a widow—at least for a while. As the early modern household work and family business were closely intertwined, it may have been more natural for a woman to become a merchant as part of the family business, to step from the helper's position to the head of the house (Oja 1937, 110). There was a handful of merchant widows active in Turku at the time, but none of them as wealthy and powerful as Valborg Innama, and none of them active after having remarried. Valborg, however, expressed consciousness of her own worth and knowledge, and went on with her business. In a letter from 1577, she dismissed some debtors who tried to settle their debts with her apparently meeker husband (Olaf Karlsson).[6] Valborg had a lot of quarrels and court cases, which, it must be emphasised, was not exceptional for any merchant of the time. Some she lost, others she won. She also complained that she had been ill-treated by both the servants of the nobility and the men at the Town Council, and that the men at the Council had crossed themselves after her and prayed that they would never see her again (Oja 1937, 100–101).

Valborg Innama kept the business in her own hands, travelled to meet the King and to the faraway market places, and she was exceptional with her interest in international and domestic trade. It appears that she wanted to seize every opportunity imaginable, and the turbulent times offered much to invest in. King John III soon launched a war against Russia, a twenty-five-year war that would last most of his reign. Although the warfare caused calamities, too, and some coastal areas were burnt by Russian troops, the war was profitable for the merchants as they now had calm trade waters southwest, and they could buy and import property from overseas to make fortunes by selling and lending the Crown victuals, equipment, and money (Oja 1937, 96–107).

Kenau the Shipbuilder

At approximately the same time, another widow was active in Haarlem, the Netherlands. She was Kenau Hasselaer, daughter of the Haarlem brewer Simon Gerritszoon Gerrits and Guerte Coenendochter Hasselaer, who had become a widow after her husband, Nanning Gerbrandszoon Borst, died ca. 1562. She was a mother of four (Guerte, Margriet, Lubbrich, and Gerbrand). Several of Kenau's brothers were shipbuilders with connections to England and Scandinavia; one was also active in early soap manufacturing. One of Kenau's sisters was married to Hadrianus Junius (1511–1575), who was a physician, classical scholar, and rector at a Latin school in Haarlem.[7] Thus, family connections paved the way for future activities and certainly provided Kenau, as well as Valborg, with social learning and tacit knowledge, often considered crucial for successful entrepreneurship (about social learning and tacit knowledge see e.g. Chell 2008, 258–261).

From the 1560s to 1580s, Kenau Hasselaer was active as a merchant widow in Haarlem and other towns nearby, focusing on shipbuilding, wood trade (from Norway), and the expanding grain trade (in the Baltic Sea Region). She made a point in referring to herself as a "shipbuilderess" (Dutch *scheepmaeckster*), not merely a widow of a shipbuilder, between 1562–1571. This activity was not unheard of for a widow in a Dutch merchant town; however, her self-consciousness was remarkable, as well as the fact that she was active in reshaping the business (Kloek 2001, 55–59; 2014, 162–164).

Most famously, Kenau Hasselaer was allegedly active in organizing female fighters against the Spanish invaders. She had been carrying on business for ten years when the Dutch provinces revolted against the rule of Philip II of Spain. Together with other townspeople, Kenau experienced the hard times of the siege of Haarlem from December 1572 until July 1573 when the city surrendered to the Spanish troops. In the first literary accounts, she was given credit for her contribution in building the defense line for the city. The story soon grew to depict her as a brave female soldier with a manly heart, leading 300 women to fight against the Spanish troops (about the representations of Kenau and the siege of Harlem, see Kloek 2001, 7–54; 2014, 165–166, 180–196).

Contemporary archival sources, however, are more contradictory and fail to prove the romantic heroism of Kenau. In the surviving court records and other administrative accounts, Kenau is not mentioned as fighting against the Spanish troops. What is admitted, however, is that she had provided the city of Haarlem with wood that had never been paid for and had to fight for the payment as late as the year 1585. It was only after her presumed death that her daughters received reimbursement for this investment. Kenau never referred to a military action, only pointed out that "as a good patriot I have sustained this town against the enemy".[8] It seems, however, that Kenau's own hometown was somehow very resentful of her.

Her family connections helped Kenau in troubled times. Her brother-in-law, Hadrianus Junius, and the business connections of siblings seemed to pave the way for future enterprises, for example, the expanding grain trade, a business that was a source of wealth for the Dutch trade during the late medieval and early modern period (about the grain trade, see van Tielhof 2002, 42–47). Through the grain trade, she also heard of a position available in Arnemuiden, and in 1574, she was appointed to be the Weighing House Master and Collector of Peat in the city of Arnemuiden. This position was a very exceptional one for a woman at the time, and it has been speculated whether it was actually a compensation for some kind of decisive action during the siege of Haarlem. At first, her appointment was not appreciated by the administration of the town: The position was confirmed by the higher administration, William of Orange (*Willem van Oranje*) and the States of Holland (a representation of two estates to the Court of the Count of Holland), not by the local institutions (about Kenau after the siege of Harlem, see Kloek 2001, 65; 2014, 167).

Like the merchants of her time, Kenau was active in taking her cases to court, and she could be a relentless dun. Several of her debtors got into heated quarrels with her, and words like "witch" (Dutch *tovenaerster*) were hurled at her. She remained a widow, defending her rights at the court by herself, while some of her female antagonists communicated through the representation of their husbands (Kloek 2001, 59–70). Kenau was not a docile person and may have been more quarrelsome than some others. Even her own son, after her death, complained that his mother and sisters were dangerous company for all men, and that men who had been close to them had died rather early. Clearly, her contemporaries often found her a nuisance, and instead of presenting her as a heroic female fighter among her neighbours, they depicted her as more or less a witch (Kloek 2001, 68).

Court cases and other disputes aside, Kenau continued to expand her business network, and when she returned to Haarlem in the late 1570s, she bought a ship for her wood trade, making some five trips a year to Norway. However, unforeseen obstacles drove her business ashore. The captain of her ship was taken hostage, and when Kenau left for Norway in 1588 to clear up the situation, she disappeared. Moreover, her ship was later identified as having been for sale in Flensburg, a port that was notorious of markets for deserted and robbed ships. It seems, then, that Kenau died in the hands of pirates, unless—as some suspected—she decided to vanish from her debtors and start a new life elsewhere (Kurtz 1956, 61–62; Kloek 2001, 72).

Valborg and Kenau as Entrepreneurs

Many depictions of Valborg and Kenau are gendered. Researcher Aulis Oja, writing in the literary style of the 1930s, has described Valborg Innama as "a self-confident and energetic Renaissance woman, the type we don't meet in medieval times or later centuries".[9] Kenau, for her part, was described as a witch and a shrew, and her first name has a meaning equaling the word "shrew" (Dutch *kenau*).[10] But what if we consider Valborg and Kenau as entrepreneurs, that is, persons capable of perceiving and successfully pursuing economic opportunities?

Although the economic conditions were different in Turku, Sweden, and Haarlem/Arnemuiden, the Netherlands, the paths taken by these two sixteenth-century women bear many similarities. The most striking thing is that they stand out at all. Valborg and Kenau were living in a period and a society where women were often told to stand by their husbands and maybe act as their substitutes. While researchers have, during the latest centuries, pointed out the fact that women were active in crafts and trade, it is likewise clear that many of these women were merely earning "a bitter living", with focus on such business as textiles, clothing, and food that were close to their typical fields of expertise in an early modern household and even afterwards (see e.g. Vainio-Korhonen 2002; Ogilvie 2003; van den Heuvel 2007).

The business activities of Valborg and Kenau were different from this pattern. Both Valborg's and Kenau's shipbuilding and overseas trade exceeded the contemporary standards of their time. Hardly anyone was expecting female merchants to make such economic investments and initiatives that they decided to undertake. Even if Dutch tradeswomen were praised by travelers in the later early modern centuries, in the sixteenth century women in Dutch international trade were few and far between. The situation would change in the following centuries, when Amsterdam became a central city for international trade, and although the amount of women tended to decline when the scale of the enterprise increased, the later centuries saw more opportunities for women in international trade (see van den Heuvel 2007, 223–265, 268). Valborg and Kenau, however, had to cope with a rather hostile and rough environment.

How precisely did they see and seize their opportunities? As documents are scarce and often short and pithy, no comprehensive analysis is possible. However, what can be observed is the fact that both Valborg and Kenau used their legal status as widows close to the maximum. In the early modern period, all members of a merchant household participated in the business in one way or another. Consequently, when the head of a merchant house died or travelled far away, the spouse would sometimes take care of the business, make it thrive, or at least attend to it before passing it over to the next generation. This, for women, meant that there was a totally proper way of entering the business on the side of their husbands, especially as widows, and occasionally taking the business beyond what had been accomplished by their late spouses. However, in a large scale trade married women seldom ran an enterprise in their own name, even if they were engaged in the business of the family (van den Heuvel 2007, 274).

Being a widow was almost a condition for certain business opportunities opening up for a woman in the sixteenth century. However, it must be stressed that in the cases of Valborg and Kenau, continuing and expanding the business implied that personal initiative was attempted and achieved by only a few women. For many women, widowhood was more likely to offer economic problems rather than investment possibilities. One could say that a certain kind of entrepreneurial personality was needed, supported by the socio-economic environment of the persons in question. Instead of making investments in international trade, many poor widows were merely forced to work or carry on petty business to earn their "bitter living". Thus, for the success of Valborg and Kenau, family background was definitely an important asset. When the first husband of Valborg died, she inherited the existing trade connections and was ready to use them for her own business. Likewise, as was seen beforehand, Kenau Hasselaer benefited from her family connections, even if some family relations were strained.

A widow's expanded legal space of action was most often seen as a temporary arrangement; however, some women clearly saw an opportunity to carry on with their own business for a long period. That Valborg kept the Innama trading house in her own hands, even after she had remarried, may have been legally justified as the Swedish town law allowed a widow to manage the inheritance of her children, regardless of whether she took a new husband or not. Obviously, the trading house was the inheritance of Valborg's children, and stepfathers were not expected to have a say on that property. However, there are not often signs of women seizing this legal opportunity.[11]

Another opportunity that both Kenau and Valborg seem to have seized successfully was making allies with authorities on a higher level than that of their hometowns. This becomes clear if one takes a look at the local disputes that these women got involved in. As previously mentioned, Kenau Hasselaer was at first not accepted as a Weighing House Master and Collector of Peat in Arnemuiden; William of Orange and the States of Holland had to interfere. Women were usually not accepted in administrative positions or councils. Even in other trade organisations such as guilds the rules and practices tended to favour male networks (van den Heuvel 2007, 271–273). Women had to resort to roundabout methods such as the special favor of a ruler or an organisation on a higher level. It seems that in some cases, women could abandon the resentful local community and ally themselves with the ruler for mutual benefit.

Likewise, it is very clear that Valborg Innama had problems fitting in among the male merchants, and her business was rather brutally vandalised several times. She complained that she had been ill-treated by both servants of a nobleman and the men at the Town Council, and that the men of the

Council had crossed themselves after her and prayed that they would never see her again. However, by supplying the troops of the King, she made herself practically indispensable to the Crown. As a creditor of the Crown, she accumulated her wealth as she was given estates as mortgage, even exemption from taxes. The King was rather docile in his actions and choice of words with Valborg, even when he wished that Valborg would give up some mortgaged property that she had received for the loans that she had given to the ruler. While King John III gave favours to the fourth husband of Valborg, it was explicitly stated that it was because of the help that his wife, Valborg, had given to the Crown (Oja 1937, 105–106). While it was relatively common that women were given favours for the services their husbands had made to their ruler, it was very exceptional that the reverse would happen (Lahtinen 2009, under "Sin makes efterleverska").

In the discussion above, it has been shown that gender, gendered expectations, and legal ramifications played a role in the lives of Kenau and Valborg. But did they themselves comment on the situation? In their own words (or in words formulated by scribes), Valborg or Kenau did not seem to put much emphasis on their womanhood; rather, they applied concepts and expressions that brought them closer to their male contemporaries. Thus, as discussed previously, Kenau referred to herself as the "good patriot", even though she never presented herself as a military hero (and most likely was not one). Valborg also presented herself as the head of the trading house, who did not approve negotiations pursued by her husband and her debtors behind her back. Some exceptions have to be pointed out, though: In her letters to the King, she occasionally used the common rhetoric of a woman in distress. When necessary, she could also refer to herself as a poor, helpless woman—thus appealing to the royal oath, the fact that the King had promised to protect widows and wives who would otherwise be considered as feeble and helpless.[12]

Valborg seems to have considered her third husband as "too soft" or ignorant of the business in contrast to herself. As creditors and duns, then, these two women seem to have been equally relentless and were considered such by others. Here, they seem to have partly run into a problem in combining the expectations related to business and gender. However, Valborg and Kenau were not afraid to embrace the ethos of the sixteenth-century business person. In taking over the business, social learning and tacit knowledge must have been crucial for them, as they hardly had any formal training (Chell 2008, 258–261). When looking for models, they had mostly examples of male businessmen to resort to. Their attitude may have been similar to that of Marie Hackman, discussed by Ulla Ijäs in this volume.

One can further suspect that approaches possibly acquired from male entrepreneurs but presented by a woman may have caused special irritation, which could explain some of the aggressive responses from town councils and debtors. On the other hand, it must be remembered that the later part of the sixteenth century was very violent both in Sweden and in the Netherlands, and that both the businesswomen and their male contemporaries had to learn to deal and cope with very uncertain economic and political circumstances, often under a constant fear of imminent warfare.

Conclusions

If one takes a look at the business world of the past, one can see both continuities and important changes over the centuries. One clear continuity is that even in past centuries, the options for doing business were more likely to be in male hands, while women often focused on petty trade or worked for their families. As is true even for later centuries, too, being born into a business family was a crucial factor that paved the way for women in business. This phenomenon has its roots in premodern history, in the times when most businesses were family businesses. The lives of Valborg Innama and Kenau Hasselaer show that the pattern was similar in trading families in Sweden and the Netherlands.

While at first thought, observing two widows coming from different countries might seem far-fetched, it is interesting to note that Valborg Innama and Kenau Hasselaer actually followed relatively similar paths in their respective surroundings. They made the most of their position as widows, whom Amy Froide (1999, 243–245) has sometimes referred to as "deputy husbands", seizing an opportunity that would almost never otherwise open up for an unmarried woman, an opportunity that not even all widows would be interested in or able to pursue.

As previous family relations and business contacts also paved the way for Valborg and Kenau, it must be emphasised that their accomplishments were not due to their individual traits only. However, both took the trade beyond the more typical short-time administrative period before passing it over to their children. While this agency was not totally unexpected, one can also see from the reactions of their community that while Valborg and Kenau were held in high esteem on the state level, many neighbours clearly saw them as troublemakers crossing the border of what was considered acceptable.

To some extent, the problems faced by Valborg and Kenau echo present day observations that women entering the business world face a double challenge. They may be presumed to fail by definition because of their gender, and if they actually embrace the model of an individual entrepreneur, they may be seen as misfits because their activities do not fit gendered expectations. Given the societal expectations and limited resources allotted to many women, it seems that a special entrepreneurial attitude, capable of seizing opportunities, was needed in order to make these women the unexpected heroic entrepreneurs of their time. The obstacles that they faced may also help to reveal the long continuities in business culture that tends to turn a blind eye to female entrepreneurs.

Notes

1 Early modern name forms have typically varied from one period and one scribe to another. In sources, Valborg Innama is often referred to "Valborg of Innama" (Sw. *Valborg Innamas*) and sometimes historians have used the Finnish name form "Valpuri Innamaa"; however, Valborg was most likely part of the Swedish speaking merchant group and all the sources are written in Swedish. Likewise, Kenau has also been referred to as "Kenu". Here I have used the name forms that seem best to fit the international readership, the Swedish form Valborg Innama and the Dutch modern form Kenau Hasselaer. The name Innama was used in a family name like manner, but it refers first and foremost to the name of the trade house, and the members of the family were often referred to with the name Innama.

2 The most comprehensive and best annotated biography of Valborg Innama has been presented in Aulis Oja's (1937) eighty-year-old article. A shorter and less exact presentation is given by Anneli Mäkelä-Alitalo (1997).

3 The most essential biographical and genealogic presentations of Kenau Hasselaer have been written by Gerda H. Kurtz (1956), M. Thierry de Bye Dólleman (1973) and Els Kloek (2001, 2014). While I have studied the original sources related to Valborg Innama, my analysis on Kenau Hasselaar's role is based on the abovementioned publications.

4 National Archives in Sweden, Letters to King John III (Skrivelser till Johan III), vol. 3, Valborg Innama's letter 12 May 1577; lists of lost items published in *Bidrag till Finlands historia IV: Spridda urkunder från tiden 1561–1570*, ed. Reinhold Hausen (Helsingfors: Finlands statsarkiv 1912), 194–196, 209–210; Oja 1937, 97–98.

5 National Archives in Finland, Bailiff's records (Fin. *Voudintilit*), KA 1071, f. 2; KA 1069, f. 18v; Oja 1937, 98–99.

6 National Archives in Sweden, Letters to King John III (Skrivelser till Johan III), vol. 3, Valborg Innama's letter 12 May 1577; Oja 1937, 97.

7 About the family relations and genealogy of Kenau Hasselaer, see Thierry de Bye Dólleman (1973, 6–16), that corrects some genealogical information given by Kurtz (1956, 42–47, Bijlage I); Kloek (2014, 157–161).

8 Dutch " als een goede patriot deser stadt Haerlem heeft helpen sustineren ende houden totten lesten toe, dat de stadt met accoort overgegaen es aen de alle gemeene vianden", Kloek 2001, 69.

9 Fin. "edustaa historiassamme itseensäluottavaa ja toimintatarmoista renessanssiajan naista, tyyppiä, jonka kaltaista emme keskiajalta emmekä kaikilta myöhäisemmiltäkään vuosisadoilta tapaa", Oja 1937, 110.

10 Kloek 2001, 7. Kenau might originally have been called Kunera, and Kenau might be a nickname referring to her character. See Kloek 2014, 197–200.

11 On medieval Swedish town law and its legislation on remarriage, see *Giftobalken*, section 11, as published in MES 1966. On division and administering of property in late medieval and early modern Swedish stepfamilies, see e.g. Lahtinen (forthcoming).

12 Examples in National Archives in Sweden, Letters to King John III (Sw. *Skrivelser till Johan III*), vol. 3, Valborg Innama's letters; discussion on the practice, see Lahtinen 2009, under "Sin makes efterleverska".

References

Bijedic, T., S. Brink, K. Ettl, S. Kriwoluzky, and F. Welter. 2007. "Women's Innovation in Germany: Empirical Facts and Conceptual Explanations." In *Research Handbook on Gender and Innovation*, edited by G. A. Alsos, U. Hytti, and E. Ljunggren, 51–71. Cheltenham: Edward Elgar Publishing.

Chell, E. 2008. *The Entrepreneurial Personality: A Social Construction*. 2nd ed. London and New York: Routledge.

Froide, A. 1999. "Marital Status as a Category of Difference: Singlewomen and Widows in Early Modern England." In *Singlewomen in the European Past 1250–1800*, edited by J. M. Bennett and A. M. Froide, 236–269. Philadelphia, Pennsylvania: University of Pennsylvania Press.

Kloek, E. 2001. *Kenau: De heldhaftige zakenvrouw uit Haarlem (1526–1588)*. Hilversum: Uitgevereij Verloren.

Kloek, E. 2014. *Kenau & Magdalena: Vrouwen in de tachtigjarige oorlog*. Nijmegen: Uitgeverij Vantilt.

Kooijmans, L. 1997. *Vriendschap en de kunst van het overleven in de zeventiende en achttiende eeuw*. Amsterdam: Uitgeverij Bert Bakker.

Kurtz, G. H. 1956. *Kenu Symonsdochter van Haerlem*. Assen: Konijnklike Drukkerij Van Gorcum & comp. N. V.—G. A. Hak & Dr. H. J. Prakke.

Lahtinen, A. 2009. *Anpassning, förhandling, motstånd: Kvinnliga aktörer i släkten Fleming 1470–1620*. Stockholm and Helsinki: Atlantis—SLS.

Lahtinen, A. Forthcoming. "Stepfamilies in Sweden, 1400 to 1650: the Family in Process Between Bloodlines and Continuity". In *Stepfamilies in Europe, 1400–1800*, edited by Lyndan Warner. London and New York: Routledge.

Lavery, J. 2006. *The History of Finland*. Westport, CT and London: Greenwood Press.

Magnus Erikssons Stadlag (MES). 1966. *I nusvensk tolkning av Åke Holmbäck och Elias Wessén*. Lund: Institut för rättshistorisk forskning.

Mäkelä-Alitalo, A. 1997. "Innamaa, Valpuri Erkintytär." In *Kansallisbiografia*-verkkojulkaisu. Helsinki: Suomalaisen Kirjallisuuden Seura, 1997–. www.kansallisbiografia.fi/kansallisbiografia/henkilo/359.

Ogilvie, S. 2003. *A Bitter Living: Women, Markets, and Social Capital in Early Modern Germany*. Oxford: Oxford University Press.

Oja, A. 1937. "Valpuri Innamaa: Turkulainen suurporvari 1500-luvulla." In *Varsinais-Suomen maakuntakirja* 6, 94–110. Turku: Varsinais-Suomen Maakuntaliitto.

Sardeshmukh, S. R., and R. M. Smith. 2016. "Eyes Wide Shut: Differential Influences of Gender on Innovation in Organizations." In *Research Handbook on Gender and Innovation*, edited by Gry Agnete Alsos, Ulla Hytti, and Elisabet Ljunggren, 129–150. Cheltenham: Edward Elgar Publishing 2007.

Thierry de Bye Dólleman, M. 1973. *Kenau Simonsdochter Hasselaer: Haar voorouders en naaste familieleden*. Haarlem: Commissie Herdenking Beleg van Haarlem.

Vainio-Korhonen, K. 2002. *Ruokaa, vaatteita, hoivaa: Naiset ja yrittäjyys paikallisena ja yleisenä ilmiönä 1700-luvulta nykypäivään*. Helsinki: Finnish Literature Society.

van den Heuvel, D. 2007. *Women & Entrepreneurship: Female traders in the Northern Netherlands, c. 1580–1815*. Amsterdam: Aksant.

van Tielhof, M. 2002. *The "Mother of all Trades": The Baltic Grain Trade in Amsterdam from the Late 16th to the Early 19th Century*. Leiden: Brill.

Weightman, G. 2008. *The Industrial Revolutionaries: The Creators of the Modern World 1776–1914*. London: Atlantic Books.

4 The Iron Lady, Elin Såger

Head of a Family Business

Jarkko Keskinen, Veli Pekka Toropainen, and Mari Välimäki

> Honourable, God-fearing and virtuous wife, Elin Johansdotter Såger . . . has been generous to the poor, has beard her misfortunes bravely, has been pious, docile, and earnest in her widowhood, has lived with her neighbors in particular harmony, unanimity and kindness.[1]
>
> —Enevaldus Svenonius, 1670

In January of 1670 the Professor of Theology and Pastor, Enevaldus Svenonius, delivered a funeral sermon where he depicted Elin Såger in accordance with the contemporary moral texts of that time as a humble, retreating, and pious wife (Ojala 2014, 162–163). However, he did not mention that Elin Såger, during her ten years, three months and eight days of widowhood, had lead the family business and three iron works as the manager of one of the largest commercial enterprises of that time in Finland. The fact that Svenonius ignored Elin Såger's achievements in the family business, demonstrated the prevailing attitude towards economically active women in the early modern period. Elin Såger lived and led the family business in a time before legislators began to restrict the legal capacity of married and unmarried women; however, the attitude toward women in business became more stringent as the seventeenth century progressed, thereby constraining their scope of action and suggesting that women should be banned entirely from the economy and economic involvement (Keskinen and Vainio-Korhonen in this volume; Pylkkänen 2005, 79–81).

Scholars from several different disciplines have produced a wide group of studies on European economic growth and institutional development (Luiten van Zanden 2009; Greif 2006). However, women and their economic agency has never been the mainstream focus in these publications. According to Rosemary Sweet, for example, economic historians have instead concentrated their interest on the man's world, wherein only merchants and divergent institutions played a central role. As a result, women in these studies become only passive objects stripped of their capacity for influence and active participation in an economy (Rosemary Sweet cited in Montenach and Simonton 2013, 1). Indeed, the research on women and their entrepreneurial activities has been marginalised and addressed only the domestic sphere or low-income work of women in urban areas (Stadin 2009, 250, 261–263; Hanawalt 2007, 261–262; Karlsson Sjögren 1998, 91–98).

In recent years, several gender historians have shown that these official norms and legislation could actually differ notably from each other, and women had far more opportunities than recorded to engage in entrepreneurial activities than the prior literature has suggested (e.g. Kay 2009; van den Heuvel 2007). In present-day economics, entrepreneurship is seen as a heroic individual and still male practice, and personal characteristics, education, and skills determine whether individuals succeed or not in their business ventures (see e.g. Drakopoulou Dodd and Anderson 2007). At the same time, the research has concentrated mainly on male business managers and their activities, and pushed women entrepreneurship into the background.

In her own time, Elin Såger was not an anomaly. Instead, she was one of the women who as head of household supported her family and also actively took part in the family business. Historians have often accentuated the meaning of social networks, community, and kin in early modern Europe. In reference to this discussion, Anu Pylkkänen (2005, 79–80) stated that the female role in the household and family business was based on the thinking that women represented her kin rather than themselves as individuals. However, women's possibilities, opportunities, and successes in business life were often not merely based on either family background or social networks. For example, Raisa Maria Toivo (2008, 147–149) noted that an individual's position within a family, local community, and in the business life also depended on personal resources and personal circumstances, such as age, skills, support, and character.

This current article focuses on Elin Såger as the manager of the Thorwöste family business between the years 1659–1669. It examines the alternatives that widows faced when their husbands died in a patriarchal society that set constraints on the female heads of a family business and its households. The analysis is based both on her personal characteristics and her immediate family and social network. Elin is not seen only as the manager of the family business or head of her household, but also as a mother to her sons and a mother-in-law to her daughters' husbands with whom she had divergent relationships and moral obligations.

The Thorwöste Family

Petter Thorwöste (Th), like many others who applied for merchant rights in seventeenth-century Sweden, was born abroad, namely, in Lübeck (Haggrén 2000). He moved to Stockholm at the beginning of the 1620s and managed to obtain an apprentice place with Mårten Wewitzer. Wewitzer belonged to the absolute upper crust of the local merchant community and conducted wide-ranging foreign trade.[2] Hence, being the apprentice in

Wewitzer's house offered Thorwöste excellent prospects for the future. During his training period Thorwöste took care of his master's business activities in Finland. Therefore, he had to stay on for several winters in Turku on the Southwestern coast of Finland, to manage iron purchases. Apparently, Thorwöste used these visits to establish new social and business relations of his own, because at the beginning of the 1630s, he moved to Turku permanently. In Turku, he signed up under Jacob Wolle, the richest merchant in town (Haggrén 2007). Wolle had acquired two sizeable iron works, Antskog and Mustio, from Southern Finland and needed an experienced bookkeeper to help him manage them (Haggrén 2000).

Apprenticeship to one of the most respected merchants gave Thorwöste an opportunity to integrate himself even closer to the local merchant community. However, in practice, this advancement was accomplished through a suitable marriage with Elin Såger. Several Swedish historians have studied the marriages between merchant families. They show that despite the age, period, or place, the members of these leading merchant families were likely to marry the descendants of socially equal or higher families (Lundblad 2007, 151–154; Åberg 1991, 107). For example Anita Göransson (1990, 540–541) suggests that marriages between merchant families were based on two strategies that aspired to maximise the benefits gained from the alliances between such families by using reductive and expansive marriage strategies. Reductive strategy aimed to keep the family resources in the family through, for example, marriages between cousins. The expansive marriage strategy strived to enhance the family resources, social connections, and know-how by marrying outside of the immediate family circles (Göransson's marriage strategies have been criticised, see Wottle 2000, 221; Ågren 2007, 94; Keskinen 2012, 84–87, 90–91).

The marriage between Petter Thorwöste and Elin Såger (Så2) in 1631 was a typical expansive alliance between two merchant families. Elin's father, Johan Såger (Så), was a highly respected member of the local community. Also, her grandfather, Petter Plagman (Pl), the burgomaster of Turku, was one of the most influential men in that town (Mäkelä-Alitalo 1998, 531). Thus, their marriage brought both important social connections and economic wealth to Thorwöste and complemented the professional skills and initial capital he had acquired during the apprenticeship. Their marriage was also typical in another sense. Socially esteemed members of the merchant community used marriages to reproduce themselves, and merchant daughters as wives played a crucial role in introducing newcomers to the local community and its customs (Lamberg 2001, 92). This task was also the case for Thorwöste who was granted merchant rights in the town in 1632 (Carpelan 1890, 99–100; see also Möller 1954, 54).

The newlywed couple bought a two-storied stone house in the immediate surroundings of the town hall and next to Thorwöste's parents-in-law. The main building included a parlour, seven smaller bedrooms, a kitchen,

Table 4.1 Seventeenth-century geneology of the Thorwöste family

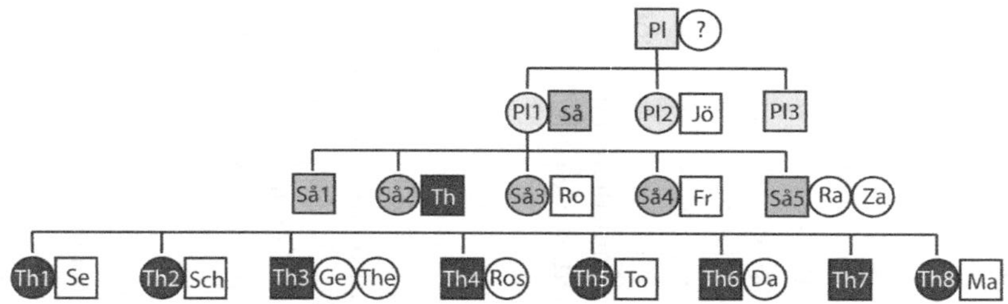

The Plagman family:

Pl	Petter Plagman	(d. 1626)
?	Unkown	(-)
Pl1	Elin Plagman	(d. 1667)
Så	Johan Såger	(d. 1632)
Pl2	Barbara Plagman	(d. 1682)
Jö	Henrik Jönsson	(-)
Pl3	Unkown son	(d. 1627)

The Såger family:

Så	Johan Såger	(d. 1632)
Pl1	Elin Plagman	(d. 1667)
Så1	Petter Såger	(d. 1685)
Så2	Elin Såger	(d. 1669)
Th	Petter Thorwöste	(d. 1659)
Så3	Anna Såger	(d. 1657)
Ro	Gottfried Roskamp	(d. 1659)
Så4	Brita Såger	(d. 1674)
Fr	Kristoffer Franck	(d. 1684)
Så5	Johan Såger	(d. 1684)
Ra	Sofia Rancken	(d. 1668)
Za	Margareta Zander	(-)

Thorwöste family:

Th	Petter Thorwöste	(d.1659)
Th1	Anna Thorwöste	(d.1683)
Se	Johan Danielsson Serlachius	(-)
Th2	Elin Thorwöste	(d. 1687)
Sch	Abraham Henrik Scheffer	(d. 1668)
Th3	Herman Thorwöse	(d. 1685)
Ge	Maria Gerdt	(d. 1678)
The	Katarina Thesleff	(d. 1705)
Th4	Johan Thorwöste	(c. 1712)
Ros	Helena Rosendahl	(c. 1687)
Th5	Margareta Thorwöste	(-)
To	Daniel Torsberg	(-)
Th6	Petter Thorwöste jr.	(d.1703)
Da	Margareta Danielsdotter	(-)
Th7	Jacob Thorwöste	(d.1671)
Th8	Maria Thorwöste	(d. 1701)
Ma	Josef Mathesius	(d. 1689)

Source: Tor Carpelan, *Åbo i genealogiskt hänseende på 1600- och början af 1700-talen*. (Helsingfors 1890).

a bakery, and a shop (Toropainen 2016, 255; see also Laitinen 2017). The large house was needed, because the household grew rapidly. Taking care of a large household and its daily chores must have been hard work for Elin, but she did not do it all alone. The household included hired accountants, seamen, apprentices, shop-assistants, hired-men, wet nurses, and maids. Already in 1635, this household had ten members making it among the largest in town (Ranta 1975, 177).

In burgher families, the firstborn was typically born approximately twelve months after the wedding. Over the first ten years of their marriage, wives were usually pregnant every other year (Vainio-Korhonen 1998, 162–163). Elin Såger gave birth to ten children, from which two boys died in childbed (Mäkelä-Alitalo 1998).[3] Their firstborn, Anna (Th1), was born in 1632 (or 1633), Elin (Th2) in 1634, Herman (Th3) in 1635, Johan (Th4) in 1636 and then Margareta (Th5), Petter (Th6), Jacob (Th7), and Maria (Th8) whose dates of birth are unknown. Hence, Elin was eighteen years old when she had her first child and over thirty when her final offspring was born (Haggrén 2000; Toropainen 2016, 164).

The death of Elin's father, Johan Såger, in 1632 was a springboard to success for Thorwöste, who then rose rapidly to join the local merchant elite. As Johan Såger Junior (Så1) was still under age Thorwöste was able to invest Johan's portion of the heritage into his own business ventures.[4] The growth of the shipbuilding industry in Western Europe had made tar burning a highly profitable source of livelihood in seventeenth-century Finland. Thorwöste wanted his share of this business, and so he started to export tar to European commercial centres (Ranta 1975, 249–250). At first the tar was produced in Ostrobothnia, but eventually, he established his own tar-burning pit in Turku. Apart from the tar barrels Thorwöste also exported grain and iron, and his imports consisted of wines, fabrics, salt, and various colonial goods (Haggrén 2000).

Thorwöste was also involved in the shipping business and purchased an ocean liner from The Netherlands in 1638. Three years later he bought, along with his brother-in-law, Petter Såger (Så1), and the local merchant. Petter Jesenhausen, another large ship from Lübeck. In addition, he built a smaller vessel in Vaasa for Baltic Sea trading. Eventually, Thorwöste took part in every large ship-building project in town and soon became the owner of the largest merchant fleet in Finland (Haggrén 2000; Möller 1954, 144).

Finnish foreign trade suffered a slight reversal at the beginning of 1640s. At first, the Swedish Crown decided to confiscate merchant vessels for military use, and so Thorwöste was forced to give up his larger vessel to transport the Crown's freight. Secondly the Crown reorganised the national tar trade in 1648 by monopolising it for a trading company in Stockholm. Thorwöste, the leading tar exporter in town, was selected to represent the merchant community of Turku in the Diet in 1649, where he tried to oppose the monopolies but in vain (Kaukiainen 2008, 86–87; see also Åström 1988; Möller 1954, 78–79; von Bonsdorff 1889–1904, 376–377).

As a consequence, Thorwöste apparently decided to look for more secure investment sources, like his old friend, Jacob Wolle, also did. Wolle had been among the first Finnish merchants to become interested in iron works at the beginning of the 1630s. He had established the Antskog ironworks in Pohja and managed to negotiate a six-year lease on the Mustio ironworks in Karjaa when previous leaseholder fell into financial bankruptcy. Over the next few years, Wolle invested substantial sums of money in his ironworks, and unfortunately ran into financial difficulties (Haggrén 2007).

In 1640, Thorwörste agreed to loan over 9,000 Swedish copper thalers to Wolle against the ownership of the Antskog ironworks. As the debt fell due next year, the extent of Wolle's insolvency became apparent to Thorwöste (Hausen 1901, 164). Feeling betrayed, Thorwöste complained to the *Bergskollegium*, which after a long and convoluted process, finally decided to move both the Mustio and Antskog ironworks to Thorwöste's ownership. He then started to develop both the iron production processes, actual produced products, and their sales.[5] At first, he established a new iron work Fiskars next to Antskog to produce more high-quality bar iron. Unlike Wolle, Thorwöste did not settle for semi-finished products. Instead his ironworks started to produce nails, pots, and cannonballs.[6] Wolle had exported most of his iron to Holland. Thorwöste found new fertile market areas in the Finnish, Estonian, and Latvian markets (Haggrén 2000, 2007).

The downside was that these investments took a lot of capital—capital that had to be borrowed from somewhere. Therefore, Thorwöste fell deeper and deeper into debt during the 1650s. At the same time, the European market area experienced a recession that lowered the profits that could be gained from iron sales. Moreover, in 1656, Turku was burned down in a fire that lasted for 15 hours and destroyed 450 townhouses (Ranta 1975, 593; see also Laitinen 2017, 37, 76, 166). The Thorwöste family townhouse was among the badly damaged houses. Hence, Petter Thorwöste found himself in the same sort of financial situation as the previous owners of the ironworks. Consequently, when Thorwöste died in 1659, he left his widow and his children a good reputation, but substantial debts till to be paid.

Sons as Sheet Anchors of Widowhood

In the early modern burgher communities, married couples typically had a notable age difference, which stemmed from two factors. First, the majority of the burghers aimed at getting a profession, i.e. their burgher rights, before getting married. Although men started their professional training around the age of fifteen, it often took another fifteen years to attain these rights. Therefore, most of the burgher men were over thirty when they entered the marriage market. Secondly, burgher daughters usually got married right after they reached sexual maturity (Keskinen 2012, 94; de Moor and Luiten van Zanden 2009, 122–123; Tilly and Scott 1987, 32; see also Pylkkänen 2005; Korpiola 2009).

Elin Såger had been seventeen, when she married the thirty-two-year-old Petter Thorwöste. The couple managed their common household and notable business together for twenty-eight years before Elin was widowed at the age of forty-five (Carpelan 1890, under "The family Såger"). As a wife, she had been subordinate to her husband. According to the then predominant law, unmarried and married women were seen as legally incompetent (Lahtinen 2007, 34). The guardianship of an unmarried woman belonged to her father, a widowed mother, or the closest male relative. Whereas, a married woman was represented by her husband, who was also the head of their household (Erickson 1995, 237).

This legal status was not just the case in Sweden, as both legislation and societal norms constrained women throughout Europe in the early modern period. It restricted their access to both work and property ownership. Married women were not allowed to conduct trade or make legally binding contracts without their husband's permission (Montenach and Simonton 2013, 2–3). Patriarchal hierarchy within the society and in the household rested on the Protestant Reformation and the Table of Duties (*Die Haustafel*) which placed a woman under her husband's authority in the domestic sphere. In this presumed ideal, the wife's principal task was to govern the household and obey her husband, whereas her husband was responsible for the support of the family and the household surrounding it (Lindström 1993, 11–14; Ojala 2014, 162–163; Bull 2004, 195).

In the early modern period, the practice of the burgher profession rested heavily on household organisation. Although the law forbid unmarried and married women to independently take part in business activities without their guardian's consent, several historians have proven that legislation and everyday practices actually differed notably from each other (there were also cultural, regional, and temporal differences, see van den Heuvel 2013, 116–133.). Women as wives and daughters participated in numerous ways in trading and assisted their fathers and husbands in the family business, and thus, they also had a considerable impact on everyday society (Keskinen 2016, 145–148; Stadin 1997, 202; Vainio-Korhonen 2010, 242–254). Despite the official norms, the society expected wives to participate and support their husbands in family business activities (Keskinen and Vainio-Korhonen in this volume). Therefore, burgher daughters usually got a rigorous education. First, they were taught to read and write, maintain bookings, speak foreign languages, and manage tasks that were needed to be managed in the burgher professions (Stadin 2009, 254–255; Andersson 1998, 13, 57; van den Heuvel 2007, 47–48).

The nature of Elin Såger's involvement in the Thorwöste family business is today difficult to estimate. On one hand, the official representative of the family was Thorwöste, and Elin Såger only appears for the first time in public records six months after her husband had passed away (Toropainen 2016, 196). On the other hand, Elin had her upbringing in one of most prestigious merchant families in that town (Möller 1954, 92–93). Therefore,

Elin had the opportunity to gain a formal education alongside her brothers and thus good premises for supporting her husband in the family business activities as well. The education and practical experiences gathered during her childhood and marriage gave Elin Såger the background as well as the knowledge to continue the family trade after her husband died.

More and more, widow-women gained new social and economic positions within their family, local community, and society. Contrary to their earlier lives, widows had a right to make legally binding contracts, own and control properties, act as guardians for their own children, and continue the family trade (Keskinen 2016, 146; van der Heijden, Schmidt, and Wall 2007, 224; Johansen 2004, 178). However, Julie Hardwick (1992, 134), who has studied widowhood in seventeenth-century France, has stated that widows often found themselves situated disconcertingly across the gender boundaries, as several cultural and economic factors still restrained them and kept them from utilising the opportunities the law seemed to offer. In other words, widows were not granted actual merchant rights. Instead, they simply could act as representatives of their late husband's privileges.

There were basically four survival strategies for widows to use to cope with their changed living condition following the death of their spouses—remarry, pass the business to someone else, go out of business, or continue the business on their own (Stadin 2009, 251–252). A marriage to a merchant widow offered young and budding merchants an excellent opportunity to acquire an already established reputation, a financially secure status and integrate themselves into the local merchant community (Bull 1998, 139). Therefore, there was usually a certain amount of demand for young widows in the local marriage market. Remarrying was clearly related to a widow's age. Younger widows tended to remarry fairly quickly, whereas widows between the ages of thirty and fifty were more likely to continue as heads of their household and the family business (Fauve-Chamoux 2001, 244).

Elin Såger, who was widowed at the age of forty-five, thus had nothing to gain from remarriage (Johansen 2004, 178–179; Keskinen 2012, 95–96, 104). Her old age prevented her from giving birth to new descendants and weakened her position in the marriage market. After getting married, she would also have submitted herself once again to male authority and would have lost the guardianship of her six still underage children.[7] She could pass the baton of the family business to neither her sons nor her sons-in-law. Her sons were still too young and did not yet have the proper education for the task, and handing the family business to sons-in-law would not only have moved the authority outside her own household, but also cut the ground from under her other children's feet. Going out of business was also not an option for Elin Såger, because the estate was so highly indebted that it endangered the very existence of the household and her own and her children's future well-being. Therefore, she refused to distribute the estate and decided to continue the family business (Nordström 1962, 158–159).

Saving her husband's life work from the creditors called for purposeful actions to set the business back in order. Thus, Elin Såger immediately got down to business by writing a heartbreaking letter to the *Bergskollegium* wherein she explained the condescending attitude that she as a widow had to face in business life from treacherous shipmasters, disobedient miner foremen, dishonest customs officers, and rivals in the mining industry (Nordström 1962, 159–160). Earlier research has shown that this behaviour was fairly common in cases of bankruptcy or insolvency, as debtors often tried to lay the blame on external circumstances on someone else and plead for a reduction of their debts (Nyberg 2006, 168–169). Also, early modern contemporary writings have suggested the common role model of a humble, retreating, and pious widow—a canon that could then be easily exploited when writing a petition to the authorities (see e.g. Ojala 2014, 173–186).

Elin Såger had one advantage on her side. Her own mother had taken care of the Såger family business since 1632, when her husband Johan Såger died (Carpelan 1890, under "The family Såger"; on Elin Plagman's activities in Turku see Toropainen 2016). Therefore, it was likely Elin Såger knew exactly what she was doing when she wrote her petition to the *Bergskollegium*. And her decision worked. The authorities took pity on Såger. She was given tax relief and other benefits which helped her keep the business running. This case manifests clearly how widows had a legal right to represent themselves and their property in public. However, these practices changed during the seventeenth century. Sheilagh Ogilvie (2003, 258) has stressed that various communal institutions and juridical practices started to set constraints for widows when they wanted to continue the family business. One of these constraints presupposed that a widow had to be represented in legal matters by a male proxy (Ojala 2014, 175; Johansen 2004, 182; Karlsson Sjögren and Lindström 2004, 249).

Hence, widows like Elin Såger lived in between two legal traditions or in the liminal space that existed between the two gender roles and where they could be pushed away from the public scene and business (Lanza 2008, 4–5). Although the highest authority of the family business was now invested in Elin Såger, she could not operate it alone. At first, she got help from her late husband's long-term bookkeeper, Elias Ekman, who took care of the legal matters in Turku. Åsa Karlsson Sjögren (1998, 109–114) argues that especially wealthy and influential merchant widows could plead a case in court themselves if need be. Thus, Elin Såger appeared herself in lower court from time to time between 1661 and 1668, but gradually, it became her oldest sons, Herman and Petter, who represented the family in the court (Toropainen 2016, 260; see also Karlsson Sjögren 1998, 112).

In time, the sons' contributions started to grow in the family business as well. The family straight from the beginning had invested in their children's education by hiring a German schoolmaster. The oldest son, Herman, continued his studies first at the Academy of Turku and then the University of Uppsala. As the oldest son was directed toward an academic career, Petter

Thorwöste prepared his second son, Johan, to be his successor and made sure that he got a suitable education. After a formal school education, father urged Johan to apply for the merchant rights from the Town Council of Ekenäs in 1651. Ultimately, Petter did not manage to complete his son's training, as he died suddenly in 1659. Therefore, the baton could not be passed directly to Johan, and his mother became the head of the family business (Möller 1954, 92; Haggrén 2000).

The Thorwöste family had done extensive business and was one of the largest private employers in Finland during the seventeenth century. Their trade complex included three ironworks, two mines, and a merchant house in Turku that owned several ships and an iron shop. All required quite a large labour force. Already in 1656, the Antskog (thirty-five), Svartå (thirty-seven), and Fiskars (eight) ironworks alone had eighty male workers (Toropainen 2016, 267–268). In addition, Elin Såger had to take care of their families, apprentices, accountants, shipmasters, seamen, and several hired men and maids. It was obviously a task she could not do alone. So, she decided to keep the highest authority in the family business, but divide her responsibilities between the family members.

Elin Såger took over the Antskog ironworks and moved there permanently at the beginning of the 1660s. Herman's scope of responsibilities lay in the merchant house in Turku. Johan was given the directorship of the Svartå and Fiskars ironworks where he received help from his brother, Petter (Nordström 1962, 158; Nikander 1929, 12). Despite this division of labour, Elin soon discovered that early modern business culture had strong gender division. Although the ironworks were privately owned, the Swedish Crown controlled and supervised them as a *raison d'état* with various craft guild regulations. These regulations caused problems for Elin Såger, as the smiths, who in principle were independent craftsmen although they were hired by the ironworks, openly challenged her authority and refused to take orders from her and were caught stealing coal and iron from the works. These disputes lead to court proceedings, which further increased the tension between the owners and their labour force (Nordström 1962, 162–165).

Further hardships seemed to come one after another, as the 1660s were a difficult time for the iron industry in Sweden. Elin tried to enhance their position by writing several petitions to *Bergskollegium* wherein she applied for support or relief for her iron works. She also wrote several complaints wherein she blamed Carl Billsten, her late husband's close business associate, and her own sons-in-law for malevolence toward her and her family business. In addition, misfortune seemed to follow the family in the form of shipwrecks, accident, machine breakages, and fires in the ironworks. In other words, despite efforts by Elin and her sons, the family business could not pick up the pieces—and the family's weight of debt kept increasing (Mäkelä-Alitalo 1998).

Challenging the Sons-in-Law

In addition to their four sons, Petter Thorwöste and Elin Såger also had four daughters whose marriages played a crucial role in the family business. Two of the Thorwöste daughters married at the beginning of the 1650s. Anna Thorwöste entered matrimony with Johan Danielsson Serlachius (Se) and Elin Thorwöste with Abraham Henrik Scheffer (Sch). Johan Danielsson Serlachius worked as a Mine Master (sv. *bärgsmästare*) and thus became a crucial connection for the family business to the mining administration of the Swedish Realm. Abraham Henrik Scheffer, on the other hand, was the son of the local burgomaster, and as a merchant himself belonged to the local merchant elite. Scheffer was also Petter Thorwöste's business partner, as they had joined together in commerce in 1644.[8]

These marriages were all strategically important (Ågren 2007, 89–90). Anna Thorwöste's marriage with Johan Danielsson Serlachius represented an expansive marriage strategy, wherein the aim was to broaden the family, but also the business, connections. This marriage reinforced Petter Thorwöste's standing in the mining industry. Elin Thorwöste's marriage to Abraham Henrik Scheffer represented a reproductive marriage strategy, and reinforced the connections between the Thorwöste and Scheffer households and brought them even closer as business partners (on the marriage strategies see Ågren 2007, 100–110).

The marriages of the oldest daughters also represented the typical early modern elite marriage pattern wherein the man was in his late twenties or early thirties and the woman was in her early twenties (Andersson 2005, 57–58); Abraham Henrik was thirty-three when he married Elin who was seventeen, and Anna was in her late teens at the time of her and Johan Serlachius' wedding. In addition, the marriages of the oldest daughters renewed the marital pattern of Elin Såger and Petter Thorwöste; Elin was seventeen when she married Petter who was thirty-two years old.

The marriages of Anna and Elin were negotiated by Petter Thorwöste and Elin Såger. King Magnus Eriksson's Town Law stated that both father and mother were the guardians of their daughters and a fiancé should approach them both in order to begin the marriage negotiations. However, the Lutheran Church accentuated the voluntariness of both the bride and the groom, and thus, marriage was not just a deal between the groom and the woman's parents (MES 1966, Giftermålsbalken I, 38; Korpiola 2005, 3–4).

When Petter Thorwöste passed away, he had still two unmarried daughters. After his death, Elin was the head of the household and the guardian of her underage children. One can interpret the Town Law thusly that Elin was also her daughters' marriage guardian (MES 1966, Giftermålsbalken I, 38). However, according to the Law of the Land, she could not act as the marriage guardian for her daughters. According to the Law of the Land, the closest relative on the father's side of the family should act as her guardian (Pylkkänen 1990, 308–311; Stadin 2009, 89). It is not quite certain which of these laws was applied in Turku. However, in the case of the family Thorwöste, there were no relatives on the father's side in town, for Petter Thorwöste had moved to Turku from Germany. In these situations, the Law of the Land stated that the mother's father should act as the guardian, however, Elin Såger's father, Johan Såger, had also passed away. Thus, one of Elin's brothers was entitled to act as the marriage guardian. The job fell to Elin's brother, Johan Såger (Junior).[9] Thus, the marriages of the younger daughters were either solely negotiated by Elin or determined within the immediate Såger family. The father's side of the family had no say in the matter. The younger daughters, Margareta and Maria Thorwöste, married during the 1660s, and their marriages became quite different than those already established by the older Thorwöste sisters.

Margareta and Maria Thorwöste were older than their sisters when they married. Their husbands were neither socially nor economically as esteemed as the husbands of their older sisters. Margareta married in 1663 to the Treasurer Daniel Torsberg (To), and she was approximately twenty-five years old. Maria married a newly ordained priest, Josef Mathesius (Ma) in 1667.[10] The couple were nearly the same age; Maria was twenty-five and Josef, twenty-seven. Margareta and Maria's marriages were more equal in terms of age than those of their older sisters'. However, at the same time, the younger sisters were more dependent on support from the parental house than their older sisters had been. Daniel Torsberg and Josef Mathesius had not had enough time to establish their own stable standing in the society like their brothers-in-law had done when they married (Ågren 2007, 88).

Margareta's and Maria's marriages were also established using different strategies than those for the marriages of Anna and Elin. It is obvious that Elin Såger's goal was not to reinforce the family business with these marriages. However, Margareta and Maria Thorwöste's marriages were expansive in the sense that they were established outside the burgher estate. Daniel Torsberg was an official, and thus he did not officially belong to any of the Swedish four estates. Josef Mathesius was a priest and belonged to the clergy and was a priest at least of a second generation (Kotivuori 2005; Carpelan 1890, 100). With these marriages, the family connections extended to new estates and families. It is possible that Elin Såger had had enough of sons-in-law who meddled in her family's business, and for that reason, she let her younger daughters enter into matrimony with men with absolutely no connections to the ironworks or trade.

The relationship between Elin Såger and her four sons-in-law was very different. Sources reveal that Elin's relationship with Abraham Henrik Scheffer and Johan Danielsson Serlachius were not without their difficulties. As mentioned above, Scheffer and Petter Thorwöste were business partners for a long time and Thorwöste had become indebted to Scheffer. Thorwöste had tried to reconcile his debts with his son-in-law before his death, but without any luck. Also, Elin tried to reconcile the debt soon after her husband's death, but in the end only succeeded in reconciling the debt in 1664 (Toropainen 2016, 258). The relationship between Elin and Abraham Henrik Scheffer did not, however, become friendly after the debt was settled. Elin wrote to the Town Court of Turku that Scheffer had questioned the way she ran the ironworks. Why then was Scheffer so interested in how Elin ran the ironworks if he had received his claim and the debt was fully settled?

According to the Town Law, both sons and daughters inherited equally and received equal shares of the inheritance (MES 1966, Ärvdabalken I, 56). Thus, all the Thorwöste children—four sons and four daughters—would inherit equally, and as the husband was the one who had managed his wife's fortune, Scheffer was interested in how the business of the family Thorwöste was run. After the distribution of the estate part of the Thorwöste family, its business would become the fortune of Elin Thorwöste and thus also part of the family Scheffer's fortune, albeit not an integrated part of it. According to Swedish legislation, land and property was not the husband's fortune or property, but stayed in the ownership of the wife when the couple married or when the wife inherited from a relative. Even though the husband managed the property, he could not sell it without the permission of his wife and her family (Karlsson Sjögren 1998, 54–55). When questioning Elin Såger's ability to run the ironworks properly, Abraham Henrik Scheffer demonstrated that he was interested in how his wife's and their children's future fortune was being taken care of.

Elin had moved in 1661 to live in one of the ironworks owned by the family, Antskog, in order to supervise the production. She now stated that her departure from the ironworks was impossible, and she asked Abraham Henrik Scheffer and her other two sons-in-law to come and inspect the ironworks and bookkeeping. Scheffer told the Town Court that he only wished that the running of the ironworks would be brought to a good condition and thus declined her offer to come and inspect the books. Instead, Scheffer authorized his brother-in-law, Johan Danielsson Serlachius, to do the inspection.[11]

Serlachius held a position as *Bergmästare*, which meant that he observed mining and sat as a judge for the ironworks situated in the southwestern parts of Finland. Thus, he went regularly also to the ironworks owned by his mother-in-law and judged the cases that were brought to the mining court. Elin Såger considered Serlachius to be too gentle when sentencing the workers at her ironworks and complained about him to the *Bergskollegium* (Nordström 1962, 158–159). However, the treatment of the workers was not the only conflict between Elin Såger and Johan Danielsson Serlachius. They also disagreed on the settlement of the inheritance of Petter Thorwöste. Elin Såger was not willing to distribute the estate after her husband's death. Johan Danielsson Serlachius was interested in the distribution, and as was mentioned above Abraham Henrik Scheffer was not fully convinced of the management of the ironworks (Nordström 1962, 161). These two sons-in-law were interested in getting their hands on the estate via their wives' share in the estate. Elin managed to keep them out until the end of the 1660s.

In addition to worrying how the family fortune was being taken care of, Scheffer and Serlachius wanted also to test Elin Såger's authority as the head of the Thorwöste household and the head of the family business. In sixteenth-century Sweden, it was not uncommon that any change in the management of the household through the death of the master resulted in testing or questioning the authority of the widow. Often former trading partners would test the authority of the new mistress or the permanence of the ongoing trading agreements (Lahtinen 2007, 65).

In addition to questioning how Elin Såger took care of the family business, Henrik Abraham Scheffer indirectly caused setbacks for the family business. For example, in 1663 a ship rented by Elin Såger was confiscated in the port of Stockholm upon its arrival. The owner of the ship, a merchant called Michel Larson, was indebted to Abraham Henrik Scheffer, who ordered the confiscation. Even though Elin got the ship back the next year, the confiscation caused difficulties for the business. Thus, Elin claimed compensation from Scheffer in the Town Court for the trouble the confiscation had caused her.[12] In addition to these reversals related to her sons-in-law, there was a fire at one of the ironworks in 1664 and then another the next year (Nordström 1962). All these economical and material setbacks caused trouble for the family business, and according to W. E. Nordström these setbacks, together with Elin's failing health, eventually compelled her to agree to the distribution of the estate.

The estate was now deeply in debt, and while Johan Danielsson Serlachius had previously been very eager to distribute the estate, he now opposed the distribution. In 1667, Elin Såger asked for help from the *Bergskollegium* to get the distribution done. However, Serlachius never showed up for the distribution, so it could not be performed. According to Serlachius, the finances of the family business were confusing, and he also suspected that Elin would favor her sons, Johan and Petter Thorwöste, over her other sons and daughters in any distribution. Thus, he was afraid he would end up with a heavy burden of debt on his hands, and the sons would inherit all that was valuable. For these reasons, he prolonged the distribution by not turning up for the division. The situation ended by Johan Danielsson Serlachius renouncing his wife's share to her father's inheritance.

Abraham Henrik Scheffer did not play an active part in the prolongation of the distribution, as he passed away before the distribution was executed. However, his wife, Elin Thorwöste renounced her share of her father's inheritance (Nordström 1962, 160–161; Reenpää 1981, 31–32; Autio 2006). The two other sons-in-law, Daniel Torsberg and Johannes Mathesius, decided to stay out of the estate as well as the oldest son, Herman Thorwöste. Thus, when the estate was finally divided in 1669, it was done between the Elin Såger's three sons, Johan, Petter, and Jakob Thorwöste. Johan Thorwöste took over the Antskog and Fiskars ironworks and two-thirds of the family debt, while Petter Thorwöste inherited Svartå and one- third of the estate's debt. Further, Johan promised to take care of his mother and her household. Johan also took on his brother Jakob as his partner to run the ironworks. The distribution of the estate seemed to have satisfied several foreign creditors as well, as they surrendered their claims, which improved the family's overall financial state (Nikander 1929, 13).

The Iron Lady

Despite the fact that women were ubiquitous in seventeenth-century society, the prior research has too often neglected their role in the family business. This analysis goes beyond the stereotypical view of female entrepreneurs as widow-proprietors to focus on the wealthy merchant widow, Elin Såger, and her scope of action in the family business after her husband's death. It illustrates how the contemporary legislation, patriarchal organisation of society and family, and different norms and customs of the commercial milieu provided both opportunities and constraints for women for them to become involved in economic activities (Simonton 2013, 97–103).

Widows as head of the household and family businesses thus appeared to live in a liminal space halfway between the conventional gender roles and the male generations. Family businesses were presupposed to be transferred from father to son or to sons-in-law. Widow entrepreneurs often troubled the society. They personified the patriarchal social order by behaving as men. They held a place of authority in their families, households, family businesses, and in their local communities. Moreover they managed wealth and possessed the kind of legal personhood that was not possible at that time in that culture for unmarried or even married women to hold (Lanza 2008, 5).

The article argues that Elin Såger did not represent the canon of humble, retreating, and pious widows as described by Enevaldus Svenovius in her funeral sermon. Instead, Elin Såger had a fierce temperament, was sharp-witted, and more than capable to make fast decisions as needed. Besides, she came from a wealthy and influential merchant family which had provided her with the prerequisites needed for managing an extensive business. Elin Såger possessed the skills and social and economic capital, and she brought all these to the family business through her marriage. She developed these skills even further in her marital partnership with Petter Thorwöste, and then made good use of them in her widowhood (Simonton 2013, 102).

In spite of her favourable personal characteristics, Elin Såger could not take full advantage the opportunities that legislation provided her. Instead, her scale of scope in business was constantly tested by the practices embedded in a network of male ties (Hardwick 1992, 133). As a consequence, she resorted to the support provided by the family members. Her sons, Herman,

Johan, and Petter Thorwöste, were not just under her authority. They had also a moral duty and commitment to help their mother manage the family business. Johan Thorwöste, who had originally been educated to take over the business, also had a personal incentive to take an active part in the family business.

Not all the members of the family became assets to Elin Såger. The expansive marriage strategy of that time as applied to her two oldest daughters caused problems for her. As long as Petter Thorwöste was alive, his sons-in-law, Johan Danielsson Serlachius and Abraham Henrik Scheffer, were valuable business partners. His death transformed them into heirs who then began to pursue the vested interests of their own families and have a closer interest in the family business. Although the sons-in-law could not question Elin Såger's legal right and authority to act as the head of the Thorwöste family and family business, they repeatedly did challenge her ability to lead the family business.

The case of Elin Såger clearly demonstrates that widow entrepreneurs could and did participate in the early modern business world. After leading a large family-owned enterprise for ten years, Elin died in August of 1669. Her sons continued to develop the family business further, so the name Såger was gradually forgotten and her efforts to grow Finnish economic history vanished into the dark. Only the name Thorwöste continued to live on.

Notes

1 "Ehrborne, Gudfruchtige och Dygdesamma Matrona hustru Elin Johans Dotter Såger . . . warit gifmild emoot dhe fattige, i mootgången toligh, uthi sitt Änckiestånd from, seedigh och alfwarsam, med sina näste grannar och Rågrannar uthi synnerligh sämia, eenigheet och wänskap lefwat". (Svenonius 1670)
2 Wewitzer was ennobled under the name Rosenstierna (Elgenstierna 1925–36).
3 According to Mika Kallioinen (2005, 113–115) one fifth of the born children died before their first birthday in the Early-Modern period.
4 When Johan Såger junior became of age his mother demanded in court that Thorwöste should pay back the heritage portion 2,705 copper thalers (Möller 1954, 250–251).
5 The resolution applied only the ownership of the iron works. Debt was decided in court later on as the Turku Court of Appeal in 1654 ordered the heirs' of Wolle to pay 20,000 Swedish thalers to the Thorwöste family.
6 Thorwöste tried on several occasions to get privileges to produce cannons, but his petitions were denied.
7 Mother didn't get the guardianship without consent from the immediate male family members (Pylkkänen 1990, 308–310).
8 Kansallisarkisto (KA, National Archives of Finland), Turun raastuvan oikeuden tuomiokirjat (TRO), 23.3.1664, 179; Carpelan 1890, 69–70, 99–100.
9 LL, Giftermålsbalk 1; Carpelan 1890, 91–94, 99–101.
10 KA, TRO, 29.2.1664, 176–177; Kotivuori 2005; Carpelan 1890, 101.
11 KA, TRO, 23.5.1664, 342–343.
12 KA, TRO 18.5.1663, 290–291; KA Turun kämnerinoikeuden tuomiokirjat (TKO), 22.2.1663, 39–41

References

Åberg, M. 1991. *En fråga om klass? Borgarklass och industriellt företagare i Göteborg 1850–1914*. Göteborg: Göteborg universitet.

Ågren, K. 2007. *Köpmannen i Stockholm: Grosshandlares ekonomiska och sociala strategier under 1700-talet*. Uppsala: Uppsala Universitet.

Andersson, G. 1998. *Tingets kvinnor och män: Genus som norm och strategi under 1600- och 1700-tal*. Uppsala: Uppsala universitet.

Andersson, G. 2005. "Forming the Partnership Socially and Economically: A Swedish Local Elite, 1650–1770." In *The Marital Economy in Scandinavia and Britain 1400–1900*, edited by M. Ågren and A. L. Erickson. Aldershot: Ashgate.

Åström, S.-E. 1988. *From tar to timber: Studies in Northeast European forest exploitation and foreign trade 1660–1860*. Helsinki: The Finnish Society of Sciences and Letters.

Autio, V.-M. 2006. "Serlachius (1600–)". In *Kansallisbiografia*-verkkojulkaisu. Helsinki: Suomalaisen Kirjallisuuden Seura, 1997. www.kansallisbiografia.fi/kansallisbiografia/henkilo/6738.

Bonsdorff, C. G. von. 1889–1904. *Åbo stads historia under sjuttonde seklet I–II*. Helsingfors.

Bull, I. 1998. *De trondhjemske handelshusene på 1700-tallet: slekt, hushold og forretning*. Trondheim: Norwegian University of Science and Technology.

Bull, I. 2004. "Profession, Absolutism and the Role of Widows." *Scandinavian Journal of History* 29 (3–4): 193–208.

Carpelan, T. 1890. *Åbo i genealogiskt hänseende på 1600- och början af 1700-talen*. Helsingfors.

Drakopoulou Dodd, S., and A. R. Anderson. 2007. "Mumpsimus and the Mything of the Individualistic Entrepreneur." *International Small Business Journal* 25 (4): 341–360.

Elgenstierna, G. 1925–36. *Den introducerade svenska adelns ättar-tavlor med tillägg och rättelser*. Stockholm: Kungliga boktryckeriet P.A. Nordstedt & Söners Förlag.

Erickson, A. L. 1995. *Women and Property in Early Modern England*. London: Routledge.

Fauve-Chamoux, A. 2001. "Marriage, Widowhood and Divorce." In *The History of the European Family Vol. 1: Family Life in Early Modern Times 1500–1789*, edited by D. I. Kertzer and M. Barbagli. New Haven and London: Yale University Press.

Göransson, A. 1990. "Kön, släkt och ägande: Borgerliga maktstrategier 1800–1850." *Historisk Tidskrift* 110 (4): 525–544.

Greif, A. 2006. *Institutions and the Path to the Modern Economy: Lessons from Medieval Trade*. Stanford: Stanford University.

Haggrén, G. 2000. "Thorwöste, Petter." In *Kansallisbiografia*-verkkojulkaisu. Helsinki: Suomalaisen Kirjallisuuden Seura, 1997–. https://kansallisbiografia.fi/kansallisbiografia/henkilo/417.

Haggrén, G. 2007. "Wolle, Jacob." In In *Kansallisbiografia*-verkkojulkaisu. Helsinki: Suomalaisen Kirjallisuuden Seura, 1997–. https://kansallisbiografia.fi/kansallisbiografia/henkilo/3909.

Hanawalt, B. 2007. *The Wealth of Wives: Women, Law, and Economy in Late Medieval London*. New York: Oxford University Press.

Hardwick, J. 1992. "Widowhood and Patriarchy in Seventeenth Century France." *Journal of Social History* 26 (1) (Autumn): 133–148.

Hausen, R. 1901. *Utdrag ur Åbo domkyrkas räkenskaper 1634–1700: Bidrag till Åbo stads historia XI–XII*. Helsingfors.

Johansen, H. M. 2004. "Widowhood in Scandinavia: An Introduction." *Scandinavian Journal of History* 29 (3–4): 171–191.

Kallioinen, M. 2005. *Rutto & Rukous: tartuntataudit esiteollisen ajan Suomessa*. Jyväskylä: Atena.

Karlsson Sjögren, Å. 1998. *Kvinnors rätt i stormaktstidens Gävle*. Uppsala: Swedish Science Press.

Karlsson Sjögren, Å., and P. Lindström. 2004. "Widows, Ownership and Political Culture: Sweden 1650–1800." *Scandinavian Journal of History* 29 (3–4): 241–262.

Kaukiainen, Y. 2008. *Ulos maailmaan! Suomalaisen merenkulun historia*. Helsinki: SKS.

Kay, A. C. 2009. *The Foundations of Female Entrepreneurship: Enterprise, Home and Household in London, 1800–1870*. New York: Routledge.

Keskinen, J. 2012. "Oma ja yhteinen etu: Kauppiaiden keskinäinen kilpailu ja yhteistyö Porin paikallisyhteisössä 1765–1845." PhD diss., University of Turku.

Keskinen, J. 2016. "Personal Catastrophe, Communal Misfortune: Bankruptcy in an Eighteenth-Century Merchant Family." In *Catastrophe, Gender and Urban Experience, 1648–1920*, edited by H. Salmi and D. Simonton, 139–156. London and New York: Routledge.

Korpiola, M. 2005. "Marrying off Sons and Daughters: Attitudes Towards the Consent of Parents and Guardians in Early Modern Sweden." In *Less Favoured—More Favoured: Proceedings from a Conference on Gender in European Legal History, 12–19th Centuries*, edited by G. Jacobsen, H. Vogt, I. Dübeck, and H. Wunder. Copenhagen.

Korpiola, M. 2009. *Between Betrothal and Bedding: Marriage Formation in Sweden, 1200–1600*. Leiden: Brill.

Kotivuori, Y. 2005. "Josef Mathesius (no 1065)." In *Ylioppilasmatrikkeli 1640–1852*, online publication. https://ylioppilasmatrikkeli.helsinki.fi/henkilo.php?id=1065.

Lahtinen, A. 2007. *Sopeutuvat, neuvottelevat, kapinalliset: Naiset toimijoina Flemingin sukupiirissä 1470–1620*. Helsinki: SKS.

Laitinen, R. 2017. *Order, Materiality, and Urban Space in the Early Modern Kingdom of Sweden*. Amsterdam: Amsterdam University Press.

Lamberg, M. 2001. *Dannemännen i stadens råd: Rådmanskretsen i nordiska köpstäder under senmedeltiden*. Stockholm: Stockholmia förlag.

Lanza, J. 2008. *From Wives to Widows in Early Modern Paris: Gender, Economy and Law*. Aldershot: Ashgate.

Lindström, D. 1993. "Skrå, ära och hantverkarkultur i Sverige ca 1350–1900—kring arbetarkultur före industrialismen." *Historisk Tidskrift*, no. 1.

Luiten van Zanden, J. 2009. *The Long Road to Industrial Revolution: The European Economy in a Global Perspective, 1000–1800*. Leiden: Brill.

Lundblad, S. 2007. *Hedersam handelsman eller verksam företagare: Den ekonomiska kulturens omvandling och de ledande ekonomiska aktorerna i Gävle 1765–1869*. Uppsala: Uppsala Universitet.

Magnus Erikssons Stadslag (MES). 1966. *I nusvensk tolkning av Åke Holmbäck och Elias Wessén*. Lund: Institut för rättshistorisk forskning.

Mäkelä-Alitalo, A. 1998. "Såger, Elin". In *Kansallisbiografia-verkkojulkaisu*. Helsinki: Suomalaisen Kirjallisuuden Seura, 1997–. https://kansallisbiografia.fi/kansallisbiografia/henkilo/5121.

Möller, S. 1954. *Suomen tapulikaupunkien valtaporvaristo ja sen kaupankäyntimenetelmät 1600-luvun alkupuolella*. Helsinki: SHS.

Montenach, A., and D. Simonton. 2013. "Gender, Agency and Economy: Shaping the Eighteenth-Century European Town." In *Female Agency in the Urban Economy: Gender in European Towns, 1640–1830*, edited by D. Simonton and A. Montenach. New York and London: Routledge.

Moor, T. de, and J. Luiten van Zanden. 2009. "Girlpower: The European Marriage Pattern and Labour Markets in the North Sea Region in the Late Medieval Period." In *The Long Road to the Industrial Revolution: The European Economy in a Global Perspective, 1000–1800*, edited by J. Luiten van Zanden. Leiden: Brill.

Nikander, G. 1929. *Fiskars bruks historia: minnesskrift*. Åbo: Fiskars aktiebolag.

Nordström, W. E. 1962. *Svartå bruks historia*. Svartå: Ab Svartå Bruk Oy.

Nyberg, K. 2006. "Financiella nätverk—kredit—och egendomsförhållanden". In *Kopparkungen: Handelshuset Björkman i Stockholm 1782–1824*, edited by K. Nyberg. Stockholm: Stockholmia förlag.

Ogilvie, S. 2003. *Bitter Living: Women, Markets and Social Capital in Early Modern Germany*. New York: Oxford University Press.

Ojala, M. 2014. *Protection, Continuity and Gender: Craft Trade Culture in the Baltic Sea Region (14th–16th Centuries)*. Tampere: University of Tampere.

Pylkkänen, A. 1990. *Puoli vuodetta, lukot ja avaimet: Nainen ja maalaistalous oikeuskäytännön valossa 1660–1710 [Half the bed, locks and keys: Woman and household economy in the light of legal practice 1660–1710]*. Helsinki: Lakimiesliiton kustannus.

Pylkkänen, A. 2005. "Forming the Marital Economy in the Early Modern Finnish Countryside." In *The Marital Economy in Scandinavia and Britain 1400–1900: Women and Gender in the Early Modern World*, edited by Maria Ågren and Amy Louise Erickson. Aldershot: Ashgate.

Ranta, R. 1975. *Turun kaupungin historia 1600–1721*. Turku: Turun kaupunki.

Reenpää, L. 1981. *Serlachiuksen suku*. Helsinki: Otava.

Simonton, D. 2013. "Widows and Wenches: Single Women in Eighteenth-Century Urban Economics." In *Female Agency in the Urban Economy: Gender in European Towns, 1640–1830*, edited by D. Simonton and A. Montenach, 93–115. New York and London: Routledge.

Stadin, K. 1997. "Hade svenska kvinnorna en stormaktstid? Stormaktstidens svenska stat och konstruktionen av genus." *Scandia* 63 (2): 193–225.

Stadin, K. 2009. *Stånd och genus i stormaktstidens Sverige*. Lund: Nordic Academic Press. First published 2004.

Svenonius, E. 1670. *Dulce Amarum Mortis*. Åbo: Petter Hanson.

Tilly, L., and J. W. Scott. 1987. *Women, Work & Family*. New York and London: Routledge.

Toivo, R. M. 2008. *Witchcraft and Gender in Early Modern Society: Finland and the Wider European Experience*. Aldershot: Ashgate.

Toropainen, V. P. 2016. "Päättäväiset porvarskat: Turun johtavan porvariston naisten toimijuus vuosina 1623–1670." PhD diss., University of Turku.

Vainio-Korhonen, K. 1998. *Käsin tehty: Miehelle ammatti, naiselle ansioiden lähde: Käsityötuotannon rakenteet ja strategiat esiteollisessa Turussa Ruotsin ajan lopulla.* Helsinki: SHS.

Vainio-Korhonen, K. 2010. "Kaupan ja käsityön ammattikasvatus." In *Huoneentaulun maailma: Kasvatus ja koulutus Suomessa keskiajalta 1860-luvulle*, edited by J. Hanska and K. Vainio-Korhonen, 221–257. Helsinki: SKS.

van den Heuvel, D. 2007. *Women & Entrepreneurship: Female traders in the Northern Netherlands, c. 1580–1815*. Amsterdam: Aksant.

van den Heuvel, D. 2013. "Guilds, Gender Policies and Economic Opportunities for Women in Early Modern Dutch Towns." In *Female Agency in the Urban Economy: Gender in European Towns 1640–1830*, edited by D. Simonton and A. Montenach, 116–133. New York and London: Routledge.

van der Heijden, M., A. Schmidt, and R. Wall. 2007. "Broken Families: Economic Resources and Social Networks of Women Who Head Families." *History of the Family* 12 (4): 223–232.

Wottle, M. 2000. *Det lilla ägandet: Korporativ formering och sociala relationer inom Stockholms minuthandel 1720–1810*. Stockholm: Stockholms universitet.

5 Merchant Trade

A Family Affair

Cathryn R. Spence

On 2 June 1576 Katherine Aikman, who was the wife of William Aikman, a merchant burgess based in Dieppe, France, and also "procuratrix" for her spouse in all "causes and affairs with the realm of Scotland", received from a man named George Harkit the sum of 500 francs. The 500 francs was divided in two sums—£29 Flemish money, which was to go to her husband in Dieppe, and £178 6s 8d Scottish money, which was to go to her in Scotland.[1] As this case illustrates, with its combination of Scottish, Flemish, and French connections, Scottish merchants in the early modern period were actively trading with Europe. Not only money, but a wide variety of items—including cloth, wine, skins and hides, and amounts of merchandise—circulated between Scotland, England, and the European continent. These transactions, which could amount to significant sums—befitting the importance and the risk of overseas mercantile trade at this time—were complicated affairs. As such, they often required the involvement of multiple parties and a great deal of trust. Perhaps nowhere was this trust more apparent than between the husband and wife of a mercantile couple.

This chapter considers the wives who were engaged in mercantile activity in early modern Scottish towns, particularly between the years 1560 and 1640. During this period in Scotland, women participated in mercantile activity in two ways. A small number of high-status women were active, usually with their husbands or as widows, as merchants in the import-export trade. As exporters, these women shipped large quantities of goods to England and Europe. As importers, they brought goods into Scotland that were then resold in smaller amounts to local merchants and other, small-scale retailers. Cloth, leather, skins, and hides were among the exports, while cloth and wine were common imports. A larger number of women participated in mercantile activity in a second manner—through the retail of imported and ready-made goods. These women, who came from high, middling, and lower social statuses, sold cloth, wine, and miscellaneous items defined in the records as "merchandise" in small amounts to a wide range of consumers.

Rights and Roles in Trade

As this chapter will argue, cooperation between merchant husbands and wives was integral to the smooth running of businesses that traversed multiple countries and involved significant capital outlay. In addition, compounding the physical and economic challenges of overseas trade were certain social barriers. In early modern Scottish towns, only merchant burgesses were allowed to engage in overseas trade, and all burgesses were required to be married (McMillan 1984, 15). While women could attain merchant burgess status through their fathers (the status being a hereditary one in some instances), in reality men carried out most mercantile trade—at least officially. Through what was known as "right of wife", men could marry into the position of burgess, allowing them to begin trading overseas or to take over the legal responsibilities for a business their wife brought into the marriage (Brown 1985, 29; McMillan 1984, 15).[2] In the latter case, the wife, from the perspective of surviving documents, seems to cease all involvement with the business, though in reality this may not have been the case.

Regardless of who brought the business to the marriage or who was making the decisions, it was only men who travelled abroad for trade or acted as factors in England or on the European continent. It was extremely rare for women of any nationality to travel overseas to conduct trade, as the voyage was seen as dangerous and not suitable for women. However, the wives of merchant burgesses often acted with their husbands or in their husbands' steads by helping to take care of business at home, selling merchant wares or merchandise from shops or stalls, or carrying on trade after the deaths of their husbands. Therefore, while perceived as the preserve of men, in reality efforts in the mercantile sector of the economy used the combined efforts of merchant families. As this chapter will show, a number of high-status Scottish women were active, usually in concert with their husbands or singly as widows, as merchants in the import-export trades of early modern urban Scotland.

Women's contributions to the running of mercantile families in the late medieval and early modern periods have been increasingly recognised by historians in recent decades. Just as the rural-based family relied on the actions of all members of the household to succeed, so too did families who lived in towns and were involved in the import or export of goods rely on the combined efforts of the husband and wife. Women who married merchants engaged in overseas trade seem to have often come to the position almost hereditarily, in that the wives of merchants were often born to the position as the daughters of other merchants. In this regard, women contributed in a variety of ways. At the outset of a marriage they might provide their husbands with wealth, connections, and status. Heide Wunder (1998, 89–90) argues that "the daughters of merchants were prepared form a young age for their future field of work" in early modern Germany, either in the homes of their parents or in the homes of other merchants. Merchant daughters would often be charged with keeping the books of their fathers' businesses, a task they would later perform for their merchant husbands. The practice of the daughters of merchants marrying the sons of other merchants and into other merchant families has also been uncovered elsewhere. Barbara Hanawalt (2007, 83), writing of merchants in late medieval London, noted that such men were "high-status persons in English society and sought out alliances within their circle". Jennifer Kermode (1998, 321), in her discussion of merchant families in York, Beverley, and Hull in the medieval period also notes that daughters of merchants tended to marry other merchants, thus helping to "retain wealth and commercial expertise within the merchant class" through extensive marriage networks.[3] This has also been observed in previous studies of Edinburgh's merchant community. James Brown (1985, 54–55), in his study of the approximately 300 merchants and their families that made up Edinburgh's merchant elite between 1600 and 1638, noted similar practices and identified multiple merchant daughters who themselves married merchants. In addition to the skills and connections they brought to their marriages, these merchant wives would have had both a privileged position and vested interest in promoting and maintaining the businesses in which their husbands engaged, as their fortunes were also bound up in these transactions. Their economic interests sometimes predated their marriages, and often continued after their marriages had ended.

The presence of Scottish women in merchant trades has begun to be examined in recent years, although the latter half of the sixteenth century and much of the seventeenth has been overlooked. In terms of the roles of Scottish women in mercantile trades, Martin Rorke (2005, 81–96; 2008, 447–462) has investigated their roles in overseas import-export trade between 1300 and 1600 using custom books, which recorded exporters and their customable exports, which did not include all types of exports. Customable exports were limited to wool, skins, hides, coarse woollen cloth, salmon, sea-fish, coal, salt, and re-exports. Customs books recorded women acting as exporters either by their first and maiden names, or, more commonly, as the widow of a deceased husband. Rorke's study is therefore limited to a consideration of women who acted as traders in their own names, or as widows, rather than also considering the roles that the wives of male merchants named in these books might have played in the trade that operated in the name of their husbands. To be fair, discerning the economic roles of wives during this period is not easy. In debt litigation, for instance, the names of husbands are recorded in all debts, regardless of who initiated the debt. It is not always possible to determine if a wife was the primary actor, with her husband listed as a matter of convention, if both partners acted in concert, or if the husband was the primary actor. However, the details of the case do sometimes indicate who actually conducted the transaction.

Rorke's study could only include the role of women with regard to the export of a limited number of goods, and no imports, as records of imports to Scotland were not kept prior to 1597. Nevertheless, Rorke (2008, 452) was able to identify a number of female exporters, noting a peak in those from Edinburgh in the 1530s and 1540s, when approximately fifteen women per year exported wool and forty exported hides, skins, cloth, fish, or some other export, accounting for 10 and 5 per cent, respectively, of the export of these goods out of Edinburgh's port at Leith. In the late 1530s there were approximately 800 exporters active in Edinburgh per year. In other words, Rorke (2005, 89–92) writes, "during the boom there were around fifty women exporters each year, shipping about seven per cent of Edinburgh's exports". Between 1550 and 1580, however, the number of exporters who were women in Edinburgh had fallen to thirty per year. By the 1590s, when there were approximately 400 individuals exporting from Edinburgh per year, less than ten were women (Rorke 2005, 92).

Certainly, Rorke (2005, 96) makes a strong case for the declining presence of women as overseas exporters in Scotland over the course of the sixteenth century, but he does state that "it would be wrong, however, to see women as retreating entirely from the formal economy or from trade". He notes that most Edinburgh women who were both widows and exporters in the third quarter of the sixteenth century disappeared from the records after they remarried, and that these remarriages allowed the new husbands of these women to participate in overseas trade. In particular, he highlights the examples of Cuthbert Ramsay, who married Janet Fleming, and John Provand, who married Katherine Henryson. Both of these men, and their wives, will be discussed later in this chapter, and Rorke (2005, 96) admits that "it is conceivable that the strong bargaining position of the women allowed them to enjoy an active commercial role within these new partnerships". Further, Rorke acknowledges the roles many women who were exporters may have continued to play as retailers of imports long after their careers as exporters had ended.

Women also acted as merchants in the import-export trades in Edinburgh in the latter half of the seventeenth century. Helen Dingwall (1999, 155), in an examination of the Edinburgh and Leith port books for the later seventeenth century, uncovered "a small but consistent number of women, designated as 'merchants', signing for cargoes on their own behalf, and not on the behalf of their husband or other male merchant". In all, Dingwall (1999, 156) found approximately eighty women listed as importers or exporters in the port books, compared to several hundred male merchants who were active in the same period. Further, Dingwall notes that the goods controlled by women were often of smaller quantities than the sometimes considerable quantities imported or exported by men. Women who were merchants prior to 1690 tended to act as importers or exporters of cloth and textiles, which Dingwall speculates may have allowed their husbands to concentrate on "heavier" import-exports, including iron and wood. After the 1690s, women were increasingly active as merchants in the import of "a much wider range of goods, many of which were destined to stock the shelves of retail shops, owned or rented by women". Both Rorke and Dingwall clearly see the relationships between women acting as merchants and women acting as retailers as intertwined, both in regard to those merchants who became retailers at the end of their merchant careers, and those merchants who were active in supplying the goods that other women sold as retailers from their booths and shops. Their respective studies illustrate the continuing and active presence of women as both merchant wives and widows in the import-export overseas trade from the sixteenth to the late seventeenth centuries, and it is logical that women would have remained active in these trades in the decades that lie between these two studies.

One source that can be useful in uncovering the activities of women in merchant families are the inventories of testaments. These can be used to determine what goods women owned in large quantities at the time of their deaths. Significant quantities of cloth or skins and hides, for example, valued to hundreds or even thousands of pounds, indicate a woman who was active in the import or export of these items. References in testaments to the necessities associated with overseas trade, including shares in ships and men known as "factors" who were based overseas, can also indicate that a woman acted as a merchant.[4] Another useful source is Scotland's burgh court debt litigation, which can reveal evidence of wholesale and large-scale selling to others, and so can be used to explore merchant activity. These sources prove that women in Scotland during the sixteenth and early seventeenth centuries were active in the import and export of a variety of goods—namely cloth, skins and hides, and wine. Through this evidence, this chapter will show that a significant number of wives and widows were active with, or independently of, their merchant husbands in the import and export trade in Scottish towns during the early modern period. The mercantile trade in early modern Scotland was, therefore, very much a family affair.

Wives as Importers

Even as trade was a family affair in early modern Scotland, the various subcategories that made up trade—whether importing, distributing, or exporting—were nevertheless strongly gendered. In these three aspects of trade lay key roles that fell to either husbands or wives. The sale of cloth, for example, was an area of trade in which the roles of husbands and wives diverged markedly.

The cloth trade was crucially important to the economy of late medieval and early modern Scotland, and its import and export could be a lucrative business. As early as the twelfth century, coarse, undyed cloth was manufactured in the Scottish countryside, with finer, dyed cloth manufactured in the towns (Gemmill and Mayhew 1995, 350). By the thirteenth century, however, the higher quality cloth found in the urban markets had come to be dominated by Flemish imports, although Scottish cloth continued to play a role. In the fifteenth century, low quality Scots cloth began to be exported, chiefly through Edinburgh, but also as a Dundee speciality aimed particularly at the Baltic (Gemmill and Mayhew 1995, 352). By the post-Reformation period, various types of cloth (including silk, satin, taffeta, velvet, and canvas) were imported into Scotland from a variety of locations, including England, France, and Spain, while cheaper cloth was produced in Scotland both for home use and export. This is borne out in information contained in the testaments of women who listed large amounts of cloth, or debts for cloth, in these documents. Testaments can give an indication as to how extensively a woman was involved in the cloth industry at the time of her death through inventories (in which amounts and types of cloth and clothing, sometimes in larger quantities, were listed), debts owed to the woman for cloth, and debts owed by the woman for cloth.

A significant percentage of testaments written by women in this period—as great as one third of the testaments written by women in Edinburgh, Scotland's largest and premiere town in this period, and the port through which the majority of Scotland's imports travelled—listed amounts and types of cloth in their inventories (Spence 2016, 65). The amounts of cloth in the inventories of these women could range from the very small, comprising only a few ells (or lengths) of cheap Scottish cloth, to the very large, comprising significant amounts and multiple varieties of cloth that had been imported into Scotland. These latter inventories, comprising significant amounts and multiple varieties of cloth, speak to a woman's role in mercantile activity in a number of ways—through large amounts of cloth valued to several hundred or thousand pounds, the listing of types of cloth not produced in Scotland, a mention that the woman owned the share of a ship or had a factor, or a combination of these elements. Large amounts of cloth in an inventory indicate that a woman was trading actively in cloth at the time of her death, while smaller amounts suggest that she either was active at one time and had since sold the cloth she had once held to others, or that she had purchased cloth from a wholesaler or distributor, and intended it for resale.

Maryanne Kowaleski (1986, 152) and Marjorie McIntosh (2005, 225), writing about England in the late medieval and early modern periods, both note that opportunities to import and export cloth were limited to the most successful high-status female merchants, who had "unusual access to cash, credit, and international connections". The same seems to have been true in early modern Scotland, as the merchant women with the largest and most extensive inventories, indicating considerable wealth and status, while few, were those who were involved in the import and distribution of cloth. Elizabeth Stevenson, who died in December 1569, was quite extensively involved in the cloth industry with her husband, Alexander Park, who was himself one of Edinburgh's leading merchants in the latter half of the sixteenth century (Lynch 1981, 373).[5] The inventory of Elizabeth's testament contains a long list of various amounts and types of cloth, including serge, red and black velvet, black and purple satin, and red, green, yellow, and purple taffeta. The inventory of her goods was valued at over £3,300. This sum jumps to an impressive £12,000 thanks to the list of debts owed to her. These include a variety of debts owed by men identified as tailors who had likely purchased the cloth Elizabeth and her husband were bringing into Edinburgh.[6] Another woman able to lay claim to an inventory of this size was Katherine Henryson, the wife of John Provand, who died in August 1587.[7] At the time of her death, Katherine's inventory was valued at £6,000, but the total value of her testament rose to nearly £23,000 once all of the debts owing to her (and her husband, John Provand, who gained his overseas trading privileges through his wife [Rorke 2005, 96]) had been taken into account. The majority of Katherine's extensive testament is taken up with various amounts of cloth and debts. The inventories of both Elizabeth and Katherine indicate that these two women were both very much involved with their husbands in the import and export of cloth during this period. The fact that these detailed inventories and debts are listed in the wives' testaments suggests that these wives maintained active roles in the acquisition and distribution of these goods.

Janet Dick, who died in February 1568, was another Edinburgh woman who was obviously involved in the cloth industry with her husband, John Hamilton.[8] The inventory of Janet's testament contains an extensive list of various amounts and types of cloth owned by her and her husband together, including worsted, velvet, satin, and taffeta, the value of which was calculated to £1,300.[9] Not all of the types of cloth mentioned in Janet's inventory were native to Scotland. There is evidence in the inventory that she and her husband were importing cloth from England, Holland, and France, as, in addition to the fine cloths already mentioned, the phrases "certain remains of Holland cloth", "tanny Inglis worsale", and "lyons cavase" all appear in her inventory.[10] As a result, John and Janet would likely have needed to own a share of a ship, or to hire the use of a ship.

Wives as Shipowners

In the fifteenth and sixteenth centuries, transporting cargo usually entailed owning a share of a ship—no cases of entire ownership are extant in Scotland and possession of ship usually referred to a one-half, one-quarter, one-eighth, or one-sixteenth share (Sanderson 1983, 190; Ditchburn 2001, 10). For example, Helen Quintin, who was the wife of a mariner and merchant burgess in Leith and Edinburgh, listed her share of one-eighth of a ship called the "Lion of Leith" and one-eighth of another ship in the inventory of her testament in 1589.[11] Issobell Tait owned one-quarter of the ship known as the "Grace of God" when she died in 1586. Grissell Grig, wife of William Symson, a merchant burgess in Pittenweem, owned one-eighth (one-half of one-quarter) of a ship called the "James" of Pittenweem and one-quarter of a ship called the "Michael" of Pittenweem when she died in 1594.[12] Margaret Lauder owned one-eighth of one ship, one-sixth of another ship, and one-quarter of two more ships when she died in 1626.[13] Elizabeth Jackson listed one-sixth of a ship from Anstruther in her inventory in 1625; Isabel

Wilkie listed one-eighth of two ships, one called "The Robert" and the other called "The Blessing", in her inventory in 1632; and Barbara Muir listed her share of one-sixteenth of a ship in the inventory of her testament in 1637.[14]

Further up the Scottish coast, in the town of Dundee, evidence of ship ownership is found in the town's burgh court records. On 24 July 1600 three wives made up three-fifths of the owners of a ship called the "James" involved in a case with Margaret Kinneir, the widow of a mariner named Thomas Brok. In that case, two of the wives owned one-eighth of a ship and a third owned one-sixteenth of it.[15] The five owners of the ship were each found to owe Margaret, the creditor in the case, a share of the deceased Thomas's hire in helping to sail their ship. Each part owner was responsible for his or her share of the hiring fee. In the case of those who owned one-eighth of the ship, their share of the fare amounted to £5 12s 6d, and 53s 6d for those who owned one-sixteenth. From the information contained in the case, it is unclear if the wives mentioned owned the shares of this ship in their own right, or were acting in their (perhaps absent) husbands' steads. Either situation, however, shows clearly that these wives were engaged in the ownership and administration of the ship. In another case, entered into the Dundee records on 8 August 1600, William Fristo, the skipper of the ship called "Gift of God" was absolved from a claim pursued against him by Isabel Robertson, who owned one-sixteenth of the ship.[16] Isabel's claim against William alleged that he had sold some parts of the ship that belonged to her owners, as well as him having interfered with English cloth, oatmeal, and beef that had been transported in the said ship and also belonged to her owners. In this case, Isabel's lack of a relational identifier indicates that she was a singlewoman of some capacity and acting independently. Why she was acting alone, and did not have the support of the other owners, is unclear.

Returning to the practice of importing and exporting cloth, in general, the women who were most extensively involved in the import of cloth and imported the greatest volumes and varieties of luxury cloth into Scotland also tended to be those who were married to the richest and most prominent merchant burgesses in the burgh. That these women produced such detailed testaments and were able, in some cases, to bequeath the tools of their business (for example, the share of a ship) to their children indicates the crucial contributions they brought to these businesses. Helen Quintin, who owned one-eighth shares in two ships, bequeathed both of these shares to her youngest son in 1589.[17] Grissell Grig left her shares of ships to George and Thomas Dundas, although she did leave the use, handling, and profit of the ships to her husband, William Symson.[18] Since George and Thomas have a last name different to that of Grissell's husband, it is possible that these two men were Grissell's sons from a previous marriage, and that she was taking steps to prepare for their futures as merchants with this bequest.[19] Without these shares of ships, owned and controlled by wives, these family businesses would not have been able to engage in international trade to the extent they did.

Other women, who listed smaller and cheaper amounts of cloth in their inventories, still played an important role in the cloth trade. They may not have imported large amounts of cloth into Scotland, but they likely played a role in the distribution of that cloth. Evidence contained in testaments shows that wives were involved, more frequently, in the import and export of cloth on a smaller scale, typically dealing with smaller amounts of velvet, satin, or taffeta, as well as the less-refined and more coarse types of cloth, including black, harden, buckram, and buckasie.[20] Beatrice Wallis, who was married to David Beverage, a burgess, and died in January 1568, listed a wide variety of amounts and types of cloth, ranging from nine and a half quarters of violet velvet, valued at £8, to half a steik of white bukasy, valued at 35s, and two steiks of "auld bukrem", valued at 27s each.[21] Janet Fleming, who was married to Cuthbert Ramsay, also a burgess, and died in October 1570, in addition to listing a variety of fancier cloth in her inventory, listed no less than ten different amounts of black cloth, all presumably—as they merit no other distinction—the cheap black Scottish cloth that was the standard at this time.[22] Janet was known to be an overseas exporter. She was listed in the customs books for Edinburgh in 1558 both under her own name and as "Uxor Craik" (Rorke 2005, 86n25). While "uxor" often indicates "wife of", in this case the term more likely means "widow of", indicating that when Janet traded under her own name, her first husband was already dead (Rorke 2005, 85). Further, Janet's second husband, Cuthbert, began to act as an exporter himself only after his marriage to Janet, indicating he achieved the right to do so through her (Rorke 2005, 96).

Wives as Distributors

Once cloth had been imported into Scotland, women in mercantile families continued to be involved with its sale. When Marion Reid, the wife of William Leyis, a merchant burgess in Edinburgh, died in May 1589 she listed in her inventory numerous types and amounts of cloth, as well as merchandise, all of which was contained in the booth owned by her and her husband. Altogether, the items in their booth were valued to £771 16s 8d. In another example, in March 1604 Thomas Hunter was determined by the burgh court of Edinburgh to pay £10 to Jonet Wood and John Aitkin, her husband, for the price of English cloth bought specifically by Thomas from Jonet two years previously.[23] Returning to Dundee in January 1611, John Hall was ordered to pay 8 merks for cloaking cloth bought by him from Marjorie Jack and James Cockburn, her spouse.[24] Acting as importers, owning shares of ships, and participating in the sale of items, it is clear that women could, and did, have influence in this important branch of early modern Scottish mercantile trade.

Infrequently, wives are found more explicitly involved with the sale of cloth on their husbands' behalfs. On 28 March 1598, for example, Laurence McGill, an advocate, was determined to owe George French, a merchant burgess, and Katherine Nisbet, his wife, £40 for the price of good cloth bought by them from him. However, three months later—in May 1598—the debt was deleted from the records at Katherine's request, she "having special power of her spouse to receive sums of money" and acknowledging receipt of payment.[25] A year later, in December 1599, George and Katherine would again appear in the records; that time they were owed £00 by William Wallace, another merchant burgess, for English cloth.[26] Katherine and George were therefore clearly working together with regard to the import and sale of cloth, and Katherine had the ability to act independently of her husband—although as a result of his acknowledgement and permission—when she needed to do so.

This involvement of wives is mirrored in another aspect of Scotland's import trade—that of wine. Then as now, wine could not be produced in Scotland, and so it had to be imported, usually from France. While women did not travel outside of Scotland as part of this trade (or, indeed for any trade), they did perform important functions from within Scotland. In particular, women acted with their husbands in the import and sale of wine. In May 1624, for example, John Edgar, a merchant, and Katherine Russell, his wife, were owed £117 10s by Alexander Glen, also a merchant, for half a tun of French wine sold by them to him.[27] When Issobell Wilkie died in February 1632, in her inventory was listed five tuns of French wine valued to 200 merks per tun, or 1,000 merks overall.[28] And, when Susanna Finlaw died in the 1642 her inventory contained amounts of French wine that were valued to £395.[29] These volumes of wine were clearly not for personal consumption.

Since wine, as a perishable product, is less likely to appear in inventories than other items, it is often necessary to seek it out in records of debts in testaments and in debt litigation. This is helped by the fact that, once imported, merchants had the task of selling their wine on to others. The servant of Hector Purves and Issobell Adair, for example, sold half a tun of French wine to Katherine Christieson, the wife of James Lennox, for £120. James and Katherine were determined by the court to pay for this half tun of wine in July 1635.[30] When Elizabeth Jackson died in 1622 among the debts owing to her was a debt for £329 16s 4d. This debt was identified as being "by John Putill for wines".[31] In keeping with the tasks usually undertaken by merchant wives, most sales of wine imported by merchant burgesses were made by their wives to others. In 1618, a single woman named Christian Studieman was determined to owe William Muirhead, a merchant burgess, and his wife, Barbara Cant, £70 in complete payment of £120 for puncheons of French wine bought specifically by Christian from Barbara.[32] While both husband and wife are included as the creditors in these debt cases, it is often specified that the transaction was conducted by the wife.

Many wives clearly handled distribution on a significant scale, independently of their husbands. In the importation and distribution of wine we see one of the clearest examples of a marital division of labour.

Merchant couples who imported wine could therefore sell it in large amounts, as in the cases just cited, or in smaller amounts. Most often these smaller amounts were sold by a female servant, as administered by the wife, who would be tasked with selling wine (and perhaps other types of drink) in small measures to individual patrons in the streets. This approach had the benefit of providing a necessary and desired service to the community and also supplementing the larger-scale sales of a wine merchant. It also provided a source of income, particularly for female servants. Alexander McMath, a merchant, and Katherine McMorane, his wife, for example, employed Margaret Henry as a servant for the purpose of selling their wines. In December 1617 Margaret was determined by the court to owe the couple £297 13s for the wine she had sold that belonged to them.[33] Often, as with buying and selling amounts of wine that had entered the country, the task of employing female servants to sell wine in small measures fell to the wives in these merchant couples.

Wives as Exporters

While most women acted as importers—a function influenced both by expectations placed on their sex that they would not travel internationally and expectations placed on them maritally that they would be present to oversee the dealings of the families at home—some women did act as exporters of certain mercantile goods. In particular, women acted as exporters of hides and skins. The skins produced by the slaughter of live animals were important to Scotland's economy during this period, whether those skins and hides were dried and salted for export or tanned and turned into leather for home use (Spearman 1988, 139). Animal skins and hides were one of Scotland's major exports to France, the Low Countries, and, in particular, the Baltic in the latter half of the sixteenth century (Ditchburn 2001, 162). As noted by S. G. E. Lythe (1960, 159–160), '[i]n a typical year in the 1560s and 1570s about a million skins and hides passed eastward through the Sound [in the Baltic]. Of these, on the average, a quarter came from Scotland.' In the years following the 1570s, the Scottish export to the Baltic fell somewhat, averaging approximately 120,000 skins and hides per year in the years immediately preceding and following 1600. By this time, approximately 85 per cent of the trade in skins and hides went through Edinburgh (McNeill and MacQueen 1996, 253). The skins and hide trade revived in the 1620s, and the number of skins and hides exported from Scotland to the Baltic per year was pushed back up over the quarter million mark (Lythe 1960, 160).

In Scotland, as elsewhere, the trade in skins, hides, and leather was typically the province of men, but women did make up a small but significant percentage of these traders. Issobell Tait, who died in January 1586 and was the wife of Thomas Harvie, a merchant burgess in Irvine on the west coast of Scotland, listed in her inventory 26 dakers of dry hides worth £390, 11 and a half dakers of leather valued to £153 6s 8d, and three dakers of salt hides worth £45.[34] Similarly, Jonet Richardson, the wife of Thomas Lothian, a merchant burgess of Edinburgh, listed in her inventory made upon her death in 1589 2,500 sheep skins valued to £1,125 and 15 dakers of hides valued to £270.[35] Altogether, the amount of skins and hides listed in Jonet's inventory amounted to £1,395—almost 90 per cent of Jonet's inventory (which was valued to £1,557 6s 8d).[36] Katherine Pursell, who died in March 1623 and was the wife of a merchant burgess named William Muir, listed in the inventory of her testament more than 3,300 skins and fourteen and a half dakers of cow hides.[37] Together, these items were valued to nearly £2,000—two-thirds of Katherine's total inventory. Similarly, Elizabeth Arthor, who died in December 1648, listed in her inventory 300 sheep skins, 2,000 lamb skins, and 2,000 other skins.[38] Together, these skins were valued to £720, nearly a quarter of Elizabeth's £4,000 inventory. The variety of items listed in Elizabeth's inventory in addition to skins—including amounts of cloth, paper, iron, and sugar—as well as items identified as "inventory to Holland" (valued to £318 4d) and an amount of Flemish money (valued to £2,120) all provide evidence that indicates Elizabeth was involved in the import and export trade, as well as the sale of these items, perhaps with her husband or, given that he is not identified as a merchant burgess, independently.

That women held such large quantities of skins and hides in their inventories indicates a clear involvement in the trade of these items. For some of these women, whose husbands had already died, it could be argued that they had simply inherited the remnants of a business, rather than having been actively involved in that business throughout their lives. This cannot readily be disproved. Nevertheless, after the deaths of their husbands, these widows would have still found themselves involved in the trade, as they were forced to arrange for the sale of significant amounts of inventory.

Conclusion

Discerning the extent of women's involvement during their marriage brings us back to the difficult problem mentioned earlier in this chapter—as husbands bore the legal responsibilities for their families' economic endeavours, the names and actions of wives are largely absent from sources. One might expect, in fact, for wives to be completely invisible. However, this is not the case. A careful reading of debt cases will sometimes show that it was specifically the wife who conducted transactions on behalf of the family. It is also very common for both husband and wife to be named in a case, which is suggestive that the wife's presence may indicate more than a passive involvement in the transaction.

With regard to importing and selling wine, debt cases show wives taking the leading role in its distribution after it had been imported, selling wine in large quantities to others for resale. And, in testaments, wives routinely listed quantities of cloth, skins, and hides that are indicative of mercantile trade. These sources provide evidence of wives contributing to the mercantile family through transactions amounting to thousands of pounds. Yet, we know that in the majority of cases, a wife's involvement in the family business would have left no written record at all. It will likely never be possible to determine what percentage of wives were involved in their families' businesses, or how much control wives exerted in these affairs, but it is safe to conclude that the significant involvement detailed in this chapter is only the tip of the iceberg, with the greater volume lying unseen beneath the records.

Notes

1 National Records of Scotland [hereafter NRS], B22/8/2.
2 As Joyce McMillan (1984, 15) notes, "The burgh council stipulated that no apprentice could become a burgess until he had served his master or another freeman for a further three years after completing his training, unless he married a burgess' daughter, in which case he could claim his burgess-ship immediately". There was therefore significant impetus to marry a burgess's daughter for craftsmen and artisans, and it was likely a similar case for members of the merchant class!
3 Mary Prior (1985, 100, 102) has noted that merchant daughters in early modern Oxford married immigrants of the same or similar trades to their fathers and brothers, assimilating them into the community.
4 A factor was a person legally authorised to undertake business on another's behalf, particularly overseas.
5 Alexander Park was discerned to pay £60 in the tax roll of 1565, which was an effort to raise a loan of 10,000 merks for the purchase of the superiority of Leith. The average contribution made by merchants was £11 6s, so Park's contribution of £60 is notable.
6 NRS, CC8/8/1/708–13.
7 NRS, CC8/8/18/106–26. Katherine Henryson was the wife of one of the merchants identified by Margaret Sanderson (1983) as one of the six merchants whose value exceeded £1,000 sterling. Katherine was the wife of John Provand, the value of whose goods Sanderson cites as being £1,886. This figure is apparently arrived at by Sanderson using the testament of John Provand's wife, Katherine, as she alludes to Katherine's testament in her article, and as John Provand's testament is not extant among the records of the Edinburgh Commissary Court. Provand was a leading merchant of the 1580s. In the tax roll of June 1583 Provand was discerned to pay £25. The average assessment was just over 33s 4d (Lynch 1981, 378).
8 John Hamilton was another leading merchant in Edinburgh in the late sixteenth century. In the tax roll of September 1565 (the same tax roll which names Alexander Park, mentioned above), Hamilton was determined to pay £50 (Lynch 1981, 373).
9 NRS, CC8/8/1/139.
10 NRS, CC8/8/1/138–9.
11 NRS, CC8/8/20/347.
12 NRS, CC8/8/26/643.

13 NRS, CC8/8/53/584.
14 Elizabeth Jackson (NRS, CC8/8/52/688), Isabel Wilkie (NRS, CC8/8/56/27), Barbara Muir (NRS, CC8/8/58/104).
15 Dundee City Archives [hereafter DCA], Burgh and Head Court Books, Volume 21.
16 DCA, Burgh and Head Court Books, Volume 21.
17 NRS, CC8/8/20/347.
18 NRS, CC8/8/26/644.
19 While in the early modern period Scottish women did not assume the surnames of their husbands when they married, any children from that marriage did. Hence, it is unlikely that George and Thomas Dundas were the sons of William Symson, but it is possible (especially given the nature of this bequest) that they were the sons of Grissell and a previous husband.
20 Harden was a very coarse cloth made from "hards" or the refuse of flax or hemp. Buckram was a stiff cloth made of cotton, and occasionally of linen. Buckasie was a kind of fine buckram. (www.dsl.ac.uk)
21 NRS, CC8/8/1/116.
22 NRS, CC8/8/2/160–5.
23 Edinburgh City Archives [hereafter ECA], Register of Diets, 1603–06.
24 DCA, Burgh and Head Court Books.
25 NRS, B22/8/7/208v-209r.
26 NRS, B22/8/8.
27 ECA, Register of Diets, 1622–25.
28 NRS, CC8/8/56/27.
29 NRS, CC8/8/60/167.
30 ECA, SL234/1/12.
31 NRS, CC8/8/52/688.
32 ECA, Register of Diets, 1615–19.
33 NRS, B22/8/18, 349r-v.
34 NRS, 8/8/18/32.
35 NRS, CC8/8/23/205.
36 NRS, CC8/8/23/206.
37 NRS, CC/8/8/52/124.
38 NRS, CC/8/8/65/147.

References

Brown, J. J. 1985. "The Social, Political and Economic Influences of the Edinburgh Merchant Elite, 1600–1638." PhD diss., University of Edinburgh.

Dingwall, H. 1999. "The Power Behind the Merchant? Women and the Economy in Late Seventeenth-Century Edinburgh." In *Women in Scotland, c. 1100–c. 1750*, edited by E. Ewan and M. Meikle. East Linton: Tuckwell Press.

Ditchburn, D. 2001. *Scotland and Europe: The Medieval Kingdom and Its Contacts with Christendom, c. 1214–1545*. East Linton: Tuckwell Press.

Gemmill, E., and N. Mayhew. 1995. *Changing Values in Medieval Scotland: A Study of Prices, Money, and Weights and Measures*. Cambridge: Cambridge University Press.

Hanawalt, B. 2007. *Wealth of Wives: Women, Law and the Economy in Late Medieval London*. Oxford: Oxford University Press.

Kermode, J. 1998. *Medieval Merchants: York, Beverley and Hull in the Later Middle Ages*. Cambridge: Cambridge University Press.

Kowaleski, M. 1986. "Women's Work in a Market Town: Exeter in the Late Fourteenth Century." In *Women and Work in Preindustrial Europe*, edited by B. Hanawalt. Bloomington: University of Indiana Press.

Lynch, M. 1981. *Edinburgh and the Reformation*. Edinburgh: John Donald.

Lythe, S. G. E. 1960. *The Economy of Scotland in its European Setting, 1550–1625*. Edinburgh: Oliver and Boyd.

McIntosh, M. K. 2005. *Working Women in English Society, 1300–1620*. Cambridge: Cambridge University Press.

McMillan, J. K. 1984. "A Study of the Edinburgh Burgess Community and its Economic Activities, 1600–1680." PhD diss., University of Edinburgh.

McNeill, P. G. B., and H. L. MacQueen, eds. 1996. *Atlas of Scottish History to 1707*. Edinburgh: The Scottish Medievalists and the Department of Geography, University of Edinburgh.

Prior, M. 1985. "Women and the Urban Economy: Oxford, 1500–1800." In *Women in English Society, 1500–1800*, edited by M. Prior. Oxford.

Rorke, M. 2005. "Women Overseas Traders in Sixteenth-Century Scotland." *Journal of Scottish Historical Studies* 25 (2): 81–96.

Rorke, M. 2008. "Trade and Traders: Edinburgh's Sixteenth-Century Exporting Community." *Historical Research* 81 (213) (August): 447–462.

Sanderson, M. 1983. "The Edinburgh Merchants in Society, 1570–1603: The Evidence of Their Testaments." In *The Renaissance and Reformation in Scotland*, edited by I. B. Cowan. Edinburgh: Scottish Academic Press.

Spearman, R. M. 1988. "Workshops, Materials and Debris: Evidence of Early Industries." In *The Scottish Medieval Town*, edited by M. Lynch, M. Spearman, and G. Stell. Edinburgh: John Donald.

Spence, C. 2016. *Women, Credit, and Debt in Early Modern Scotland*. Manchester: Manchester University Press.

Wunder, H. 1998. *He Is the Sun, She Is the Moon: Women in Early Modern Germany*. Cambridge and London: Harvard University Press.

6 Marie Hackman—A Female Manager in the Family Firm Hackman & Co

Ulla Ijäs

Introduction

This chapter focuses on the early nineteenth-century businesswoman and manager Marie Hackman (b. Laube, 1776–1865). Marie Hackman lived all her life in Vyborg, at that time a small town 150 kilometres northeast of St. Petersburg. During her lifetime Vyborg belonged to the Russian Empire, and by the time of her death Vyborg had become the second largest town in the Grand Duchy of Finland. Marie Hackman's family connections gave her links to the German merchant class around the Baltic and in German port towns, but also with the German lower nobility in St. Petersburg and the Russian Baltic provinces (Koskull 1937, 56–71; Kuisma 2004, 449–450).

Marie Hackman's father, Johan Friedrich Laube, was an ennobled civil servant from Altenburg, Germany, while her mother Helena Haveman's family was involved in the timber trade in several Baltic port towns and in Lübeck. In 1799, Marie married Bremen-born merchant Johan Friedrich Hackman (1755–1807) in Vyborg, a union which produced two sons, Johan Friedrich Jr. (1801–1879) and Carl Alexander (1806–1846). Marie Hackman lost her husband in 1807, but afterwards continued the family business with the help of paid clerks until her eldest son took over the business in the 1820s.

This chapter demonstrates what it meant to be a female manager in a nineteenth-century family firm in Finland, in the eastern parts of the Baltic region. It explores both how and why a female manager of a family firm manifested her status in her consumption choices. The study argues that Marie Hackman made consumption choices like any other merchant house owner, even though they were typically men. Marie Hackman's consumption choices illustrate how she built her identity as the family firm's owner and manager. The importance of good taste and sociability as key motivations behind these choices will be discussed. What we consider, in contemporary terms, as belonging to the private sphere—i.e. purchases for one's personal use—cannot be separated from the public role of an entrepreneur when studying a late eighteenth- and early nineteenth-century context.

Hence, gender as a social concept will be illustrated, and the myth behind the "masculine" entrepreneur will be explored.

The aspects of material culture and consumption have been emphasised here for specific reasons. First, they allow approaching societal conditions and illustrating what it meant to be an entrepreneur. Second, when studying early modern entrepreneurs, typically there are no documents which include self-reflections, or in this case others reflecting on Marie Hackman as an entrepreneur. Evidence of her attitudes, emotions, and experiences concerning herself (as an entrepreneur) can only be found in her material belongings and in the documents which illustrate her purchases. Marie Hackman did not, for example, reflect upon her inner feelings in her letters, nor did she leave behind any diaries or personal notebooks. In this study, material purchases illustrate both the societal surroundings and the reciprocity inherent in the early modern business.

The concept of an entrepreneur is almost implicitly male, while a woman's role in the family business has remained under-investigated. In a family firm, women are often seen as helpers and private family leaders, but seldom placed in top positions in the business sphere (Hamilton 2006, 253–271; Martinez Jimenez 2009, 53–64; see also Lahtinen in this volume). Until relatively recently, if women ran their own business, they would have concentrated on providing food and care (Vainio-Korhonen 2002; Ogilvie 2003; Lahtinen in this volume). Despite the lively discussion about women's roles in enterprising or business families in history, scholars in business studies still maintain the narrative of the heroic male entrepreneur, while women remain invisible. Eleanor Hamilton (2006), for example, refers to Kate Mulholland's (1996, 123–149) sociological analysis of the creation of "entrepreneurial masculinities", where she argues that patriarchal strategies shape the role of women. In the field of history, and particularly gender history, the patriarchal subordination of women is questioned, and scholars have shown that despite the legal obstacles women participated in business life in several ways and, hence, one cannot speak about the inclusive subordination of women or the patriarchal rule as a monolithic ideology of the early modern period (Hamilton 2006; Mulholland 1996; Phillips 2006).

In this chapter, the term "family business" or "family firm" is used to describe the enterprising activities of a family. The business was owned and managed by the family members. The contemporaries, however, used the term "my house" or "our house" when referring to the business. This expression came from the concept of a merchant house (trading house); it could include a joint enterprise of several merchants, or be just a single merchant who ran the business on his own. In early modern society, the families' relevance to the economic system was fundamental; all business was family business, since the families and businesses were bound inextricably together (Müller 1998).

The studied time period extends from the 1790s to the 1850s, and the empirical data was collected from the archives of Hackman & Co, which are kept in the Central Archives for Finnish Business Records, and from the private archives of the Hackman family in the Åbo Akademi University Manuscript Collection. I have used letters and accounts that were kept for both business and private purposes. From these sources, I have also collected both qualitative and quantitative data, which will be analysed later in this chapter.

Women in Family Firms

Kirsi Vainio-Korhonen (2002, 15), in her study on female entrepreneurs in Finland, has referred to what she terms "classical" entrepreneur studies, and argued that in these studies the typical entrepreneur is usually characterised in very masculine terms. He is a resourceful pioneer, a creative and competitive man. Beatrice Craig (2015, 2) has demonstrated that the scholarship on business history is derived from early twentieth-century studies, such as Werner Sombart's (1863–1941) and Joseph Schumpeter's (1883–1950) theories, which make businesswomen "unthinkable" and focus on "the ultimate alpha male" entrepreneurs. Referring to Mark Cassons studies, Craig points out that the contemporary authority on entrepreneurship distinguishes self-employment from entrepreneurship. There are not many women in the latter group. Schumpetrian entrepreneurs are "creative destructors", and driven by their will to conquer and succeed for the sake of success itself. A lack of interest in the wives, daughters, or sisters of this masculine "entrepreneur-hero" has resulted in the invisibility of women in business studies and histories (Hamilton 2006; see also Colli, Fernández Pérez, and Rose 2003). Recently, discussion about breaking the myth of the heroic entrepreneur has arisen. Sarah Drakopoulou Dodd and Alistair R. Anderson (2007, 341–360) argued that one should not solely focus on entrepreneurs as individualised persons but, instead, studies should align with a socio-economic perspective and, thereby, break the myth.

In short, one should study family businesses as a matter of (group) identity and lifestyle. Andrea Colli (2003, 41) has written about the communal identity of European family firms, based on the traditional bourgeois *Gemeinschaft*. Unlike in the United States, the focus in Europe was on family-owned firms rather than corporations. In Europe, families were identified with the firm which brought them their subsistence, and, at the same time, the family was the main source of income, labour, and knowledge. This is in contrast to the United States, where enterprises were commodities, which could be bought or sold (about the communal values of family firms in Finland see Keskinen 2012).

By conceptualising both the family business and gender in time and place, one might overcome the obstacles of anachronism when speaking about "the identity of a businesswoman" or "the identity of a family entrepreneur" in studying the nineteenth-century business families and their female managers (Colli 2003, 19; Ahlberger and Lundqvist 2007, 9–26). This contextualising and conceptualising will also help us to avoid assuming the myth of the heroic male entrepreneur as the norm, or an idealised idea, and to reflect this idea in early modern societies without taking into account the different nature of businesses in the past.

The Case Study: Hackman & Co

Marie was the eldest child in the Laube family. She had two younger brothers, who were sent to study in the St. Petersburg military academy and then in field regiments, and it appears quite obvious that, from an early age, it would be she, instead of her brothers, who would continue the family business. The family strategy was to find an industrious husband for Marie, so that the sons could carry on their careers in the service of the Imperial army, which was at that time was a more prestigious and profitable career choice. A career in trade was uncertain, while a career in military service led to ennoblement after 25 years. Here, the gender of the business successor does not play the most important role. In fact, a woman could transmit the family assets to the next generation, and by choosing the right, hardworking, and intelligent husband for her, the family could spread their network to new towns. This strategy can be called expansive, and it was realized in 1799 with the marriage of Marie to the German merchant Johan Friedrich Hackman (Bull 2002, 193–210).

When Marie was being trained as a young woman to take care of her family estates and businesses, and when after that she actually did so, there is no evidence that anyone questioned her ability. For example, she traveled numerous times to St. Petersburg for business purposes. When her husband died in 1807, she continued the business transactions and, in 1812, she declared that she would continue the business "under her own name". She also later stated that, during the five years following her husband's death, she had been the only managing director of the firm.[1] Although these statements do not describe her in heroic terms, nor do they reveal any particular attitudes towards womanhood. These letters were written only because Marie Hackman officially declared who had the right to represent the company in public. In other words, the name of the person who was responsible for the debts and assets of the company had to be known (Lahtinen in this volume).

In all her actions, Marie Hackman put the well-being of her family and the success of the family firm first. Her actions in business were not based on individual profit-seeking and "heroic" maneuvers, but well-reasoned decisions which would benefit the family and the business. In her consumption choices, she never exceeded her financial resources or risked the family firm. Her actions were typical for her time; the importance of the social reproduction of a family was one of the most important aims of an entrepreneur. Social reproduction was a goal for male entrepreneurs, too, as Leos Müller (1998) has suggested. Hence, the family should never be threatened by poor investments in material goods, cash, credit, or people, including those married into the family. Without a well-functioning, reproductive family there could not have been a successful family firm (Colli 2003, 75; Müller 1998).

The legal premises of family businesses in nineteenth-century Vyborg were complex. Russian law and customs were used simultaneously with Swedish ones in Vyborg and its provinces. Some old medieval laws, such as the town law, also prevailed, while new Russian *ukases* were introduced during the eighteenth century. The Russian imperial order of 1785, for example, stated that anyone who could pay certain fees to the state could enter trade. According to his or her (women were also allowed to enter into business) annual fees, a merchant belonged to a certain guild with special privileges. The Russian concept of an entrepreneur might have been less gendered than entrepreneurship in most European countries at the time (see Ulianova 2009, 23–24). Export trade and factory ownership were allowed only to the members of the first guild, Marie Hackman among them. The guild system was abolished when Vyborg was annexed to the Grand Duchy of Finland in 1812. After that, the Swedish law of 1734 and trading ordinances were introduced, and the Swedish-style burgher rights limited entrepreneurship to men in towns, i.e. to the burghers. One must also consider, however, not only the legal premises, but also the socio-cultural aspects. Marie Hackman was born into a German family, and the business was usually organized in the same way as in the old home country. Even though the law might have allowed women to start their own enterprise, only a few, if any, German women in Vyborg took the opportunity.

Marie Hackman was in her early thirties when she lost her husband. J. F. Hackman died in June of 1807, and it is said that she had no knowledge of running the business at that time. However, this impression comes from twentieth-century male historians who have studied the firm Hackman & Co (Tigerstedt 1940–52; Enbom and Sandelin 1991). Apparently, they could not contextualise Marie Hackman within her own time and, instead, reflected the late nineteenth- and twentieth-century bourgeoisie ideal of housewives onto early nineteenth-century society. When studying Marie Hackman's life and her management more closely, it is evident that she had both the knowledge and the capacity to manage the business. Although she never had any formal schooling, her mother introduced her to the management of a large household. Her father was constantly absent on his duties in St. Petersburg—he was a businessman and a secretary at the provincial court. This meant that Marie's mother had to take care of the daily management of the family businesses, since Marie's brothers were sent to study in St. Petersburg and there were only the women left at home in Vyborg (about this typical pattern at the time, see e.g. Fairchilds 2007, 73).

Female management of Russian estates was typical; not only did women manage the household, but they supervised the farming and participated in business transactions. This is usually explained by the fact that women in Russia could own and inherit immovable goods, which was not typical in other parts of Europe (Ulianova 2009; Pickering Antonova 2013, 74–94, 228–234). Scholars who study the Nordic countries have highlighted that the possibilities and capabilities for women to work were better than in many parts of Europe (Christiansen and Markkola 2006, 9–30). Hence, some results based on the studies of British scholars, for example, cannot be extended to Russia or to Finland. The division between the public and private realms, and women's exclusion from the public life of business in Britain, was an earlier phenomenon than in Finland, for example. This was established already in the eighteenth century, hand-in-hand with the advent of industrialisation, which was also realised much later in both the Nordic countries and in Russia. Only recently have British historians argued that the whole picture of female entrepreneurship in eighteenth-century Britain was more complex; women were in fact active in many fields of business, as Nicola Phillips (2006) has argued.

Consumption Choices of a Female Entrepreneur

As a widow, Marie Hackman was obviously in charge of all purchases made for either private use or for the family business. As such, she represented both the masculine merchant and the feminine mistress of a household when furnishing her house. We should highlight, however, similarly to Amanda Vickery (2009, 300–301) in her work *Behind Closed Doors: At Home in Georgian England*, that such a gendered dichotomy might arise retrospectively, when trying to construct a picture of consumption in a certain historical time and space. Even when an object was marketed to men or women, we cannot be sure who ultimately purchased it, or who made the final decision to purchase it (Auslander 1996, 83; Vickery 2009, 300–301). Hence, the status of the household, not its individual members, should be considered. Marie Hackman purchased objects similar to her male counterparts in Tallinn, Lübeck, or Helsinki. She also employed her friends and business associates—yet another inseparable category—when commissioning goods.

This chapter illustrates the conspicuous consumption of a businesswoman, rather than how a businesswoman produced consumer goods for markets, which has been the typical case when studying businesswomen and consumption. Another typical approach to women and consumption in business families are studies focusing on the women of merchant-elite families and their activities at home; their consumption, charity, and other "leisured" tasks were achieved independently of the family business (Phillips 2006; see also Vainio-Korhonen 1998; Crowston 2013, 266–315; Craig 2015, 83–85). This impression of leisured upper middle-class/bourgeoisie women has remained since Thorstein Veblen's ([1899] 1992) sociological study, published in the late nineteenth century. He showed the world a family model that was in reality practised only among certain select urban groups in Europe and Northern America, where a woman's daily tasks were, more or less, consuming men's earnings. Veblen's critique of the American rich and their extravagant luxury consumption gave birth to the concept of conspicuous consumption, which combines a "keeping up with the Joneses" type of consumption, emulation, and the wasteful use of resources (Veblen [1899] 1992; Trentmann 2016, 13, 15). Yet, Veblen and many after him have not realised that entertaining and managing a social life were work, and a great part of this work was consumption. This type of consumption was not a woman's meaningless waste of money earned by her hard-working man; rather, the consumption had a reasonable purpose. The motivation for consumption might be attributed to status manifestation, manifestation of political, economic, or social alliances, and, of course, personal desires (Chalus 2005). Despite using the term "industrious" rather than leisured in describing the business families, the concept of conspicuous consumption can still be used; in Frank Trentmann's (2016) words, Veblen used it as "the engine of an entire social system". Display, imitation, and emulation are the terms illustrating conspicuous consumption. Group identity—what it meant to be a proper merchant, a good businessman, or more particularly a trustworthy, creditable business associate—was visualised through material culture.

The family business was the business of a family. As Nicola Phillips (2006) has highlighted, we should forget the dichotomy between public and private and, instead, focus on the overarching category of business in the studied period. Women's access to certain areas of business might have been restricted, but on the other hand their participation in areas which are considered "private" in modern terms were crucial for their business. Their appearance in fashionable clothes in fashionable places, their skills in both hosting parties and negotiating, were important for a flourishing family business. All of this can be discovered in Marie Hackman's consumption choices when her husband was still alive. It was all about "the latest fashion", and the price of the purchases was practically never an issue.[2] The social position of such a consumer becomes clear when studying a letter written in 1801. "My wife wants to show off in society", was Marie Hackman's husband's verdict when Marie insisted that he should order new accessories for a certain ball.[3] The case in point does not reveal the frivolity of young Marie Hackman, nor her leisured extravagance; as a newlywed wife, she had to dress according to her new marital status. But, more importantly, she had to dress in accordance with her husband's social status. Johan Friedrich Hackman was the most prominent merchant of their town, and was aspiring to the post of Prussian consul in Vyborg. A wife's responsibility was not only in taking care of the family life, or in managing the household duties, but to support her husband in his business and political affairs (Chalus 2005; see also Steinrud 2008; Pickering Antonova 2013; Auslander 1996, 83).[4] Complaining about his wife's desire for "showing off" was just J. F. Hackman's rhetoric; it was his way of apologising for the favour he was asking from his friend in St. Petersburg.

The purchase of Wedgwood china, white feather boas, and fashionable Spencer jackets,[5] made via a German merchant living in St. Petersburg, illustrate the importance of communal cultural norms and group identity. Not only the family business networks, but also shared ideas about taste and fashion, linked the merchants in the German-speaking communities around the Baltic. It was important to visualise these shared norms through material culture. For example, in 1813, an already widowed Marie Hackman purchased a silver bowl from St. Petersburg and wrote that she would like to have one similar to that of her neighbour, Mr. Heyno, who was—like Marie Hackman—a timber merchant with German roots.[6] The motivation for this consumption was emulation, but also in reinforcing group identity. The practise of emulation, and shared aesthetic tastes and fashions, illustrate the importance of community. In the early modern business, an individualistic, self-sufficient "pioneering hero" type of an entrepreneur was abnormal. Instead of promoting individualism, it was thought that a merchant should act according his social status. He should not exceed the line between decency and excess.

If one were to compare the family businesses of the northern Baltic with those of Germany, the common culture and material premises that prevailed in this network of German-speaking business families would immediately be evident. The same cultural consumption—the same journals, operas, and fashion styles—was pursued by the merchant families of Vyborg and Lübeck (North 2008, 2). In Vyborg, the culture of the "beau monde" can be seen on a smaller and more modest scale than in the metropolises of the time. "They had the clubs, the concerts, the balls, the masquerades, the embroidered waistcoats, the beautiful equipages", just like in St. Petersburg (Burja 1787, 77). In this case, we must, however, remember that the Vyborg elite did not relate to the Russian aristocracy in St. Petersburg, but to the German-English bourgeoisie/lower nobility elite also resident there.

In the late eighteenth century, sociability and politeness became major motivations underpinning bourgeoisie or middle-class consumption. China, silver cutlery, but also the comfortable sofas and elegant mahogany tables were used when polite society gathered (Auslander 1996, 83; Vickery 2009, 292–295). The sums spent on liquors, wines, tea, and coffee illustrates the importance of socialising in the Hackman household. One of the largest sums spent was on wine and other alcoholic beverages. The purchase of hundreds of bottles of red wine alone reveals the almost constant flow of friends and business associates who dined at the Hackman table. Traditionally, studies have emphasised the domestic nature of china and silver. When studying a family firm, one should not forget that it was the businesspeople who used and admired these objects. Associates, friends, and family formed overlapping networks. The goods might have been used in the family home, but they were still used to promote the business and to manifest status and social identity.

When Marie Hackman became the head of both the family firm and the family itself, as a widow, she continued to follow the pattern of consumption of a leader of a business family/family business. It was not her sex, but her social position that dictated her consumption practices. The most active years of the widow Marie Hackman were from 1809 to 1825, during which time the undefined household costs, food, alcohol, and her sons' education were the biggest categories of expenditure in the Hackman family. Horses and their equipage, and children's clothing, formed two other substantial categories (Ijäs 2015a, 2015b).

As a widow, if Marie Hackman had furnished her home in a very feminine way, she might have been giving a sign that she either did not understand or did not care about the masculine aspects of business culture. Working on large and heavy account books, to take a practical example, would have been impossible on a small and light table. If Marie Hackman would have had only a lightweight embroidering table (see Ilmakunnas 2016, 137–150) to hand, it might have raised doubt in her business partners' minds that she did not want, or was unable, to concentrate her efforts on business. Using money wisely and purchasing objects approved as social status symbols—those goods which were tasteful and fashionable—was perhaps even more crucial for a widow than for a businessman. A man in business could bend the boundaries of proper behavior without the fear of losing his standing in the eyes of his fellow businessmen. In business, as in the society as the whole, men had more opportunities, but this does not mean that men could freely choose their material belongings. A businessman's dress and dwelling should follow his social status and, foremost, his marital status; a notion that was mentioned by J. F. Hackman while he was still unmarried.[7]

One of the overlapping consumption categories that represents, perhaps better than any other, Marie Hackman's role and character as a business leader and a private person, and the importance of socialising, is her expenditures on gambling. If this were to be signified by a single object, it would be her gambling table. As in most European societies of the time, the lines between business and socialisation were blurred (Pickering Antonova 2013, 42). Marie Hackman, like many of her peers, loved to gamble. The purchase of new cards and gambling tables, as well as the money actually spent on gambling, is often exhibited in the family accounts (Ijäs 2015b, 209). Marie Hackman found gambling to provide the same sort of excitement for her as business did; it demanded speculation, risk taking, and fast thinking—all the characteristics which made a good businessman. Gambling was not, however, at the time, only a masculine hobby. Women, as well as men, gambled; and many did so for money. Marie Hackman considered gambling such an important part of business life that she encouraged her eldest son to spend more time at the gambling table than at playing the piano (Tigerstedt 1940–52, 323). Socialising over a game of cards was an essential part of business life, and it could teach one a lot about an opponent's character—for instance, the willingness to take risks and to negotiate. Marie Hackman paid attention that her sons did not lose their whole fortune at cards; hence, she cut off her youngest son's allowance when he was in his early 20s because of his excessive gambling. Gambling, as any other consumption sector, must remain within certain limits. Consumption should not be too showy, nor should it be too modest. Socialising was a virtue, but spending all your money on cards or on too flashy equipage was against the rules of a good business manager.

One of the biggest categories of expenditure between the years 1809 and 1825 was her sons' education. The culture of family businesses emphasised continuity, and the next generation was introduced to the family business early on. During the school years of the younger generation, Marie Hackman purchased books, instruments, and paid for private tutors for her sons. In their adolescent years, Marie Hackman spent almost equal sums on both of her sons' clothing and education. It would have been inappropriate if the young Hackmans would have worn old and worn-out clothes, hence the St. Petersburg tailors and fashionable clothes. Private tutors helped them to master the Russian, French, and German languages, and mathematics and geometry, but also music and dancing. This implies the lifestyle of the merchant elite; it was important not only to know how to calculate and do the books, but also how to socialise, and how to dress like a proper businessman.

Conclusions

In the research focusing on actual history rather than abstract economic theory, the "heroic male entrepreneur" model has been challenged, and scholars have shown that socio-economic circumstances affected both the male and female members of a family firm. In the world of nineteenth- century family businesses, when a woman inherited a business from her late husband and decided to continue it, she was treated as a fully legitimate manager. She had legal authority over the business, unless she remarried, which Marie Hackman never did. Instead of gender, social status might be a more helpful category in understanding the history of family firms. The importance of credit, trust, social status, and reproduction were crucial for the family firms. The consumption choices of family members both supported the current activities of the family firm and the continuation of the firm in future generations. Maintaining and improving social status via the consumption of objects which implied common cultural values increased trust within the business network. Asserting one's status by purchasing an expensive chandelier, for example, demonstrated that the family firm did not have financial problems, and hence was a trustworthy business partner. In this picture, the gender of the consumer did not play the crucial role. Instead, it was the social status that mattered; the crystal chandelier, for example, carried connotations of taste, fashion, and social networks shared by the purchaser and her peers. Marie Hackman built up her intertwined roles of both business manager and private person via these consumption choices.

When studying Marie Hackman's consumption as a business manager, it can be demonstrated that she was shopping in the same shops as the other managers, who were typically men. She acquired similar goods to those of married male merchants, i.e. those with their own house, and drove four-horse carriages just like her male counterparts. On the other hand, Marie Hackman also followed a pattern of consumption similar to any woman of the same social background; she shopped for the latest fashions and the comfortable domestic goods which were popular among polite society all over Europe. The family business demanded this; she had to show that she belonged to a certain set of society, and that she knew what belonging to this social group demanded of her. Fashionable clothes, large, solid writing desks, and well-educated sons represented the financial stability of the family business.

In all her actions, she put the family business first. Hence, no consumption, not even gambling, should be excluded from consideration. Frivolity or bad housekeeping in any sector of life, or by any member of the family, would be devastating for the business. This means that in the early modern family businesses, the idea of a Schumpetrian "creative destructor" was unthinkable. The business was not based on individual profit-seeking, but on the common good, enforced by communal values.

Marie Hackman was not merely a helper in the family firm, nor did she limit her agency to the private sphere. In the early modern family business, the public and private spheres were overlapping categories, as illustrated in this chapter. Women were crucial partners in family businesses. Their capability to socialise, to entertain, and foremost—to reproduce—were essential. The young Marie Hackman's desire to "show off her new dress" was a part of a business strategy. A fashionably dressed wife was a merit to any upcoming merchant. A wife's duty was to support her husband in his business and political aspirations, and this support was demonstrated in her outfit.

Group identity and shared cultural norms were enforced by consumption choices. These choices reinforced the network of German merchants, and hence strengthened their opportunities in trade and politics around the Baltic region. Thus, the purchase of a new steel-grey Spencer jacket, as was the case in 1801, from a fellow German in St. Petersburg, was not merely a favour to a friend. It was a sign that this friend was a special trustee, to whom he could commit this delicate task. His—or perhaps his wife's, which remains unknown in the letter—taste, sense of fashion, and trustworthiness was being weighed. At the same time, Marie Hackman and her husband will remain indebted to this friend, and hence the St. Petersburg friend may assume that his needs will be fulfilled whenever he asks in turn. This reciprocity, as demonstrated here, was not limited to business ventures. It also encompasses private life as well. At the time, these two realms were inseparable. In the early modern world of business, lone-wolf or pioneer types of entrepreneurs would not have succeeded, since business was based on cooperation at every level of the entrepreneurs' lives. The myth of a heroic male entrepreneur, with his individualism and extraordinary characteristics, was born in different societal circumstances, wherein trade was organised on different premises.

In her consumption habits, for most of her life Marie Hackman exhibited both masculine and feminine traits. Did she have any other choice? She represented the family firm in all aspects of her life and, since she was the only manager of the firm, she had to act according her status, despite her biological sex. Gender as a social category might help to explain this. Gender was and is more flexible than just one's biological sex; it can be negotiated within different social occasions, and at different times and places.

Notes

1 ELKA, Hackman & Co, B 21, 31 December 1812; Ijäs 2015a, 197–198.
2 ELKA, Hackman & Co, 17 July 1800, Bruun, St. Petersburg; 8 May 1804, Setterwall, Stockholm.
3 ELKA, Hackman & Co, B 12, 5 April 1801, Bruun, St. Petersburg.
4 Swedish ethnologist Marie Steinrud (2008) has studied Marie Hackman's peers in Sweden in her study. She provides an exhaustive survey of women's duties in the Tersmeden family, which owned iron ore mines in Sweden. In her study, Steinrud focuses on the public/private dichotomy, like many other scholars of the field. Katherine Pickering Antonova (2013) has studied gendered spaces in the early nineteenth century Russian noble estate.
5 ELKA, Hackman & Co, B 12, 29 March 1801, Bruun, St. Petersburg; B 15, 25 March.1802, Zagel, St. Petersburg; Ijäs 2015a, 2017.
6 ELKA, Hackman & Co, B 30, 13 December 1813 Clementz & Berg St. Petersburg.
7 ELKA, Hackman & Co, B 1, 19 August 1791, Frans Schumacher St. Petersburg.

References

Ahlberger, C., and P. Lundqvist. 2007. "Varans vägar och världar—en inledning." In *Varans vägar och världar: Handel och konsumtion i Skandinavien ca 1600–1900*, edited by C. Ahlberger and P. Lundqvist, 9–26. Göteborg: Historiska institutionen i Göteborg.

Auslander, L. 1996. "The Gendering of Consumer Practices in Nineteenth-Century France." In *The Sex of Things: Gender and Consumption in Historical Perspective*, edited by V. de Grazia with E. Furlough. Berkeley, Los Angeles, and London: University of California Press.

Bull, I. 2002. "Inheritance in Family Business: The 'Long' Merchant Family: Problems Concerning Generation Change." *Scandinavian Journal of History* 27 (4): 193–210.

Burja, A. 1787. *Observations d'un voyageur sur la Russie, la Finlande, La Livonie, la Curlande et la Prusse.* Nouvelle edition, revue & corrigeé. Maestricht: Jea. Edme Dufour, & Ph. Roux, Imprimeurs-Libraires, associés.

Chalus, E. 2005. *Elite Women in English Political Life, ca 1754–1790.* Oxford: Oxford University Press.

Christiansen, N. F., and P. Markkola. 2006. "Introduction." In *The Nordic Model of Welfare: A Historical Reappraisal*, edited by N. F. Christiansen, K. Petersen, N.

Edling, and P. Haave, 9–30. Copenhagen: Museum Tusculanum Press, University of Copenhagen.

Colli, A. 2003. *The History of Family Business 1850–2000*. Cambridge: Cambridge University Press.

Colli, A., P. Fernández Pérez, and M. B. Rose. 2003. "National Determinants of Family Firm Development? Family Firms in Britain, Spain, and Italy in the Nineteenth and Twentieth Centuries." *Enterprise & Society* 4 (1) (March): 28–64.

Craig, B. 2015. *Women and Business Since 1500: Invisible Presences in Europe and North America.* London: Palgrave Macmillan.

Crowston, C. H. 2013. *Credit, Fashion, Sex: Economies of Regard in Old Regime France*. Durham and London: Duke University Press.

Drakopoulou Dodd, S., and A. R. Anderson. 2007. "Mumpsimus and the Mything of the Individualistic Entrepreneur." *International Small Business Journal* 25 (4): 341–360.

Enbom, S., and C. F. Sandelin. 1991. *Ett handelshus i Viborg: Hackman & Co. 1880–1925*. Helsingfors: Hackman.

Fairchilds, C. C. 2007. *Women in Early Modern Europe, 1500–1700*. Harlow, UK and New York: Pearson/Longman.

Hamilton, E. 2006. "Whose Story Is It Anyway? Narrative Accounts of the Role of Women in Founding and Establishing Family Businesses." *International Small Business Journal* 24 (3) (June): 253–271.

Ijäs, U. 2015a. "Favourites of Fortune: The Luxury Consumption of the Hackmans of Vyborg, 1790–1825." In *Gender and Luxury in the Modern Urban Economy: A European Perspective*, edited by M. Kaartinen, A. Montenach, and D. Simonton, 190–205. London and New York: Routledge.

Ijäs, U. 2015b. "Talo, kartano, puutarha: Kauppahuoneen omistaja Marie Hackman ja hänen kulutusvalintansa varhaismodernissa Viipurissa [The House, the Mansion, the Garden: Merchant House's Owner Marie Hackman's Consumption Choices in Early Modern Vyborg]." PhD diss., University of Turku.

Ijäs, U. 2017. "English Luxuries in the Nineteenth Century Vyborg." In *A Taste for Luxury in Early Modern Europe: Display, Acquisition and Boundaries*, edited by J. Ilmakunnas and J. Stobart. London: Bloomsbury.

Ilmakunnas, J. 2016. "Ompelupöytä—naisten arkinen ylellisyysesine 1700- ja 1800-luvun Euroopassa." *Historiallinen Aikakauskirja* 2: 137–150. [With an English abstract: Work table: An everyday feminine luxury object in eighteenth- and nineteenth-century Europe.]

Keskinen, J. 2012. "Oma ja yhteinen etu: Kauppiaiden keskinäinen kilpailu ja yhteistyö Porin paikallisyhteisössä 1765–1845." PhD diss., University of Turku. [With an English summary Private and Public Interests: Cooperative Competition in the Merchant Community of Pori 1765–1845.]

Koskull, J. 1937. "Släkten Hackmans stamfäder i Bremen." *Suomen sukututkimusseuran vuosikirja XIX–XX 1935–1936*, 56–71. Helsinki: Suomen sukututkimusseura.

Kuisma, M. 2004. "Marie Hackman (1776–1865)." In *Suomen kansallisbiografia 3: Forsblom—Hirn*, edited by M. Klinge, A. Mäkelä-Alitalo, and A. Litzen, 449–450. Helsinki: Suomalaisen Kirjallisuuden Seura.

Martinez Jimenez, R. 2009. "Research on Women in Family Firms: Current Status and Future Directions." *Family Business Review* 22 (1) (March): 53–64.

Mulholland, K. 1996. "Entrepreneurialism, Masculinities and the Self-made Man." In *Men as Managers, Managers as Men: Critical Perspectives on Men,*

Masculinities and Managements, edited by D. L. Collinson and J. Hearn, 123–149. London: Sage.
Müller, L. 1998. *The Merchant Houses of Stockholm, c. 1640–1800: A Comparative Study of Early-Modern Entrepreneurial Behaviour*. Uppsala: Uppsala University Press.
North, M. 2008. *Material Delight and the Joy of Living: Cultural Consumption in the Age of Enlightenment Germany*. Translated by P. Selwyn. Aldershot and Burlington: Ashgate Publishing.
Ogilvie, S. 2003. *A Bitter Living: Women, Markets, and Social Capital in Early Modern Germany*. Oxford and New York: Oxford University Press.
Phillips, N. 2006. *Women in Business 1750–1800*. Woodbridge: The Boydell Press.
Pickering Antonova, K. 2013. *An Ordinary Marriage: The World of a Gentry Family in Provincial Russia*. Oxford: Oxford University Press.
Steinrud, M. 2008. *Den dolda offentligheten: Kvinnlighetens sfärer i 1800-talets svenska högreståndskultur*. Stockholm: Carlssons.
Tigerstedt, Ö. 1940–52. *Ett handelshus i Wiborg: Patriciesläkten Hackmans öden 1790–1879*, I–II. 2 vols. Stockholm: Wahlström & Widstrand.
Trentmann, F. 2016. *Empire of Things: How We Became a World of Consumers, from the Fifteenth Century to the Twenty-First*. London: Allen Lane.
Ulianova, G. 2009. *Female Entrepreneurs in Nineteenth-Century Russia*. London and Brookfield: Pickering & Chatto.
Vainio-Korhonen, K. 1998. *Käsin tehty: miehelle ammatti, naiselle ansioiden lähde: käsityötuotannon rakenteet ja strategiat esiteollisessa Turussa Ruotsin ajan lopulla*. Helsinki: Suomen historiallinen seura.
Vainio-Korhonen, K. 2002. *Ruokaa, vaatteita, hoivaa: Naiset ja yrittäjyys paikallisena ja yleisenä ilmiönä 1700-luvulta nykypäivään*. Helsinki: Suomalaisen Kirjallisuuden Seura. [With an English Summary: Food, Clothes Care—Finnish Female Entrepreneurs from 1750 to the Present-Day]
Veblen, T. (1899) 1992. *The Theory of the Leisure Class*. With an introduction by C. Wright Mills. New Brunswick: Transaction Publishers.
Vickery, A. 2009. *Behind Closed Doors: At Home in Georgian England*. New Haven and London: Yale University Press.

Section II

Notions of the Visibility and Invisibility of Women

7 Moving Between Visibility and Invisibility

Understanding Social and Family Business Spheres

Henrietta Nilson and Ulla Hytti

Introduction

The family firm is an institution that has historically been forced to adapt to social and juridical environmental situations. Because the leadership and day-to-day running of the firm is embedded in the social entity of the family, a complex understanding of the family business calls for a more inclusive approach towards different family members. One such family member is the wife. Coming from history in which women were denied ownership of family firms (Karlsson-Stider 2000), the wife has been described as the one doing the paper work in the firm, being the caretaker that is not viewed by others (Hollander and Bukowitz 1990), and also the person who requires perfection and control (Vera and Dean 2005). These different roles can create ambiguity (Dumas 1989) in relation to the various social spheres: in the family firm (co-worker), in the family (mother, wife), or in the surrounding social setting (friend, activities). Wives have often taken multiple roles when it comes to earning the family income, such as working in the family firm as well as holding outside employment. Even if wives have been acknowledged by their contribution to the family's well-being and the firm's wealth, they have often been absent from public records regarding salary and titles (Martinez Jimenez 2009), and frequently went without any compensation at all (Rowe and Hong 2000). This absence has led to a discussion about wives and women from an invisibility aspect (Lyman, Saganicoff, and Hollander 1985).

"Invisibility" of women in family business research can have different meanings. It can be referred to as *not being allowed to work in the business but doing so anyway* (Karlsson-Stider 2000). That is, legal restrictions hindered women from publicly declaring a stake but their labour was indeed critical for the family firm (Bersbo 2012). This kind of invisibility is, in some regards, equal *to being hidden*, which also can be compared to the power of ruling norms in the society, as shown, for example, in the absence of titles and salary (Martinez Jimenez 2009). A second kind of invisibility is the *lack of a description of activity*. For instance, within entrepreneurship research the heroic male is the ruling norm undermining the role of women

(Hamilton 2006), and interest in studying women who achieve leadership positions in family firms has been surprisingly low (Nelton 1998). A third form of invisibility and visibility is also mentioned as *a kind of neglect*. There are examples where women are discriminated due to their gender (Wang 2010) and their professionalism is overlooked which leads to feelings of invisibility (Cole 1997). Furthermore, the family business institution also nurtures neglect in the action of women's socialisation processes. This is affected by society's prejudices (Salganicoff 1990) as well as the lack of opportunity to take over the firm in a succession process (Haberman and Danes 2007), where sons have been the first choices as heirs (Sentuti 2009). The neglect of daughters in the succession process is also about not allowing them time to become prepared for the visibility leadership in a family firm demands (Kram and McCollom-Hampton 2003). Daughters in family firms sometimes also suffer from being compared to their parents, especially when mothers rule the family firm. To live in *the mother's shadow* is to be constantly compared by non-family members to the mother who leads the family firm which makes the situation coloured by invisibility (Vera and Dean 2005). The description of (in)visibility is faceted and difficult to grasp, yet they are phenomena that contribute to womens' and wives' everyday life in family firms. This chapter follows Hamilton's (2006) suggestion to take a closer look at the alternative gender discourse and practises that make family businesses a unique phenomenon. The aim of this chapter is to explore:

> *How moving in-between visibility and invisibility in different social and family business spheres is done to secure a self-rewarding and empowered role.*

In order to address this aim, the chapter is organised as follows. First, we will introduce our idea of (in)visibility as a theoretical construct by relying on Asplund's (1987) theory of social responsivity. Second, we inform of our methodological approach and ways of gathering and analysing the research materials before moving into presenting our findings in the form of Vera's story. The chapter closes with our discussion of arenas for moving between visibility and invisibility to highlight the theoretical insights from the empirical materials and with the concluding remarks where we will summarise the main contribution of the chapter.

(In)visibility—A Theoretical Development

The faceted use and the multiple meanings of the term "(in)visibility" (that is, visibility and invisibility) in earlier research made it necessary to ground the term theoretically and find a standpoint for its interpretation (Nilson 2015). The present study uses the social theory of responsivity by Johan Asplund (1987) and further develops it from earlier research about (in)visibility (Brighenti 2007, 2010). The theory's point of departure is in the social interaction between two or more individuals and the idea that our experiences are not born from within us but are the outcome of relating ourselves to the social and physical world (Israel 1988). This calls for a social responsivity "where one part's action is a response to the other's stimuli" (Asplund 1987, 10). The process of social responsivity is seen to be spontaneous but not pre-programmed, such as a reflex. A person can be "responsive spontaneously and *at the same time* critical or at least can reflect about her or his own behaviour and the actions to which he or she reacts as well as to others' reactions to her or his own actions" (Israel 1988).

In this social process there are arenas or special units[1] for the involved to communicate and pay attention to each other that invite some people but exclude others (Asplund 1987). The invited are socially responsive towards each other but asocial towards the rest of the world to a different degree. The social responsivity between a mother and an infant is an example of such a special unit. Alternatively, a phone call between two close friends can form such an arena for those involved and invited that spontaneously excludes others (Asplund 1987). Visibility and invisibility are conditioned and constructed in these arenas of social responsivity (Nilson 2015). Visibility is invited by positive attitude with smiles, attention, glances, and gestures towards the person who is being welcomed into the arena. For example, the entry of an individual into a family business meeting could be recognised with affirmation and offering of a chair. The person in question is thus rendered visible enabling feelings of belonging to the arena (also Hytti et al. 2017). On the other hand, invisibility is reinforced in the form of neglect, such as turned backs or the avoidance of eye contact and exclusion of the individual (Nilson 2015), if for example trying to engage in a conversation about the family business. Thus, in the exclusion from the arena the invisibility is reinforced. For the rest of this chapter, the above-mentioned interpretation is the one used regarding the phenomena of (in)visibility.

Methodology: Consciousness About (In)visibility

It is necessary to give careful thought about the chosen method when conducting research on phenomena like (in)visibility, as neither the words nor the phenomena by themselves are frequently used or spoken about in everyday life (Nilson 2015). In the present study, dialogue is used from a Freirean (1970, 1974) perspective, which involves holding a dialogue as a way of knowing (1970) and making platforms where consciousness about phenomena is possible. In this specific case the life story (Johansson 2005) and interactive dialogue (Freire 1970, 1974) were used as a grounding for the participants to increase their consciousness.

The present study was initiated with an invitation to Vera, a mother of four children and a part of a family business. Vera was considered an interesting participant as she, now in her late 70s, had a lifelong experience of a family firm—from childhood to adulthood—working together with her family members, and hence we expected that she would have some knowledge about being (in)visible. However, since (in)visibility as phenomena are relatively unfamiliar for us—something that we do not regularly think, it was necessary to create platforms for consciousness. Therefore, the starting point for this was to ask her to tell her life story (Johansson 2005) in an interview. The initial question for Vera was: *Can you please tell me about your life in the family firm, from the very beginning up till now?* As the aim with the interview was to let her speak freely, there were no prepared questions or guidance for Vera during the interview, just subtle nods to reassure her that she can continue with her story.

In the first phase a content analysis (Czarniawska 2014) was conducted by relying on the theoretical framework in the study that focused on (in)visibility. Then the story was rewritten in a short version and the words visibility and invisibility were inserted in the text and this *new* story rewritten by the first author was sent to Vera. In a first Freirean (1970) dialogue, the content of the new story was discussed between Vera and the first author where the focus was on Vera´s experience of reading about herself in terms of (in)visibility. At this phase she was asked the following question: *Can you describe your experience of reading about yourself in terms of (in)visibility?*

In a second dialogue, that took place after three years, the discussion was focused on what (in)visibility *did* to her, that is, *her* experience of the dialogue and how the story about herself in terms of (in)visibility had *affected* her life. In this dialogue she was asked to respond to the question: *Have (in)visibility done anything to you? Has something happened after you read your story about (in)visibility?*

By letting the respondent become conscious about the phenomena, both the meaning of the words and the context in which they are occurring can be discussed and understood (Nilson 2015). This is an interactive method in which the researcher is involved, and also interferes with the process (Alvesson and Kärreman 2012). A mutual learning develops in the interaction between the researcher and attendant; moreover, the knowledge production is aimed both at the practitioner and at academia (Docherty, Ljung, and Stjernberg 2008).

Vera's Story

Vera is a woman, mother (of four), wife and, during the present study, also worked in her and her husband's family firm. The life story takes it departure from her early childhood to be continued over her lifespan.

Childhood and Upbringing

> *"A girl in the manufacturer's shop was going to get married so the position was free. I begged my father on my knees to give me permission to apply for the job. I told him I would milk the cows before I leave in the morning and*

> *as soon as I get back in the evening. I knew he could not manage the milking part on his own. He turned me down—I thought it was a bit harsh; I have thought about it since."*
>
> *(Nilson 2015, 76)*

This is how Vera talks about her life as a 15-year-old girl who lived on a farm together with her parents and siblings during the 1950s in Sweden. These were times when women were still suffering from the aftermath of juridical restrictions regarding ownership in family firms (Karlsson-Stider 2000) The quote informs how the employment options were strongly constrained for women and fathers in particular were in an important position to influence them (Lamb 2000).

Vera's upbringing was coloured by manual labour. The whole family took part in the daily work on the farm and in the woods. Every family member, regardless of gender, had to make an effort. As the youngest of the siblings, Vera was expected to help her parents out. She was forbidden to accept paid work outside the farm and had to rely on her parents' good will to buy her clothes and other things she needed, in other words, payment in favours instead of money. During her spare time Vera often visited her grandparents' house to spend time with them, enjoying their company and baking cakes. The family was highly religious which was also related to complying with certain norms and expected behaviour, such as avoidance of showing off. On one of her birthdays, Vera received an accordion enabling her to immerse into the world of music.

> *"I was standing there in the living room just like that and played and played. My mother was mortified and she said, 'don't you have anything else to do?"*
>
> *(Nilson 2015, 77)*

Despite her mother's discomfort, Vera practiced even when she was supposed to be helping out with household chores. Music came to be her most important area of interest and after a while she joined the church's orchestra. Vera learned to play her instrument well and was eventually given a position in the church as a choir leader. She was an active musician and the stage became an important venue; the music was also a forceful tool for allowing her to meet new people and overcome some of her shyness.

The emotional connection to her mother was different to that of her father. Vera had some difficulties handling her mother's gloomy mood, while her father made hard work in the woods into cheerful moments to remember. He was a joker and made the work and the tough life a lot easier which she found amusing. Eventually, at the age of 21, Vera got married and moved out from the family farm. At that time her work was replaced by a milking machine that her parents finally decided to buy.

Vera's Adult Life

Vera and her husband had four children and during their upbringing Vera was a housewife. Meanwhile, her husband started a family firm where the area of business involved restoring old furniture, and worked on it part-time. In addition, he had a paid full-time position at the railways responsible for ticket inspection among other things. The couple bought an old house that was large enough for the family and the business. Vera found this compelling as the firm was close to their home and when the children grew up and were able to manage on their own, Vera took a more active part in the family business and so did two of their children, a son and a daughter.

Although the family business was located in the family home, Vera was not a part owner of the firm, she assisted her husband in the family business and at his other paid position. Vera sometimes found it challenging to work in the family firm, especially during high season and peak hours for deliveries when the working hours could stretch into the night. When demands from customers were excessive, the couple sometimes argued, taking different sides in the discussion (customer versus family business). Vera's input on both positions was neither paid nor recognised with a title; she was a worker without any formal job description or salary, a scene with a close resemblance to her childhood.

Eventually, Vera took on a part-time job cooking for elderly people in their homes. She was known as a good worker and was well-liked and appreciated by her clients. Now, for the first time in her life, she was earning her own salary and had a position. She was delighted about the money and used it to buy clothes of her own, which had always been one of her favourite pleasures.

Vera is a social yet shy person. Her social sphere was connected to her private life as well as the church and the business. She spent time with elderly people, an activity that continued throughout her whole life which started out with her relatives but expanded eventually to the clients via her job. Moreover, the church functioned as a place for social interaction in which she helped out by serving coffee at their gatherings, as well as acting as a popular entertainer. Even the family business served as a social venue were Vera could meet people and socialise. She discussed and gave customers recommendations about articles and how to restore their furniture that she found suitable. Furthermore, the family business was a venue for uniting the family and Vera especially enjoyed the coffee breaks, with discussions with her children about life and religion. This was a time of social interaction that she misses nowadays, although she points out that she is not missing the work.

Platforms and Arenas for Moving Between Visibility and Invisibility

Previous research on women in family firms has strongly highlighted their invisibility. Women are unlikely to be named successors (Martinez Jimenez

2009; Martin 2001; Wang 2010), there are stark differences in the tasks women and men perform, women are considered important in mediating between the family and the business, and women are not paid for their contributions (Martinez Jimenez 2009). However, recently research has suggested that invisibility is not absolute but relative, and women may be invisible yet hold powerful positions (Al-Dajani and Marlow 2010; Cole 1997; Hamilton 2006). Smith (2014) suggests that the matriarchal voice in the family business is strong despite the "official male leader" (Deacon, Harris, and Worth 2014). Hamilton (2006, 2013) questioned the overarching explanatory power of patriarchy for gender relations in family business. Indeed, individuals can resist and challenge patriarchal relations in the family firm, and women often take on important roles that are not necessarily reflected by their title but nonetheless they play an important part in shaping family business fortunes (Hamilton 2013; Cole 1997). In addition, Hytti et al. (2017) suggest that accessing the family business leader identity sometimes requires concealing the leader identity at certain times. Hence, invisibility can be a tool or mechanism for the women in family business assumed power.

Vera's story is illustrative of her moving between visibility and invisibility in the different arenas both in the public and private spheres. During her upbringing, Vera was *socialized into working in the family business* (Cabrera-Suarez, Saa-Perez, and Garcia-Almeida 2001; Miller, Steier, and Le Breton-Miller 2003) that she somehow had to relate to. The society's strong restrictions, along with the need to make ends meet, meant that Vera's choices and opportunities for alternative actions other than working in the family farm were extremely limited. She tried crossing the boundaries by asking her parents for approval to take on a paid job, but was unsuccessful in her endeavour—an episode she still considers unfair. Her reflections on her moving out from the family home and her work being then replaced by a milking machine, communicates a young girl's invisibility within the family farm domain. However, even if her family situation was strained, there were arenas for visibility even in this context. One such arena was her work in the woods together with her father. She enjoyed his company and primarily his happy mood and good temper, which meant that even if the work was hard for a young girl, her father was acknowledging her presence rendering her visible.

Although her parents denied her to work in paid positions, they *embraced her interest in another social sphere* (music). While objectively considered waste of time away from working in the family farm, Vera was able to spend time in practising and performing. The music helped her to become visible. That is, she could use the music and the performance as a vehicle to be highly visible in a situation that would otherwise have been very hard due to her shyness as well as existing social norms. The music has followed her ever since and these memories remain close to her heart.

An individual's role is linked to the expected behaviour within that role (Leaptrott 2005). *Informal and formal institutions such as religion and religious communities influence on the individuals* involved. Religious rules are powerful tools that sometimes may restrict individuals' social actions. Living in a deeply religious family often gives little room for stretching those boundaries as the social norms affect individuals' understanding of feasible actions, and how they construct their identities (Stenholm and Hytti 2014). Vera had the opportunity to circumvent the religious society's restrictions about not showing off by taking advantage of the stage offered in the church in two different ways: as a performer and as an active and legitimate agent in the church gatherings. This enabled her to be highly visible without annoying or embarrassing anyone in her family or herself. The platform served as a social and amusing arena that the whole religious community could embrace. Additionally, becoming an active volunteer worker in the church offered Vera another "stage" on which to perform. Her roles as an entertainer and volunteer were legitimate roles within the church. The church as an arena served as a social setting for Vera to communicate with other people and be visible in a socially accepted way. This could be interpreted as a form of identity or role switching and moving in and out of visibility by relying on different identities or roles. The social norms might have made it difficult for her to become visible if playing for example folk songs but her role as a musician playing religious music in the church enable her to navigate the social norms, temper the disruptions, and ensure visibility (Hytti et al. 2017).

Vera got married at an early age and history seemed to repeat itself when she again found herself working in a family business setting without any salary or title (Rowe and Hong 2000). This has been discussed in research as a kind of invisibility; however, Vera, like many mothers in family firms, used the family business as an arena for allowing them to become visible (Barrett and Moores 2009). In Vera's case, she *enjoyed the social contact with customers* when giving them advice about items and she took the opportunity to become highly visible, which made her a force in the family firm to be counted on. Moreover, as part of the church community, she could socialise with people, getting them to know about her family's business. In this way, the religious community became an arena for making business in which people of the same faith do business with each other.

Furthermore, *getting a paid position outside the family firm* opened a new arena for visibility for Vera. Vera was a highly valued co-worker and colleague. From an early age she had been very fond of elderly people, with whom she eventually also got to work. Vera very much liked this job and she earned some money at the same time. The position was a venue for freedom and (financial) autonomy in the sense of being able to do something fun with the money.

Previous research has established women as "nurturers of the next generation of leaders" (Dugan et al. 2008) and the importance of their unique offerings such as their "*emotional leadership*" was emphasised (Salganicoff 1990; Martinez Jimenez 2009). Vera, like many mothers in family firms, saw that the only way to meet their children or spend family time together was to be in the firm. Hence, in this position of the emotional leader and caretaker for the family Vera created moments of discussions around the dinner table. In this way, the meal times became a platform for visibility for all family members. These are moments created within the family business boundaries that could hardly have occurred if the family members were engaged in different professions. This highlights the uniqueness of the family business context, and offers one explanation why family members continue to operate in the family business despite not given official or visible roles.

A family business is a complex combination of different roles for the involved family members (Lansberg 1983). Within the family business, the question of identity and the ability to successfully construct a legitimate and credible identity for the different stakeholders, including the subject him or herself, is far more complex than in non-family businesses. This is due to the more numerous group memberships and roles that are salient, and relationship ties that are more complex in family businesses than in non-family businesses (Milton 2008). In Vera's case she does not seem to be suffering from role confusion—quite the opposite. She switches between private family and family business roles and she is visible or invisible as norms dictate. However, in the process she has also allocated some space for herself and for what she finds interesting and fun. Within the organisation there is a degree of choice (Kanter 1993) and in Vera's case she has chosen the fun—and to highlight what she sees as the good side of things. While certain roles or positions have been denied from or closed for her, it does not mean that her life would have been gloomy and pre-determined by others. By navigating the various social norms and expectations from her community and family, and moving in between visibility and invisibility she has been able to hold many positions and roles that she considered near and dear to her heart (Barrett and Moores 2009).

As Kanter (1993) noted, firms often have a shadow organisation, an ongoing parallel activity that leaves people unnoticed and peripheral. While this chapter is depicted as a Vera's story, it is possible to see also other stories, such as the partnership story. *Being a married couple and running a business together* is often built on mutual trust and the ability to share everyday tasks, which also demands a sense of equal partnership (Ponthieu and Caudill 1993). In Vera's case, she backed up her husband in the family firm, but also in his paid position; on the other hand, Vera's husband did not jeopardise their income by quitting his full-time paid job.

Vera has acted like wives to entrepreneurs often do: she has advised their customers and presented a visible team image together with her husband (Kanter 1993). However, unlike other examples in which wives tend to put their own needs and interests second, Vera has used her ability to *compartmentalise* (Cole and Johnson 2007) *between family, business, and social spheres*, which has enabled her to take advantage of all the different arenas for visibility that were offered. Nowhere in Vera's story are there regrets about the choices she made in her life; on the contrary, she is grateful for all the things she has experienced and enjoyed. Her satisfaction is clearly expressed and seems to be connected to equity more than to equality (Marshack 1993). Hence, we argue that the visibility of men and invisibility of women in family businesses may also be exaggerated if not scrutinised (Smith 2014; Deacon, Harris, and Worth 2014).

Concluding Remarks

The overriding story dealing with women in family businesses seems to underline their invisibility evidenced by women's difficulties in getting access to the leadership positions or being paid for their work (Martinez Jimenez 2009). In the present study, we discuss that this is not the only view but it depends largely on whose perspective this is viewed from, and a "small yet important story" seems to emerge from between the lines (Dey and Steyaert 2010). Through Vera's story we illustrate how she—by moving between visibility and invisibility—in the intertwined spheres of social life and the family business was able to secure a self-rewarding and empowered role. The chapter also suggests a need for reconsidering the primacy of (official) work roles in comparison to the family or social roles as sources of (life) satisfaction for the individuals in the family business. Research on family business should avoid equalling access to family business leadership as a sole measure of success for the individual family members or as a sole avenue to have an important role in the family and family business. The chapter has highlighted the importance of social spheres as an important arena for assuming agency and securing visibility.

Note

1 In his original Swedish text Asplund (1987) applied the concept of a "responsorium".

References

Al-Dajani, H., and S. Marlow. 2010. "Impact of Women's Home-Based Enterprise on Family Dynamics: Evidence from Jordan." *International Small Business Journal* 28 (5): 470–486.

Alvesson, M., and D. Kärreman. 2012. *Kreativ metod—skapa och lösa mysterier*. Malmö: Liber.

Asplund, J. 1987. *Det sociala livets elementära former*. Göteborg: Korpen.

Barrett, M., and K. Moores. 2009. *Women in Family Business Leadership roles: Daughters on Stage*. Cheltenham, UK and Northampton: Edward Elgar.

Bersbo, Z. 2012. *Rätt för kvinnan att blifva människa—fullt och helt: Svenska kvinnors ekonomiska medborgarskap 1921–1971*. Växjö, Kalmar: Linnaeus UniversityPress.

Brighenti, A. 2007. "Visibility: A Category for the Social Sciences." *Current Sociology* 55: 323–341.

Brighenti, A. 2010. *Visibility in Social Theory and Social Research*. Hampshire: Palgrave Macmillan.

Cabrera-Suarez, K., P. Saa-Perez, and D. Garcia-Almeida. 2001. "The Succession Process from a Resource- and Knowledge-Based View of the Family Firm." *Family Business Review* 14: 37–47.

Cole, P. 1997. "Women in Family Business." *Family Business Review* 10 (4): 353–371.

Cole, P., and K. Johnson. 2007. "An Exploration of Successful Copreneurial Relationships Postdivorce." *Family Business Review* 20 (3): 185–198.

Czarniawska, B. 2014. *Ute på fältet, inne vid skrivbordet*. Lund: Studentlitteratur.

Deacon, J. H., J. A. Harris, and L. Worth. 2014. "Who Leads? Fresh Insights into Roles and Responsibilities in a Heterosexual Copreneurial Business." *International Journal of Gender and Entrepreneurship* 6 (3): 317–335.

Dey, P., and C. Steyaert. 2010. "The Politics of Narrating Social Entrepreneurship." *Journal of Enterprising Communities: People and Places in the Global Economy* 4 (1): 85–108.

Docherty, P., A. Ljung, and T. Stjernberg. 2008. "Interaktiv forskning—utveckling, användning och spridning av kunskaper." In *Gemensamt kunskapande—den interaktiva forskningens praktik*, edited by B. Johannisson, E. Gunnarsson and T. Stjernberg. Växjö: Växjö University Press.

Dugan, A. M., S. P. Krone, K. LeCouvie, J. M. Pendergast, D. H. Kenyon-Rouvinez, and A. M. Schuman. 2008. *A Woman's Place: The Crucial Roles of Women in Family Business*. Marietta, GA: Family Business Consulting Group.

Dumas, C. 1989. "Understanding of Father-Daughter and Father-Son Dyads in Family-Owned Businesses." *Family Business Review* 2 (1): 31–46.

Freire, P. 1970. *Pedagogy of the Oppressed*. New York: Continuum International Publishing Group.

Freire, P. 1974. *Education for Critical Consciousness*. New York: Continuum International Publishing Group.

Haberman, H., and S. Danes. 2007. "Father-Daughter and Father-Son Family Business Management Transfer Comparison: Family FIRO Model Application." *Family Business Review* 20 (2): 163–184.

Hamilton, E. 2006. "Whose Story Is It Anyway? Narrative Accounts of the Role of Women in Founding and Establishing Family Business." *International Small Business Journal* 24 (3) (June): 253–271.

Hamilton, E. 2013. *Entrepreneurship Across Generations: Narrative, Gender and Learning in Family Business*. Cheltenham: Edward Elgar Publishing.

Hollander, B., and W. Bukowitz. 1990. "Women, Family Culture and Family Business." *Family Business Review* 3: 139–151.

Hytti, U., G. A. Alsos, J. Heinonen, and E. Ljunggren. 2017. "Navigating the Family Business: A Gendered Analysis of Identity Construction of Daughters." *International Small Business Journal* 35 (6): 665–686.

Israel, J. 1988. "Social Responsivity as Elementary Human Action." *Acta Sociologica* 31 (3): 231–240.

Johansson, A. 2005. *Narrativ teori och metod, med livsberättelsen i fokus*. Lund: Studentlitteratur.

Kanter, R. M. 1993. *Men and Women of the Corporation*. 2nd ed. New York: BasicBooks.

Karlsson-Stider, A. 2000. *Familjen och firman*. Stockholm: Ekonomiska forskningsinstitutet vid handelshögskolan.

Kram, K., and M. McCollom-Hampton. 2003. "When Women Lead: The Visibility-Vulnerability Spiral." In *Reader in Gender, Work and Organization*, edited by R. Ely, E. Foldy and M. Scully. Oxford: Blackwell Publishers.

Lamb, M. E. 2000. "The History of Research on Father Involvement: An Overview." *Marriage & Family Review* 29 (2–3): 23–42.

Lansberg, I. 1983. "Managing Human Resources in Family Firms: The Problem of Institutional Overlap." *Organizational Dynamics* 12 (1): 39–46.

Leaptrott, J. 2005. "An Institutional Theory View of the Family Business." *Family Business Review* 18: 215–228.

Lyman, A., M. Salganicoff, and B. Hollander. 1985. "Women in Family Business: An Untapped Resource." *SAM Advanced Management Journal* (Winter): 46–49.

Marshack, K. 1993. "Coentrepreneurial Couples: A Literature Review on Boundaries and Transitions Among Copreneurs." *Family Business Review* 6 (4): 355–369.

Martin, L. 2001. "More Jobs for the Boys? Succession Planning in SMEs." *Women in Management Review* 16 (5): 222–231.

Martinez Jimenez, R. 2009. "Research on Women in Family Firms: Current Status and Future Directions." *Family Business Review* 22 (1) (March): 53–64.

Miller, D., L. Steier, and I. Le Breton-Miller. 2003. "Lost in Time: Intergenerational Succession, Change and Failure in Family Business." *Journal of Business Venturing* 18: 513–531.

Milton, L. P. 2008. "Unleashing the Relationship Power of Family Firms: Identity Confirmation as a Catalyst for Performance." *Entrepreneurship Theory and Practice* 32 (6): 1063–1081.

Nelton, S. 1998. "The Rise of Women in Family Firms: A Call for Research Now." *Family Business Review* 11 (3): 215–218.

Nilson, H. 2015. *Snacka om (o)synlighet: Familjeföretagarens nästa drag [Talk about (in)visibility—next move for the family firm]*. Växjö: Linnaeus University Press.

Ponthieu, L., and L. Caudill. 1993. "Who's the Boss? Responsibility and Decision Making in Copreneurial Ventures." *Family Business Review* 6 (1): 3–17.

Rowe, B., and G.-S. Hong. 2000. "The Role of Wives in Family Businesses: The Paid and Unpaid Work of Women." *Family Business Review* 13 (1): 1–13.

Salganicoff, M. 1990. "Women in Family Business: Challenges and Opportunities." *Family Business Review* 3 (2): 125–137.

Sentuti, A. 2009. "The Other Side of Succession: Female Entrepeneurs and the Intergenerational Transfer in Small and Medium Family-Owned Firms: Some Italian Empirical Evidence." *EIASM 5th workshop*, Research on management practices in family firms, Hasselt, Belgium.

Smith, R. 2014. "Assessing the Contribution of the 'theory of matriarchy' to the Entrepreneurship and Family Business Literatures." *International Journal of Gender and Entrepreneurship* 6 (3): 255–275.

Stenholm, P., and U. Hytti. 2014. "In Search of Legitimacy Under Institutional Pressures: A Case Study of Producer and Entrepreneur Farmer Identities." *Journal of Rural Studies* 35: 133–142.

Vera, C., and M. Dean. 2005. "An Examination of the Challenges Daughters Face in Family Business Succession." *Family Business Review* 18 (4): 321–345.

Wang, C. 2010. "Daughter Exclusion in Family Business Succession: A Review of the Literature." *Journal of Family & Economic Issues* 31: 475–484.

8 'All the Days of Their Lives'

Women, Business, and Family

Deborah Simonton

> Let us suppose, then, that we take our stand in the centre of Castle Street in the year 1800, and that we are looking due west. We have on our right hand the New Inn, the Tolbooth, and the Town-House; and on our left the houses on the south side of Castle Street on the same line as at present. But between these two lines, instead of the open prospect to the west which is now so much admired, we can see before us only a big block of common-looking houses, having shops in the ground floor, which completely obstructs the view.
>
> (Robbie 1893, 552)

In 1801, John and David Abercrombie sold a tenement and all its pertinences to Aberdeen City Council. This property, one of the "common-looking houses", blocked the major new road Aberdeen was to build as part of its major renewal scheme. At the end of May the previous year, their maternal grandmother and surviving proprietor, Margaret Morice, had died. Her house sale is essentially a footnote in history. However, the story behind this property was of an upwardly mobile family, which had built a thriving bakery business in the active commercial and political centre of town. The chapter focuses on the parallel stories of the business and the personal lifecycle of the Morice family, which can be traced through the corporation records of eighteenth-century Aberdeen. There are virtually no business or personal records for the firm or family, but public records allow us to examine the dynamic of the business as a partnership of the couple, John and Margaret, while she as a widow continued to successfully operate the bakery. It plots the family events against the business life of the family. In so doing it captures elements of how such a firm operated, how the family moved in economic and political circles and ultimately how women and the family interacted. Numerous other women shared in family businesses in Aberdeen, and their stories enrich our understanding of women's activities in other types of family enterprises. Ten years earlier, across the square, the Plainstanes, the wife of a local printer, Susan Trail, had also died, aged seventy-one. Adjacent to the square and the printing house, Margaret

McGhie shared a prestigious inn on the Plainstanes from about 1755 to 1776. Margaret McGhie, Margaret Morice, and Susan Trail's role in family business is largely obscured and there are few records to illuminate their activities. Yet these were hardly "invisible women".

Invisible Women

The perception that women were invisible workers has a long history, but one that is partly artificial. In 2005, a collection on eighteenth century Britain was entitled *The Invisible Woman*, and as recently as 2016, Beatrice Craig referred to women in business as "invisible presences" (Baudino, Carré, and Révauger 2005; Craig 2016). The editors of *Invisible Woman* justified this expression, arguing that because women's proper place was "the seclusion of domesticity . . . her identity as a worker tended to become invisible, or more accurately unrepresentable" (Baudino, Carré, and Révauger 2005, 2–3). We must be careful about overstating the significance of the "domesticity" argument for the eighteenth century (Vickery 1993). It is clear from many recent studies, as Hannah Barker (2006, 171) says about businesswomen in Manchester, Leeds, and Sheffield, "female enterprise was likely to be both accepted and rewarded, and that businesswomen could wield considerable power". Daryl Hafter and Nina Kushner (2015, 3) point out, "A true vision of economic activity in the eighteenth century shows female presence everywhere—always active, always busy, always earning. . . . So omnipresent that few remarked on the fact". The point about representation, however, is well taken, because women often were under or not recorded precisely because they were seen as subordinate to the male worker and specifically the male head of household who was also the head of the business. If the marital economy offered opportunity to many wives, it also prioritised the marital union in a way that kept the wife in second place. Arguably, then, women's invisibility is often a "matter of record" in the sense that records usually named male heads of household and therefore the business. Eleanor Gordon and Gwyneth Nair (2000, 794) argue that the nineteenth-century census excluded "wives of small businessmen from the occupational tables, although there may have been no real change in their role". Craig (2016, 1) also argues that in the late eighteenth and early nineteenth centuries, "10 to 15 per cent of western Europe's large trading firms were run by women. Historians have no difficulties finding women running important trading houses, presiding over the birth of manufacturing firms, acting as bankers, or conquering new markets for their products until the end of the eighteenth century". She points out however the difficulties in finding women in small business, where guilds attempted to marginalise women and to push them into businesses which men did not want. Where the economy was expanding, in contrast, women were perceived less as competitors and more easily found spaces.

The lives of women in the past are constructed by historians from a range of materials. We are familiar with how women create and project their own lives through letters, diaries, and oral transmission. Dealing with working women, we are accustomed to the problems of interpreting their stories through the mediation of administrative records and other people's views of them. Women of the business community occasionally wrote their stories for us, like Hannah Robertson discussed below, but usually these women must be understood and their lives collected from the opaque records that made up their daily lives. We seldom hear people's own voices in these. The *Aberdeen Journal* is a valuable source for activities in Aberdeen. Much of the paper, begun in 1746, was made up of advertisements. Advertisements, while necessarily opaque, partial, and largely impersonal, nevertheless tell us a great deal about how women established a business identity in towns during the late eighteenth century. We have some insight to what they were doing and how they projected themselves; on the other hand, these depend on wanting to advertise, and John and Margaret Morice did not (there is a growing literature on advertisements and their uses, see McKendrick 1982; Berg and Clifford 2007; Phillips 2006; Barker 2006; Stobart 2008). These are used along with an array of Aberdeen City Council *Registers*, *Baillies' Enactment Books*, and other administrative council records, like apprenticeship, tax records, and related materials. The council was concerned with managing the community so mention of individuals tended to relate only to town governance, not domestic issues or even business. Some birth, death, and marriage records exist, but are erratic since much of Scotland's recordkeeping suffered from rebellions and upheavals during the century. The Inland Revenue *Apprenticeship Books* were created for taxation purposes, and by the end of the century provided only the information tax officials needed to assess the duty due. The story of this search was posted on the NACBS blog site in 2015, and emphasised the importance of curiosity and following "breadcrumbs" (Simonton 2015). Stories of women such as Margaret Morice are the bread and butter of our research; they whet our curiosity and through them we see the lives of towns come alive. This tale is not yet finished. Margaret Morice's story, taken together with that of other businesswomen, about whom there may be yet less detail, helps us to explore how women's businesses inflected the character of eighteenth-century towns.

Sources are one aspect of the situation. Women's voices were also often muted. Thus, they may have been active in businesses and a crucial support to the entrepreneurial activities of the family business, but their actions may have been less obvious. For example, many women were responsible for the accounts and sustaining the shop, while the husband may have been more likely to be the front of the shop, and the artisan, and out and about building business, dealing with customers or agents and suppliers. London bookseller James Lackington claimed his second wife Dorcas's "attachment to books was a very fortunate circumstance to us both. . . . Accordingly, when I was out on business, my shop was well attended. This constant attention, and good usage, procured me many customers" (Lackington 1794, 326). Women also dealt with suppliers, deliveries, and tax officials, but commonly in aid of a family business that carried his name. As Barker argues, women's activities could take a variety of forms, reflecting differences of age, wealth, and skill, but these considerations could override gender. Even if wives in partnerships were often relegated to secondary positions, "the smooth manner in which widows could take control of familial concerns upon a husband's death suggests the importance of their earlier involvement" (Barker 2006, 171). As married women, those in this chapter only became "named" as widows, although they were fundamental to the business operation and the commercial ambiance of the town during their husbands' lifetimes. They operated from premises around the main square of the town, the Plainstanes, on the route from the harbour to the commercial centre. They were thus highly visible to their community, friends, neighbours, customers, and competitors, despite their invisibility in the records.

There is clear evidence of women working throughout history and certainly during the eighteenth century. Family business was one such route since "the marriage contract itself was, . . . the point of conception for potential commercial activity" (Mann 1999, 139). Women often brought skills, family traditions, and connections into marriage that contributed to business. Their active participation rested on a variety of factors, ranging from knowledge and experience, to the size and demands of the household and the operation. Barker (1997, 2006), Barker and Harvey (2003), Nicola Phillips (2006), Christine Wiskin (2003) and Penelope Lane (1999), among others, have demonstrated that women were active in English business families throughout this period. Stana Nenadic (1998, 626) argued that about a fifth of businesses in nineteenth-century Scotland were owned and operated by women. My work on women in Aberdeen (Simonton 2013), together with studies by Cathryn Spence (2016) on credit, Catriona Macleod (2015, 136–137) on Glasgow, Alastair Mann (1999) on printing trades, and Elizabeth Sanderson on Edinburgh all attest to the continuance and vigour of Scottish women in business, whether single, married, or widowed. The Port Books of Edinburgh and Leith show a small but consistent number of women designated as "merchants", signing for cargoes on their own behalf—and some men signing for women's shipments (Dingwall 1999, 155). Many had husbands working as professionals, but this did not prevent them from participating in contractual business activities.

Scots women did not operate under coverture as their English cousins did, since the two legal systems were (and are) separate and different. The concept of communion of goods operated in Scotland, implying an equal responsibility for marital property. Women could retain control over their personal items, and sometimes separate property, which historians have argued gave Scottish women access to capital and resources (Logan 1839,

187–188; Laurence 2009; Forte 1984, 107, 109–110; Barclay 2011, 51; Stair 1770, 719; Coutts 1999, 177–178). In addition, "in her domestic role as the person in charge of her master's establishment" a wife could pledge her husband's credit for "household necessities suitable to his station". He could not renounce this right without a court order (Erskine 1828, 815, 152–158). Scots law aimed to ensure the "harmonious operation" of the marital economy. Thus, as Katie Barclay (2011, 52) explained,

> Law emphasised the husband's right to manage his wife and her property, while a wife's right resided in her interest in her husband's property and the expectation that she be provided for. The law's interest in the marital union was in its role as an economic unit, not as may be expected as a procreative unit. . . . It reflected the importance of the marital economy to Scottish economy and (thus influenced) the amount of social power women could exert within marriage as well as the resources they could draw on.

Together with access to her own personal items, a variety of legal provisions and relative flexibility gave Scottish wives amongst middling- and lower-middling tradespeople more independence and responsibility (Macleod 2015, 136–137).

The Commercial Community

Tracing and interrogating business families among the middling sort offers a lens through which the operation of commercial communities like Aberdeen can be viewed and better understood. As Barker and Karen Harvey (2003, 129) argued for Manchester, women in "petite bourgeoisie" families "were not simply parasitic but facilitative". They were at the centre of commercial activities, promoting the emerging consumer culture through trading and provision of spaces like inns where business was transacted. This chapter focuses on a baking family. While lacking the cachet of a merchant family, bakers are crucial to feeding a town, but their role is rarely highlighted as central to urban development. And yet, in Aberdeen, bakers along with weavers were the most prestigious of the Seven Incorporated Trades (Bain 1887, 211). They were firmly among the urban petty traders who, like innkeepers and printers, facilitated the workings of medium-sized ambitious commercial towns.

Aberdeen was a growing and prosperous town where the expanding urban economy helped to promote a more forward-looking attitude among the citizens. It was a trading centre for the hinterland, and carried on maritime trade to Scottish and English ports, the Netherlands, Scandinavian and Baltic regions, and occasionally North America. By mid-century, the city council identified harbour improvement and better access to the countryside as urgent. Thus, in the last half of the century ten new straight streets were created. The Council paved the "Plainstanes", fronting the bakery, specifically for men to gather "by way of exchange" and a new Townhouse on the Castlegate in 1754.[1] The elite also built large fashionable civic residences on the Castlegate, which was central to the traffic of the day, the prime "drinking" location, and the focus of printing, political, educational, and economic activity. For a large part of its history, two women operated the prestigiously positioned New Inn, built to serve a pre-existing commercial and political milieu. The Masonic lodge and Townhouse formed part of the building, and the Masons proudly announced its opening in 1757:

> One of the compleatest (sic) Inns in Scotland, consisting of a Variety of commodious Rooms, good Stabling, (?) for Wheel carriages . . . and as the Possessor, Mrs Robertson, from Perth, is known to be extremely well-qualified for the Management of such a House, . . . the Society hope that Gentlemen, and others, particularly Brethern will encourage this Undertaking, as the Want of such an Inn in Aberdeen, has long and justly been complained of.[2]

A forward-looking town, the Council piped in spring water, began regular cleaning, established a fire brigade, an early lighting system, and prohibited building with thatch.[3] In 1769, Alexander Carlyle, member of Edinburgh literati, commented: "The market place, which is very large and spacious. . . . (the town hall) is very large and handsome, and much better furnish'd and kept than any we have seen in Scotland". (Carlyle, 30 August). Samuel Johnson echoed this opinion in 1773, noting, "New Aberdeen has all the bustle of prosperous trade, and all the shew of increasing opulence" (Chapman, 12–13). The bakery was located at the head of the Plainstanes with the Townhouse and New Inn a few steps away on the North, and directly in front of the Mercat Cross, while the Chalmers published and sold the *Aberdeen Journal* a few minutes away. In other words, the Morices were right in the centre of the active commercial space of Aberdeen, a visible presence indeed.[4]

Who Were the Morices?

The bakery on the Castlegate run by John Morice and Margaret Kennedy was a single generation business, but one that benefitted significantly from a combination of enterprise and location. John was born in 1705, in Echt in rural Aberdeenshire a few miles to the west of Aberdeen. His parents were William Mores and Elsphet Mathie, tenant farmers on the Forbes estate. He had five siblings, James and George, farmers, David a baker and probably his twin, William a minister, a sister, Janet, and Robert a rural cloth manufacturer, litster, and dyer (Ancestry; Johnston 1861). Margaret's origins are more obscure. She was born Margaret Kennerty, in 1710, a local name derived from Kennerty, up Deeside less than 30 kilometres from Aberdeen. When their first son was baptised, one of the witnesses was Alexander Kennedy, merchant, probably a near relative of hers. Another was John's brother, David (Johnston 1861).

Apprenticeship was required to become a baker in Aberdeen, regulations specifically declaring that "it is statute and ordained that no freeman sail be maid at no tyme hereafter without he serve lawfully prentice within the samyu be the space of six years fullie togidder as prentice and servant" (Bain 1887, 219–20). British legislation also required registration and taxation of apprenticeships at the Inland Revenue in London, except those assigned by public charge by a parish (*Board of Stamps*). However, first sons might enter the trade without formal indentures, and apprenticeship to family members or fathers was common (Bain 1887, 223). Nevertheless, John does not appear in the extant record, nor does his brother David who also became a baker. In Scotland, which was not governed by the Statute of Artificers that defined English apprenticeship, the structures and practices of apprenticeship had become more "casual". Simultaneously, more workers moved into trades in towns without formal apprenticeship and paid a small fee for the right to trade (Devine 1983, 94–5).

John and Margaret's marriage does not appear in the surviving records either, although this is not surprising. Marriage practices in Scotland often followed an "irregular" but legal pattern, which Svetlana Baloutzova explained, comprised "three categories: *verba de praesenti* (a consent to marriage), *verba de futuro* (a promise of marriage followed by sexual intercourse) and finally cohabitation by habit and repute" (Baloutzova 2013, 61). Thus couples operated on the "blindingly simple" belief that if they said they were married, they were married (Smout 1981). The Morices may have married by any of these routes and no records would remain. They probably married in 1729, when he was twenty-four and she nineteen, average ages for the time, and worked together for ten years before their first known child was born (Ancestry; Barclay 2011). This suggests they began by establishing the business since once they started having children, successive births were rapid.

John in Charge, 1734–1770

The origins of the business are shrouded in the mists of time, and probably operated from about the date of their marriage. In 1734, John was admitted to the Burgess Register as a trade burgess, as a baxter (baker), paying the standard £24 required of men who had served an apprenticeship. There were two classes of burgesses in Scotland: Guild burgesses or Merchant burgesses and Trade or Craft burgesses. Initially, no clear distinction existed between them, but as John Gibson commented in 1777, "a difference between the merchants and trades rank very early established" (Gibson 1777, 151; Bain

1887, 8, 73–81, 91–2). Stresses between them over rights and privileges grounded in their divergent interests meant craftsmen lost political power to wealthier merchants. In consequence, the Incorporated Trades of Aberdeen rigidly excluded burgesses so that when a craftsman became a burgess, he was expected to give up his craft. However, John was a Trade burgess, enabling him to continue his baking and build up personal and professional standing. In any case, in 1738, the Bakers agreed that all members who became burgesses of guild should still enjoy the same privileges as the other members of the trade.

Women often shared husbands' occupations, and so worked in a wide range of trades, side-by-side with and substituting for husbands, either short or long term, often managing an entire concern. They understood many of the same jobs as men, and could do them when required. Margaret almost certainly handled transactions, especially selling bread, though John always purchased the meal.[5] She is less likely to have baked bread, given the heaviness of the work and the coding of baking as male. According to Bain, "Notably in Aberdeen, the baking of loaf and biscuit bread has been preserved as a strict monopoly for the men bakers. According to the acts and ordinances of the Baker craft in Aberdeen, women were not allowed to bake any bread, pastry, or pies to be sold in the streets or chops" (Bain 1887, 212). Baking was heavy work and apprentices were usually older than average, because "the great Burthens they are obliged to carry out in serving their Customers requires more strength than is normally to be met with in younger Years" (Campbell 1747, 276). It also meant that Margaret was more likely to take on a range of ancillary tasks rather than in breadmaking and baking.

From 1739, with the birth of their first child, her contribution would necessarily have been curtailed, and by 1750 they had seven children, including twins (Table 8.1). Therefore, until about 1755, Margaret had childcare responsibilities, although by 1758, three children had died.[6] Certainly, the biological aspects of childbearing and rearing cannot be ignored, but childcare involved far less intensity than today. Nevertheless, the presence of children shaped the decisions women made about how to ration their time and energies. Cleaning, mending, cooking, and childcare formed only a part of women's labour. At the same time, this work could be onerous. "Considerable physical labour was required for such tasks as transporting water to meet the daily needs of families that could include eight or ten members" (Fox-Genovese 1984, 115). Urban working women had responsibility for the immediate needs of the household and business; they expected to feed and clothe their own family, apprentices, journeymen and any domestic servants that lived in. If they could not provide items directly, they bought them from the marketplace. Although many requisites were available for purchase, they still required processing; for example, urban women could expect to make butter, to preserve fruits and vegetables, and occasionally slaughter meat, or at least clean poultry.

Table 8.1 The Children of John and Margaret Kennedy Morice

Name	*Birth*	*Marriage*	*Death*	*Comment*	*Time at home*	*Ages between 1750–61*
David	1739	none	1795	At Kincardine O'Neill	1739–51	11 to 12
Margaret	1741		1752?	"Death of child of John Morice"		9 to 12
Mary	1743	none	?		1743–89, to 52	7 to 18
Laura	1744		1758?	"Death of daughter of John Morice"		6 to 14
Barbara (twin)	1747	1778	1824	At Edinburgh	1747–78, to 31	3 to 14
John (twin)	1747		1756?	"Death of child of John Morice"		3 to 9
Alexander	1750		?	No further information		Birth to 11

The degree to which women produced goods for the household, or relied upon the market was determined by several factors. One of these was the extent of urbanisation. The larger the town as well as the greater the commercialisation of the marketplace, the less likely it was that she would produce directly for her family. Aberdeen was a prosperous town with a growing middle class, and advertisements from the *Aberdeen Journal* demonstrate that a wide array of essential, as well as luxury comestibles, could be purchased. For example, in 1781, Miss Walker made and sold "Goods in the Confectionary Way; as also Preserves, Pickles, Jellies; Blamanges, Spiceries, Sweet-breads of all Kinds. Tarts, etc".[7] As she was located not five minutes from the bakehouse, on Marischal Street, Margaret had ready access to her wares. She also had other victuallers located around and on the Castlegate, which had three confectioners, three inns providing prepared food and a wine merchant in addition to their bakery. The nearest pump was a few metres away, and the Mercat Cross was directly in front of the bakery. In towns, women were not far removed from the countryside, and small livestock and vegetable gardens proliferated, which can be seen behind the houses in Figure 8.1. Where responsibilities in the workshop demanded her attentions, she could have hired a laundress or a servant. The female servant

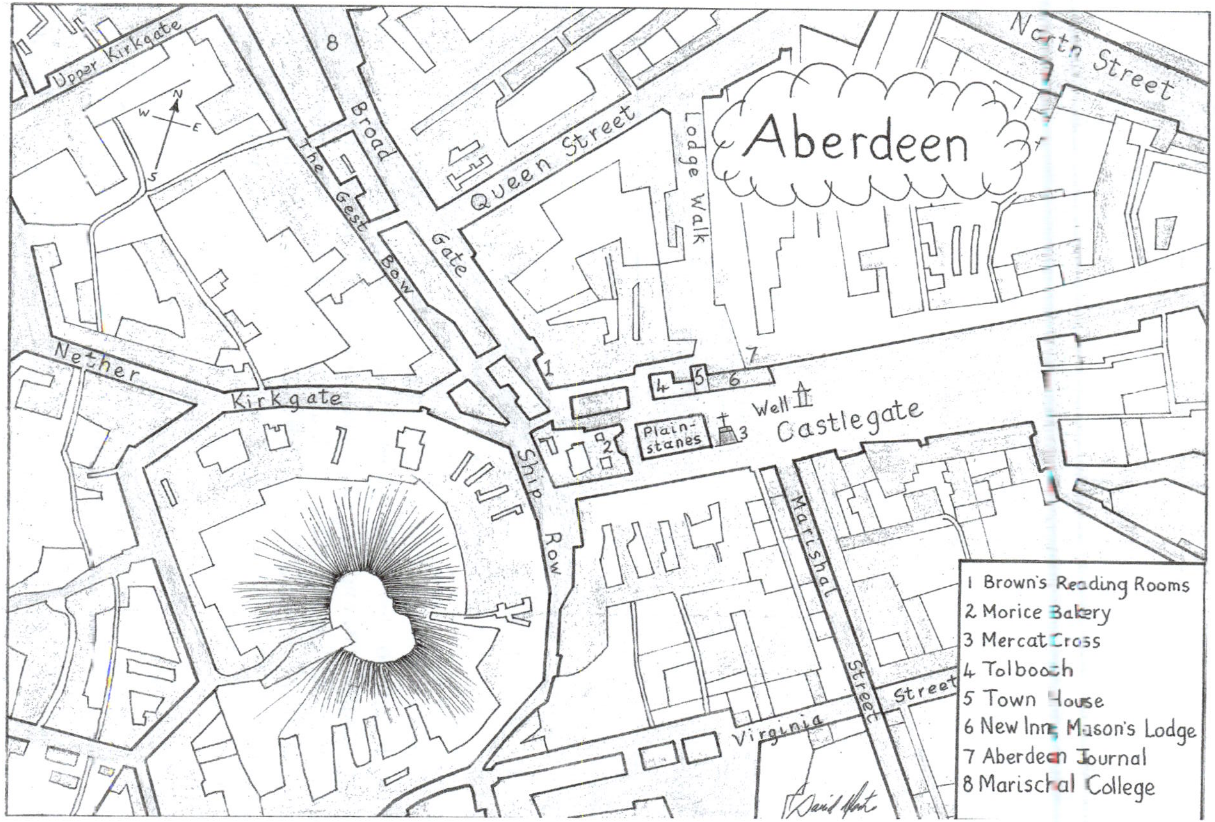

Figure 8.1 The Castlegate, Aberdeen

tax records only cover the years after John's death, but even between 1785 and 1791, Margaret paid no servant tax (Scotland's Places). Thus, household tasks fell to her, and as her daughters grew up, they probably took a share of these responsibilities.

Family strategies involved juggling the demands of business and household and thus also required planning to ensure there was adequate labour. The Morice family business was not large, but the firm was busy enough to need to replace her. John seems to have only taken three apprentices while their growing family was young, the first after their daughter Margaret was born, in 1742, and when there would have been two children under two—though he waited a year before doing so—and a further apprentice a year later about a month before their third child was born. Guild rules changed in 1732 to allow more than one apprentice, and ordered "no member to take a second (apprentice) until three years of the former apprentice's time be expired", so he was operating with the maximum number of permissible (Bain 1887, 228). His next apprentice did not start until 1755, a gap of seven years. Because of the lack of business records, we do not know if he retained journeymen, hired workers, or if his brother David worked with him.

If we look at the business from a family point of view, between 1750–1761, with only one apprentice, family labour could have helped cover the workload, although the surviving children were quite young. Children commonly worked from the time they were able, helping with small tasks and taking on more as they grew older and more competent. As an integrated process, women trained and supervised younger members of the family business, passing on skills while also caring for them. From around 1746, David, the eldest, probably attended one of the day schools in Aberdeen that catered for young men aiming for professional careers. He could have attended the Grammar School, which was rebuilt after 1750, because it was not large enough to satisfy demand (Dennison, Ditchburn, and Lynch 2002, 324). From 1756 to 1758, he attended University, and was apprenticed to advocate Gilbert Gerard in 1759 for three years (Seven Incorporated Trades of Aberdeen; NAUK). So, he was unlikely to have offered much help in the business during this time, and John's decision to take another apprentice in 1755 probably reflected this. They also had to consider his fees, since there is no record of David receiving a bursary. His apprenticeship fee was substantial, and consistent with solicitor training fees across Britain of £16 13s 4d sterling.

John's use of apprentices may also have reflected his increasing political involvement. In 1739 and again in 1744, he was elected Constable in Futtie Quarter, adjacent to the bakehouse. The wide-ranging duties of a constable meant they had to "give their appearance when and wherever said Magistrates shall appoint", to carry out a long string of responsibilities. For example, during riots in August and September of 1739, they were warned to be more vigilant, keep watch in the night, and look out for apprentices harassing custom and excise officers.[8] This was not an honorific position and it demonstrated not only council concerns and intervention in daily urban activities, but also the integrity expected and the demands placed on those appointed. His political career reached its peak in the years following the Jacobite uprising in 1745–46. In 1748, he was elected Deacon of the Bakers Guild, and served as one of two Trades Representatives on the Town Council, positions that lasted a year. The same year, he was elected Master of the Trades Hospital, a post that required, "a diligent and godly man". This position required him to organise the Trades' charity events and oversee the accounts of the Trades Hospital, which housed indigent merchants and tradesmen. He served as Deacon two further times, in 1751 and 1752 and as Master of the Hospital a further two times, in 1768 and 1769. He also appeared as a prosecution witness in a case of adulterated flour in 1763.[9]

In 1752, when the Masons built their Lodge and the New Inn, hiring Hannah Robertson as innkeeper, and as John and Margaret McGhie opened their coffee house on the Castlegate, John Morice purchased "the foreland, Bakehouse and Ovenhead . . . and all the pertinents" facing the Merket cross on the Plainstanes. It is probable that they had leased these previously, since he had been elected constable for the area adjacent to the tenement. He paid £100 sterling "as the worth, Value and Price" of the property.[10] This purchase marked the firm out as having achieved some level of wealth, standing, and prestige.

Between 1752 and 1761, both he and Margaret were available full-time. We should not ignore the fact that children died in 1752, 1756, and a third in 1758, and we can only guess at the impact of these deaths on the family and its emotional health. As one was probably young John, the second son and Barbara's twin, whom the parents might have expected to succeed them, this may have been a deep blow to their business aims. By 1761, John was 51 and Margaret was 45. From this time, John increased significantly the number of apprentices, taking ten in nine years, the first of whom was a nephew, although Margaret was available, and daughters Mary and Barbara and youngest son Alex could well have contributed to the business. John died in January 1770, aged 65. We do not know how he died, but his reliance on more apprentices could coincide with when he need the strength of youth in the shop. If John's achievements were modest, nonetheless the couple had built a substantial active business, marked by the purchase of the bake house. His gravestone in St Nicholas' Churchyard noted "In remembrance of John Morice, baker in this city, who lived respected as an honest man, and a good citizen" substantiating the picture built up through the records (Johnston 1861, xxxiv).

Margaret in Charge, 1770–1800

In January 1770, Margaret took charge of the business.[11] She was sixty years old, and had David, Mary and Barbara, and possibly, Alex aged twenty, at home. She also had some of John's apprentices still under indenture: Pat

Copeland, James Masson, Andrew Reid and Patrick Panton; the first three had about three and a half years to serve, and Panton had four and a half (only two should have been there, so some may have disappeared).[12] For the next twenty-six years, she continued trading as Margaret Morice and Co, until 1794, when she reverted briefly to her birth name. She clearly felt confident and competent to run the bakery and the traces of evidence that cover her tenure substantiate that she was successful and maintained a functioning and solid concern.

She deliberately used the company name to hold on to the prestige and commercial identity associated with her "business" persona, developed when the partnership had built up a substantial and respected undertaking. Since Scottish women usually kept their birth name, this practice of retaining a "commercial" name is notable. Innkeeper Margaret McGhie used her married name, and this was a general practice in Aberdeen amongst wives in business, like publicans, Mrs Sherrifs and Mrs Gemble. An inn or "House" as it was commonly called, had an identity with the husband's name, and retaining the premises as "Mrs McGhie's house", as the newspaper regularly referred to it, was a logical commercial option. Margaret Morice thus saw the advantage in doing so. Whilst some historians suggest that the practice of keeping their natal name indicated that women's ties were stronger to their birth family and that they were marginal to their husband's family, evidence from business families tends to challenge this. As Barclay (2011, 72) explained,

> Social observer Thomar Morer argued in the seventeenth century that the retention of their surname indicated that Scottish women were more independent of their husbands than their English counterparts. It allowed women identities that were separate from their husbands' and gave them authority as the gatekeepers to their families and any related benefits.

These women kept the business name for commercial reasons, and utilised the power that came with their sense of self and identity as well as capitalising on the strength of a business name. If there were any doubt about who was "in charge", the business name helped solidify the claim of women like Margaret Morice. Individualism as we know it was only in its infancy, and women, like men, tended to understand their place in society in reference to family. In Margaret's case, her understanding of her business situation was couched within the knowledge that in a town like Aberdeen, where who you knew and how you knew them was so important, commercial imperatives could strongly point to retaining a business name, and thus strengthening her own business position.

Her business strategies bear this out. She took no apprentices for ten years. For the first four, she had the labour and strength of those indentured to John, and regulations allowed apprentices to continue serving a widow and to obtain their freedom in the same way as if apprenticed to her husband, or any other man. By 1774–75 all four had completed their apprenticeships and may have stayed on as journeymen, providing the necessary strength and labour. The most senior, James Masson, completed his apprenticeship in 1773. At some point, she took him into "copartnership", hence the notation "and Co". This partnership may have lasted up to nine years, adding two apprentices in 1776 and 1780. The register indicates that they were indentured to "Margaret Morice and Co., bakers in Aberdeen". The plural is significant, because it would appear to have subsumed James Masson who took no apprentices in his own name. Her next apprentices started about the time that Masson announced the end of the copartnery and moved to the head of the Broadgate, some few minutes away.[13] He still was not recorded as taking apprentices, and no more is heard of him. Thomas Warrack was the first apprentice Margaret Morice and Co had taken, completing in 1786. In 1787, he was elected to represent the Bakers on the Council, and he must have been in partnership with Margaret. However, on 20 July 1787, Margaret, designating herself "Baker", placed her only notice in the *Aberdeen Journal* referring to it (Figure 8.2).

On the same day, the creditors of "Thomas Warrack, late baker, Aberdeen", were summoned to meet to "concert measure for their conduct with regard to Mr Warracks' subjects". This suggests not that he had died, but may have "skipped" town. Her notice further insisted "that all accounts due to M. Morice and Co. be paid in to her only".[14]

The company had taken two more apprentices in 1786, two more in 1789, and she continued to take apprentices regularly until 1796, the last one probably continuing until virtually her death since he was contracted until the end of December 1799. William Abel and John Ross reappeared, taking their own apprentices. So, did two of John's, Archibald Reid and

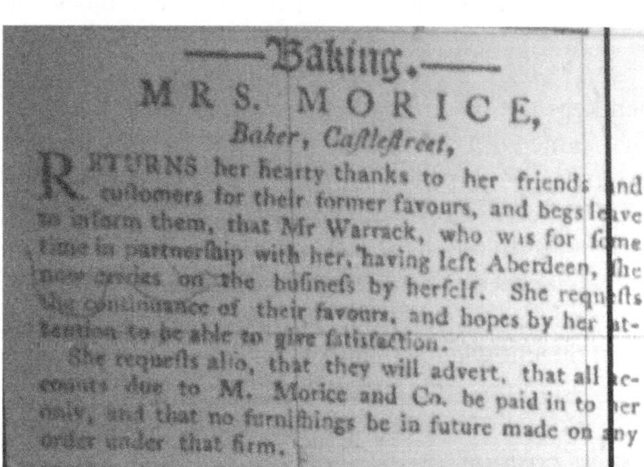

—Baking.—

MRS. MORICE,

Baker, Caſtleſtreet,

RETURNS her hearty thanks to her friends and customers for their former favours, and begs leave to inform them, that Mr Warrack, who was for ſome time in partnerſhip with her, having left Aberdeen, ſhe now carries on the buſineſs by herſelf. She requeſts the continuance of their favours, and hopes by her attention to be able to give ſatisfaction.

She requeſts alſo, that they will advert, that all accounts due to M. Morice and Co. be paid in to her only, and that no furniſhings be in future made on any order under that firm.

Figure 8.2 Margaret Morice announces the end of a partnership, *Aberdeen Journal*, 20 July 1787

Table 8.2 Margaret Morice and Co, Apprentices and Partnerships

Name	*Apprenticeship start*	*Partnerships*	*Dates*	*Activity*
James Masson	2 July 1768			
Pat Copeland	3 July 1768			
Andrew Reid	12 August 1768			
Patrick Panton	15 August 1769			
		James Masson	1773	End of apprenticeship
Thomas Warrack	1 May 1776			
William Anderson	1 May 1780			
Alexander Shepherd	31 January 1781			
Alexander Burgess	22 February 1781	James Masson		End of copartnery
William Abel	1 July 1782			
Alexander Walker	1 May 1784			
George Murray	1 June 1785		1786	
		Thomas Warrack	1787	End of apprenticeship
Robert Watson	1 April 1786	Thomas Warrack		Baker Trade Rep.
John Ross	1 November 1786			.
Andrew Robb	1 January 1789			
George McInray	1 May 1789		27 July 1789	
		Thomas Warrack		End of copartnery
George Moir	Whitsun 1791			
James Fettes	8 January 1792			
Adam Low	16 March 1795			
John Low	16 December 1796			

Thomas Abel, related to two of Margaret's.[15] As the only woman regularly recorded in the apprenticeship records, she also had the distinction of being consistently described as "baker in Aberdeen". This is notable on many levels. The bakers were prestigious in Aberdeen and Bain insisted, "the baking of loaf and biscuit bread has been preserved as a strict monopoly for the men bakers" until 1846. In 1726, the pastry bakers became so exercised at competition from women making cakes and pastry at home, like confectioners, that they decreed:

> The baxter traid taking to their consideration the great loss sustained by this traid . . . hereby statutes and ordains that no freeman of this traid in time coming shall give the use of his oven for firing the above pastrie so wrocht as aforesaid being for sale, and that under the penalty of ten merks Scots.
>
> (Bain 1887, 212, 228)

Despite Bain claiming that Aberdeen was particularly vigilant, he also "acknowledged that strict adherence to the letter of the law could not have been a cardinal virtue" (Bain 1887, 231). It is likely the guild turned a blind eye, either because of the status of the shop or perhaps because of her business persona as Margaret Morice and Co. They allowed her to continue not only because of her standing as the widow of a respected burgess and colleague, but also because of her own acumen and resilience.

John was recorded only twice in the Aberdeen *Register of Apprentices*, but his apprenticeships were registered at the Inland Revenue. She, in contrast, appeared only once in those *Apprenticeship Books* (NAUK). As a relatively prominent member of the Incorporated Trades, and their Council representative from time to time, John probably ensured his apprentices were properly recorded, even if he did not use the local record. On the one occasion when she did, she had just ended the partnership with Masson. Thus, she may have seen a "properly" registered apprentice as essential to retaining the prestige of the business. None of her three sons joined the business, while over the thirty years that she ran it, she apprenticed fifteen boys (compared with John's thirteen over twenty-five years). The five-year terms of her indentures and fees for training compared well with apprentices to male bakers across Britain, and were identical to John's.[16] Parents must have been comfortable with placing sons with her as they and the cautioners came from families of good middling standing. The premiums and numbers fell off a little towards the end when she was eighty years old; she used her own name, rather than the company only twice.[17] Since these were a baker's sons and she received no fee, they may well have represented guild "courtesy", to help an old woman, wife of a colleague and herself a colleague, to survive the last years of her life.

She co-owned the "large tenement on Castle Street" with her eldest son David. She paid Window and Inhabited House taxes during the same period that she took apprentices. She appeared in the press only once, when Warrack left; all other mentions were oblique: a partner ending a partnership, her son asking for a lease for his mother, lawyers asserting her claim to the property. She died in 1800 at the age of eighty having been partner and proprietor in the bakery business virtually "all the days of her life" beginning as a young bride of around nineteen or twenty and dying after sixty years "in the business". There is little doubt that she was a visible and well-established presence at the centre of Aberdeen's commercial space. When, shortly after her death, her two younger nephews sold the property to the New Street Trust, it marked the end of the business and of the business family. It also marked the end of the building as it was pulled down to make way for the new street, eventually named Union Street, at the junction with what is now King Street, still facing the Plainstanes.[18]

Neighbours, Publicans, and Printers

Around the Plainstanes, several business families operated, as did many female proprietors. Printing and innkeeping were trades in which women were common partners with husbands, often retaining businesses on their death as Margaret Morice had. The examples of two of her neighbours, Susan (or Susannah) Trail and Margaret McGhie, demonstrate further the ways that women worked in business families. Printing trades offer a different view of the urban artisanal community. They cover a wide spectrum encompassing booksellers, bookbinders, printers, papermakers, newsvendors, paper merchants, and so on. Throughout the trades there was a strong and recognised presence of women together with evidence of wives and widows taking independent decisions. In the print trades, however, women usually became visible as wives, and especially as widows, where they frequently carried on part or all the trade. Daughters and single women were less obvious, though frequently present. The John Johnson collection of trade ephemera held at the Bodleian includes numerous women printers, working with husbands and as widows, such as Susanna Burchett (late Miles) who advertised in the mid-century as printer and engraver, while Barker (1997, 89) suggests that females constituted roughly 8 per cent of the trade in the Northeast of England (John Johnson Collection of Printed Ephemera). Numerous female printers worked in Scotland, since the trade was less restricted than in England.

Born into a clerical family and daughter of an Aberdeen woman, at about age nineteen in 1740, Susan Trail of Montrose married James Chalmers, son of the Professor of Divinity and Printer to the Town and Marischal College (see Figure 8.3). Although she bore eight children (and buried four), much like Margaret Morice, evidence suggests she worked in the printing business, including the new *Aberdeen Journal*, begun in 1746. When her husband died, Susan took over the business and newspaper, petitioning the Council on 5 September 1764 for herself and her eldest son, James, to continue as printers to the town. The council in return "unanimously Granted the desire of the same (Susan) . . . and the longest liver of them to be Town's Printers" retaining all the profits and emoluments. This represented a vote of confidence in her abilities. Significantly, her petition and the Council response underlines the recognition of a joint operation, in which she was identified as an equal partner; she would hold all rights if she survived her son.[19] In October, James advertised that he intended to continue printing "in Conjunction with his Mother" and that "they" were to stand as candidates for the position of Printers to the County. As he remained in London, she managed the printing activities for over a year on her own. Although father and son were the public faces of the business, she was visibly involved in management during both their tenures. No histories of the paper or printing in Aberdeen however note this. She died in Aberdeen 18 May 1791, and her own paper simply noted she was an honourable woman.[20] Many men were no longer pulling the press and had become managers, and so women were well-positioned to take up similar positions in printing houses.

Figure 8.3 Susan (Susanna) Trail, age c. 19. Charles John Guthrie, Genealogy of the descendants of Rev. Thomas Guthrie, DD and Mrs Anne Guthrie (Edinburgh: A. Elliott, 1902), 119.

Inns characterise a different scenario of the victualling world of business. Hannah Roberston moved to Aberdeen from Perth when, in c.1754, the Masons appointed her to manage the New Inn. When she "begged" her bankrupt husband's permission to take up the job, he "wisely foresaw how entirely I was unqualified for such a laborious office, accustomed as I had been to all the conveniences, and elegancies of life: . . . I was however firm in my purpose, and exhorted his reluctant consent" (Robertson, n.d., 21). He played no part in running the inn, though he joined her once she released him from debtors' gaol. While this was not a family business, it gives insight to how such a woman regarded her business persona: "At first I succeeded in this undertaking, for my tavern was much frequented". She enjoyed the business, felt she was doing "good" and "allowed myself the pleasure of feeding the hungry, for nobody went empty away from my door" (Robertson, n.d., 22). As the first proprietor, she was partly responsible for establishing its reputation, and it became a well-established concern. It is unclear why she returned to Perth in 1763, but the Inn suffered a series of fires and she claims to have been pressured.[21]

Inns and coffeehouses were highly visible and central to the commercial culture of urban life. They were run by men and women who used marriage, location, service, and reputation to further their businesses. John and Margaret McGhie had opened the Laigh Coffee House in 1756 at virtually the same moment that the Masons built the New Inn.[22] In June 1763, they moved from across the Castlegate to replace Robertson at the New Inn. John's advertisement announcing the move assured potential patrons that "no pains or Expense have been wanting to fit up and furnish it in an elegant Manner, and to render it a House of Entertainment, for the Service of Town or Country, as commodious as any in Scotland".[23] In 1769, Alexander Carlyle described the New Inn as "a very good house—handsome rooms, very good service"; however, he also noted, "a little more attention to cleanliness thro' every part of the house would make it perfectly agreeable" (Carlyle, *Journal of a Tour*). Margaret remained unmentioned. When John died in early 1772, she took over. The inn was thereafter regularly described in the *Aberdeen Journal* as "Mrs McGhie's House". She conducted the full range of activities expected of a prominent inn: the "Club" met there; she sold tickets for concerts and assemblies at the Mason's Lodge; roups (auctions) regularly sold anything from the goods from a returning schooner to household inventories. Indeed, the inn appears to have been even more active during her sole tenure. Usually advocates or other senior members of the community placed adverts for events for clients, suggesting a recognised a trusted business arrangement with Mrs McGhie. When James Boswell and Samuel Johnson visited in August 1773, the inn was full, but upon hearing that Boswell, whose father used the inn, was seeking lodging, room was found for them. Johnson approvingly wrote, "we found a very good house and civil treatment" (Chapman 1924, 12). In 1776, she left the Inn and moved to "the New Street off the Broadgate" and began taking in lodgers.

Like Trail and Morice, she had clearly been part of the family operation of the inn and continued deploying her skills taking lodgers, probably when the activities of the inn had become too much. Her successor refurbished the inn and so possibly after ten years it required more investment and energy than she was prepared to handle.[24]

Partnership, Patronage, and Persistence: Concluding Thoughts

Piecing together an array of disparate records generates a picture of the Morice bakery business, which was clearly long-standing and central to the commercial area of Aberdeen. Many women managed to establish themselves in business using the tools at hand. Family business was a fundamental entrée for many businesswomen, a pattern that Morice, McGhie, and Trail utilised. While like many women they continued the businesses as widows, their role during their husbands' lives was more obscured, but there is little doubt that they had been active partners in the bakery, printing, and innkeeping family enterprises. Otherwise they could not have operated with such confidence as widows. Through business families such as Morice's, we can see how the business altered as the family grew, how they utilised apprenticeship and other strategies to promote it and how they created and sustained a place in the commercial community. Wives' activities and strategies as widows also shed light on how they probably operated during the period when husbands were alive. In all three cases, the evidence is largely tangential, but the glimpses these women give us into the past demonstrates women's position in these families and how they exploited their skills, acumen and abilities to be full partners in eighteenth-century urban family businesses. Families like this demonstrate how commercial activities functioned and how they intertwined with political, religious, and social cultures of the town. In these activities and commercial spaces, gender was not neutral; it was a fundamental aspect of how families managed business and life.

Abbreviations

ACA	Aberdeen City Archives
AJ	*Aberdeen Journal*
NAUK	*Board of Stamps: Apprenticeship Books*, Series IR 1; The National Archives of the UK.

Notes

1 ACA, *Council Register*, LXI, 569.
2 AJ, 14 June 1757.
3 *AJ*, 4 July 1763, 18 July 1763, 21 November 1763.
4 Bain; ACA, *Justice Court Book*, 26 July 1744.

5 ACA, *Enactment Books, 1749–1758*, e.g. 20 May 1757.
6 ACA, St Nicholas Church; Ancestry.
7 *AJ*, 25 June 1781.
8 ACA, *Justice Court Book*, 17 August, 25 September, 1 October 1739.
9 *AJ*, 4 October 1748, 19 November 1751, 7 November 1752, 22 August 1763, 24 October 1768; Bain 1887, 169, 171.
10 ACA, CA-13-NStT-5–16.
11 ACA, *Register of Indentures*.
12 NAUK, *Apprenticeship Books*.
13 *AJ*, 9 September 1781; ACA, *Enactment Books*, 5.
14 *AJ*, 20 July 1789.
15 ACA, *Register of Indentures*; NAUK, *Apprenticeship Books*.
16 ACA, *Register of Indentures*; Simonton 1988.
17 ACA, *Register of Indentures*, 211, 219.
18 ACA, CA/13/NStT/5–16.
19 ACA, *Council, Baillie and Guild Registers*, LXIII, 5 September 1764.
20 *AJ*, 18 May 1791.
21 *AJ*, 13 November 1759.
22 *AJ*, 7 December 1756.
23 *AJ*, 13 June 1763.
24 *AJ*, 20 May 1776, 26 August 1776, 25 November 1776.

References

Ancestry. 1997–2017. *Genealogy, Family Trees and Family History Records*. www.ancestry.com/.

Bain, E. 1887. *Merchant and Craft Guilds: A History of the Aberdeen Incorporated Trades*. Aberdeen: J & JP Edmond & Spark.

Baloutzova, S. 2013. "When a lass goes 'So round', with Her 'Tua Sides High': Oral Culture and Women's Views on Illegitimacy." In *Women in Eighteenth-Century Scotland: Intimate, Intellectual, and Public Lives*, edited by K. Barclay and D. Simonton, 55–74. Aldershot: Ashgate.

Barclay, K. 2011. *Love, Intimacy and Power: Marriage and Patriarchy in Scotland, 1650–1850*. Manchester: University Press.

Barclay, K., and D. Simonton, eds. 2013. *Women in Eighteenth-Century Scotland: Intimate, Intellectual, and Public Lives*. Aldershot: Ashgate.

Barker, H. 1997. "Women, Work and the Industrial Revolution: Female Involvement in the English Printing Trades." In *Gender in Eighteenth-Century England*, edited by H. Barker and E. Chalus, 88–100. London: Longman.

Barker, H. 2006. *The Business of Women, Female Enterprise and Urban Development in Northern England, 1760–1830*. Oxford: Oxford University Press.

Barker, H., and K. Harvey. 2003. "Women Entrepreneurs and Urban Expansion: Manchester." In *On the Town: Women and Urban Life in Eighteenth-Century England*, edited by R. Sweet and P. Lane, 111–130. Aldershot: Ashgate.

Baudino, I., J. Carré, and M.-C. Révauger, eds. 2005. *The Invisible Woman: Aspects of Women's Work in Eighteenth-Century Britain*. Aldershot: Ashgate.

Berg, M., and H. Clifford. 2007. "Selling Consumption in the Eighteenth Century: Advertising and the Trade Card in Britain and France." *Cultural and Social History* 4 (2) (June): 145–171.

Campbell, R. 1747. *The London Tradesman*. London: T. Gardner.

Carlyle, A. 1982. *Journal of a Trip to the North of Scotland*, edited by R. B. Sher. Aberdeen: Aberdeen University Centre for Scottish Studies.

Chapman, R. W. 1924. *Johnson's Journey to the Western Isles of Scotland and Boswell's Journal of a Tour to the Hebrides with Samuel Johnson, LLD*. Oxford: Oxford University Press.

Coutts, W. 1999. "Wife and Widow: The Evidence of Testaments and Marriage Contracts c. 1600." In *Women in Scotland, c. 1100–c.1750*, edited by E. Ewan and M. Meikle, 176–186. East Linton: Tuckwell Press.

Craig, B. 2016. *Women and Business Since 1500: Invisible Presences in Europe and North America?* New York: Palgrave Macmillan.

Dennison, P. E., D. Ditchburn, and M. Lynch, eds. 2002. *Aberdeen Before 1800: A New History*. London: Tuckwell Press.

Devine, T. M. 1983. "The Merchant Class of the Larger Scottish Towns." In *Scottish Urban History*, edited by George Gordon and Brian Dicks. Aberdeen: AUP.

Dingwall, H. 1999. "The Power Behind the Merchant? Women and the Economy in Late-Seventeenth Century Edinburgh." In *Women in Scotland, c. 1100–c.* 1750, edited by E. Ewan and M. Meikle, 152–164. East Linton: Tuckwell Press.

Erskine, John. 1828. *An Institute of the Law of Scotland*. Vol. 2. Edinburgh: Bell & Bradfute.

Ewan, E., and M. Meikle, eds. 1999. *Women in Scotland, c. 1100–c. 1750*. East Linton: Tuckwell Press.

Forte, A. D. M. 1984. "Some Aspects of the Law of Marriage in Scotland: 1500–1700." In *Marriage and Property*, edited by E. M. Craik. Aberdeen: AUP.

Fox-Genovese, E. 1984. "Women and Work." In *French Women and the Enlightenment*, edited by S. Spencer, 111–127. Bloomington: Indiana University Press.

Gibson, J. 1777. *History of Glasgow, from the Earliest Accounts to the Present Time*. For the author.

Gordon, E., and G. Nair. 2000. "The Economic Role of Middle-class Women in Victorian Glasgow." *Women's History Review* 9 (4): 791–814.

Hafter, D. M., and N. Kushner, eds. 2015. *Women and Work in Eighteenth-Century France*. Baton Rouge: Louisiana State University Press.

John Johnson Collection of Printed Ephemera. Bodleian Libraries. University of Oxford. www.bodleian.ox.ac.uk/johnson.

Johnston, A. 1861. *Short Memoir of James Young, Merchant Burgess of Aberdeen, and Rachel Cruickshank, His Spouse*. Aberdeen: J. Craighead.

Lackington, J. 1794. *Memoirs of the Life of John Lackington*. London: Whittaker, Treacher, and Arnot.

Lane, P. 1999. "Women in the Regional Economy: the East Midlands, 1700–1830." PhD diss., University of Warwick.

Laurence, A. 2009. "Women and the Transmission of Property: Inheritance in the British Isles in the 17th Century." *Dix-septième siècle* 244 (3): 435–450.

Logan, J. 1839. *Compendium of the Laws of England, Scotland, and Ancient Rome, for the Use of Students*. Part 1. Edinburgh: Fraser and Crawford.

Macleod, C. 2015. "Women, Work and Enterprise in Glasgow, c. 1740–1830." PhD diss., University of Glasgow.

Mann, A. J. 1999. "Embroidery to Enterprise: The Role of Women in the Book Trade of Early Modern Scotland." In *Women in Scotland, c. 1100–c. 1750*, edited by E. Ewan and M. Meikle, 137–151. East Linton: Tuckwell Press.

McKendrick, N. 1982. "The Consumer Revolution in Eighteen-Century England." In *The Birth of a Consumer Society*, edited by N. McKendrick, J. Brewer, and J. H. Plumb, 34–92. London: Hutchinson.
Nenadic, S. 1998. "The Social Shaping of Business Behaviour in the Nineteenth-Century Women's Garment Trades." *Journal of Social History* 31 (3) (Spring): 625–645.
Phillips, N. 2006. *Women in Business, 1700–1850*. Woodbridge, Essex: Boydell Press.
Robbie, W. 1893. *Aberdeen: Its History and Tradition, with Notices of Some Eminent Aberdonians*. Aberdeen: Free Press.
Robertson, H. n.d. *The Life of Mrs Robertson*. Darby: J. Drewry.
Scotland's Places. Historical Tax Rolls. Female servant tax rolls, 1785–92. Vols 3, 7, 11, 15, 19, 23, 27. https://scotlandsplaces.gov.uk/digital-volumes/historical-tax-rolls
Seven Incorporated Trades of Aberdeen. "Clerk David Morrice, 1756." www.seventradesofaberdeen.co.uk/clerk-david-morrice-1756/.
Simonton, D. 1988. "The Education and Training of Eighteenth-Century English Girls." PhD diss., University of Essex.
Simonton, D. 2013. "Negotiating the Economy of the Eighteenth-Century Scottish Town: Female Entrepreneurs Claim Their Place." In *Women in Eighteenth-century Scotland: Intimate, Intellectual, and Public Lives*, edited by K. Barclay and D. Simonton, 211–232. Aldershot: Ashgate.
Simonton, D. 2015. "Finding Margaret Morice." *NACBS Blog*. April 10, 2015. www.nacbs.org/blog/finding-margaret-morice/.
Smout, T. C. 1981. "Scottish Marriage, Regular and Irregular, 1500–1940." In *Marriage and Society: Studies in the Social History of Marriage*, edited by R. B. Outhwaite, 204–236. London: Europa.
Spence, C. 2016. *Women, Debt and Credit in Early Modern Scotland*. Manchester: Manchester University Press.
Stair, J. 1770. *The Institutions of the Law of Scotland*. Edinburgh: The heir of Andrew Anderson [Agnes Campbell].
Stobart, J. 2008. "Selling Through Politeness: Advertising Provincial Shops in Eighteenth-Century England." *Cultural and Social History* 5 (3) (September): 309–328.
Sweet, R., and P. Lane, eds. 2003. *On the Town: Women and Urban Life in Eighteenth-Century England*. Aldershot: Ashgate.
Vickery, A. 1993. "Golden Age to Separate Spheres? A Review of the Categories and Chronology of English Women's History." *The Historical Journal* 36: 383–414.
Wiskin, C. 2003. "Urban Businesswomen in Eighteenth-Century England." In *On the Town: Women and Urban Life in Eighteenth-Century England*, edited by R. Sweet and P. Lane, 87–110. Aldershot: Ashgate.

9 Statutory Invisibility

Urban Business Women's Legal and Political Rights

Jarkko Keskinen and Kirsi Vainio-Korhonen

Over the years, much research has been carried out into burgher occupations, relations between the state and the burghers, and the requirements set out by law governing the practising of trade and commerce. At a general level, the research has broadly examined the importance of occupational guilds for trade in the medieval and early modern periods in particular. In the wake of Douglass North, several researchers have seen these institutions organised among the burghers as part of an economic development process which, from the eighteenth century onwards, led to the birth of modern industrial capitalism (see e.g. Greif 2006; Epstein 2000; Ogilvie 2011).

The majority of Nordic research into the burgher occupations has concentrated on analysing the education of the burghers and the criteria they had to meet in order to trade, either from the point of view of a particular area or a single town (on research dealing with handicrafts, see e.g. Edgren 1987; Lindström 1991; Vainio-Korhonen 1994). Research on Nordic merchants was characterised for much of the twentieth century by a strong focus on economic and administrative history, as a result of which the interest of researchers was revolved around the economic and political activities of a merchant elite (Boëthius 1943; Samuelsson 1951; Möller 1954; Wuorinen 1959). At the turn of the millennium, the emphasis of research into merchants changed with the focus instead being on power, family, and marriage as well as various other social networking strategies (see Bull 1998; Kallioinen 2001; Ågren 2007; Lundblad 2007; Keskinen 2012).

Alice Clark (1919) began discussion on the topic with the publication of *Working Life of Women in the Seventeenth Century*, in which she presented the marginalised economic life of women as a result of the dawn of capitalism in the seventeenth century. A number of researchers have followed in her footsteps, discussing the role of women in pre-industrial society. At the same time, the concept has arisen that in seventeenth- to nineteenth-century patriarchal society women found themselves in a subordinate position in which legislation across Europe prevented their active, independent participation in trade (on this debate see Crowston 2008, 19–44; Ojala 2014, 41–51; for broader chronological span see Hietala and Nilsson 1999). Recently, researchers have shown that legislation and practice may differ considerably and that at different times women played a significant role in the economic life of pre-industrial society (see e.g. Simonton and Montenach 2013). In the Nordic countries, the majority of this research has concentrated on analysing the economic activity of unmarried women and the burgher widows, and the marriage and property rights of burgher wives (Stadin 2004, 249–255; see also Ågren and Erickson 2005).

This chapter examines the rights of burgher women to do business in eighteenth-century Turku, which at that time was the largest city in Finland and part of Sweden. Unlike earlier research, it focuses on a Turku merchant's daughter Maria Augustin (1749–1803), to whom her father wished to transfer the right to continue the family business on his retirement due to illness. The chapter shows how the economic policy pursued by the Swedish Crown and its aims to revise the legislation governing the burghers led to restrictions being placed on opportunities for women and their rights at the local level. Training for and working in burgher occupations was strongly linked to the family and women were involved in the family business in many different ways as wives, daughters, and widows. Despite this, more stringent legislation increasingly restricted women's opportunities to participate in the family business and made them statutorily invisible, especially in urban economic and political life.

Burgher rights were a personal privilege which, under the revised legislation, could no longer be transferred from one generation to the next and instead were granted on a case by case basis by the town's mayor and council. The new eighteenth-century legislation required that an applicant for merchant rights was male. A merchant, who, due to illness or advanced age, was prepared to relinquish his rights, did, however, need an heir for his life's work. Maria Augustin's case well illustrates the difficulties that merchant families faced if they attempted to navigate the shift in generation of a family business by ignoring normal custom and assigning rights to a daughter instead of a son.

The Maria Augustin case is a prime example of how little source material of women's activities remains available to history researchers. Despite their wide-ranging business operations, no correspondence from her father's or Maria's own merchant career has been preserved, not even account books to be read by future generations. In their absence, the chapter is based on material from official authorities—applications, statements, appeals, and court records. All of these documents are held in the Provincial Archive of Turku.

Women in Economic Life and the Law

Until 1809, Finland was part of the Kingdom of Sweden and was governed by Swedish law. In the 1340s, King Magnus Eriksson's Town Law established a common legal and administrative system for towns in the Kingdom of Sweden for the first time (MES 1966). In addition, it also set up a statutory basis for practising burgher occupations in towns. The law enshrined the principle under which all trade in the realm had to be concentrated in the towns, where only those master craftsmen and merchants who had been granted burgher rights were allowed to carry out burgher occupations. These protected rights also came with obligations for the burghers, the greatest of which was responsibility for the town's economic prosperity and tax burden. The burghers also had a right/obligation to participate in the town's administration and to send a representative from among their number from each town to the Swedish Estates assembly (*Riksdag*) (Vainio-Korhonen 2010, 221). Thanks to these preferential rights, the burghers gradually formed their own independent group, which clearly differed from other groups in urban society not only due to its rights and obligations but also due to its customs (Lindberg 2001, 28–31, 36).

The criteria for granting burgher rights were largely similar in the different towns of medieval Europe. Instead of issuing strict orders, those in power only enacted rough, indicative laws and instructions which could be adapted on a case by case basis. Thus, the town councils and burgher communities were able to modify administrative practices, forms of business, and especially the criteria for entry to the burgher estate such that they were able to independently determine those who were selected as members (Reynolds 1986, 186–187; Kallioinen 2000, 52–53).

There were two different ways of becoming a burgher without applying or paying burgher fees. In practice, all the sons of burghers born in the town automatically inherited their father's burgher rights without any separate formalities. It was also possible to obtain rights by entering into a suitable marriage. A man from outside the town could namely become a burgher if he married a daughter born in the town to a burgher family who owned a house there. In addition to this, it was possible to gain burgher rights on the basis of wealth. The law obliged all town citizens whose wealth amounted to at least three marks, to apply for burgher rights. The obligation also covered all the people who had worked in the service of the town's burghers and who had accumulated wealth worth at least twenty marks. Servants however, in addition to the application, had to pay a five öre burgher fee and guarantee that they would stay in the town for the next six years and that they were able to meet their obligations to the town's coffers accrued during this period (MES 1966, Konungabalken XV, 3–4, 5, 10; Lindström 1991, 16, 48).[1]

According to the law, it was not possible to grant burgher rights to women. However, women were able to continue running a family business as widows although they had not been granted burgher rights in their own name. The law also ordered that irrespective of estate or age, unmarried and married women were legally incompetent (Lahtinen 2007, 34). An unmarried woman's guardian was either her father, a widowed mother, or her closest male relative, whose task was to protect his ward's financial and legal interests. A married woman was represented by her husband, who was simultaneously, by virtue of the marriage, the head of the household

(Erickson 1995, 237). Magnus Eriksson's Town Law, however, allowed women to trade independently in products worth less than one öre. Thanks to inflation, the sum became so negligible over time that in practice women were officially locked outside the world of trade entirely.

Swedish historian Kekke Stadin (2004, 249–250), has stated that the view of the social status of burgher women reflected the strong link between burgher occupations and the domestic economy and the prevailing division of labour between the sexes. According to the burgher ideal, a woman should help her husband or father in the business. However, the law did not set out what this help actually meant. It would appear that women's opportunities to participate in the business run by the family varied by country, town, and even family. For example, in seventeenth-century Lübeck and Gothenburg the burgher wives belonging to the merchant elite played an active role in their families' business operations (Dalhede 2006, 271). In Holland, where the activities of the occupational groups were not as organised as in other countries in Western Europe, women's economic participation was considerably freer than in England, for example (van den Heuvel 2013, 116–133; for English practices see e.g. Ogilvie 2003, 9; Davidoff and Hall 1987, 200).

According to Veli Pekka Toropainen's (2016, 65, 213; see also Karlsson Sjögren 1998) research into the agency of urban women in seventeenth-century Finland, in the leading burgher families of Turku women participated actively not only in business but also in defending their own rights in the town court. In his view, the internal power relations within burgher families were characterised by negotiation, flexibility, and a constant re-evaluation of the division of labour based on gender, instead of official norms. In practice, this meant that the men who acted as the head of the community or family did not dispute women's rights to trade as long as it was in line with the interests of the family business and with the man's consent.

Before the law, a woman's position was clearest of all at the death of her husband. The business run by merchant families was based on the personal privilege of the male head of the family, which could not as such be transferred to the next generation. The widows of merchants formed an exception to this rule. Widows enjoyed rights that they had not been able to exercise at an earlier stage of their lives (see e.g. Simonton 2013, 93–115; Pylkkänen 2005, 76; Korpiola 2009). At the same time, women gained a new economic and social position of power in which they had the right to enter into contracts, own property, act as guardians of the family's children and continue the business of their late husband (Keskinen 2013).

Merchant Rights and Gender

In the early seventeenth century, the administration of the Kingdom of Sweden and of Finnish towns was reorganised. At this time, the focus of new administrative legislation came to be not only the administrative organisation of towns but also more stringent administration and control of customs duties, taxes, and trade, i.e. propping up the State finances. In the same context, Swedish King Gustav II Adolph issued a decree on the occupations practiced by burghers, which was clearly more detailed than the earlier Magnus Eriksson's Law. The decree ordered that all those in burgher occupations were to obtain burgher rights from the town council and swear a burgher oath. The intention was to remove the medieval practice by which citizens born in the town had the right to trade and work as craftsmen without separate burghers' rights. The majority of the towns' burghers reacted to the decree with reservations, as they viewed it as being contrary to the old Town Law and their own ancient rights (Granqvist 2016, 20–21).

The attitude to business carried out by women began gradually to change towards the end of the seventeenth century. Among other things, in a statement issued in 1679, Turku Court of Appeal judge and *lagman* (lawman) of Finland Claes Rålamb submitted that women should be banned from commerce entirely. To justify this, Rålamb asserted that the majority of women were simple creatures, lacking the experience required for trade and thus could easily be tricked. On the other hand, he considered that capable and sensible women did exist who should be permitted to do business. Rålamb's dual attitude reflected well women's position in society; as an abstract group they were considered to be incapable of managing demanding tasks, but as individuals they were viewed as having good characteristics for doing business. The prevailing patriarchal society did not permit them to operate independently, but at the same time required women to make their own efforts for the common good and the well-being of the family (Toropainen 2016, 212; Stadin 2004, 253–254).

The Civil Code of 1734 superseded Magnus Eriksson's Town Law that had been in force for almost 400 years and the decrees that had followed it. Unlike its predecessor, the Act also regulated the requirements for obtaining burgher rights in detail. The third section of the Book of commerce stated that burgher rights must be granted by the mayor and the town council. An applicant was required to be literate and have eleven to twelve years' practical experience under another merchant. If the town council's decision was positive, the applicant had to obtain two guarantors, swear a burgher's oath, and promise to live in the town for at least six years. Besides these official requirements, the law laid down that only men were able to request merchant rights (see e.g. Keskinen 2012, 54–60).

The legislation prevented women from being trained in commerce and closed the only possible route through which they could have become independent members of the burgher class.[2] Additionally, women's legal incompetence prevented them from swearing the merchant oath required to gain merchant rights. Thus, the new provisions prevented all unmarried and married women from applying for merchant rights themselves or participating in commerce. The law did not affect merchants' widows, who retained the right to continue their husband's business independently after his death. However, a widow did not take over ownership of her late husband's merchant rights, but only acted merely as the representative of these personal rights until she died or remarried, at which point she lost her right to participate in the family business (Stadin 2004, 251–252).

Historical research often presents the position of widows as a phase of life in which women gained a new kind of powerful position that they had not been able to enjoy earlier in their lives. However, the emphasis on this new legal, social, and economic freedom is based on a comparison of the position of widows and married women, producing a slightly distorted picture of the course of women's lives and their participation in family businesses. This is due to the fact that the majority of research into widows has focused on the English cultural sphere in which women were tightly subordinate to the power of their husbands. Here other European countries have presented women's rights as part of a more liberated position in which widows in particular enjoyed many rights that Englishwomen did not have (van der Heijden, Schmidt, and Wall 2007, 224).

However, the law of a society based on patriarchal order was not the only thing that placed restrictions on women's opportunities. Different cultural and economic factors limited women's involvement in family businesses even when they would have had a legal right to do so in the capacity of a widow. Not even wealth could guarantee a widow the same position within local society as her late husband, since money could not buy the cultural capital that women lacked. Thus, customs created a paradoxical situation in which married women were legally subordinate to the power of their husbands but despite this had an opportunity to participate in the family's business in many ways or even carry out an independent occupation that supported the domestic finances. As widows, on the other hand, women gained a completely new kind of freedom under the law to conduct business but the prevailing customs prevented them from efficiently putting these powers to good use (Hardwick 1992, 133–134, 143).

Political Culture and the Right of Widows to Conduct Business

With the Treaty of Nystad, which ended the Great Northern War between Sweden and Russia in 1721, Sweden ceased to be a great political power in the Baltic Sea region. At the same time, the long period of autocracy (1680–1719) ended, when Ulrika Eleonora, crowned queen of Sweden in 1719, transferred an increasing amount of power to the *Riksdag*. The greatest problem the estates now faced was a national economy that was heavily in debt. Sweden thus had to gather her resources and consider how she could regain the status of a great power that she had lost (see e.g. Nurmiainen 2009, 129–158).

In practice, the challenge faced by the new government was to create economic growth in a nation whose economy was predominantly founded on agriculture and a culture of craftsmanship. To bring in additional income, the Crown started to promote foreign trade by means of legislation. At the same time, it sought to lower the transaction costs arising from business and divide mutual resources more equally between those involved in business (Ojala 1999, 252–253; for transaction costs see e.g. North 1985, 559; Williamson 1998; see also Greif 2006).

Naturally, in a seventeenth-century class-based society, equal division of resources did not mean that they would be distributed equally across the entire population. The purpose of the legislation was to share resources more equally than before between the groups of people that the Crown had granted the privilege to conduct business. The Crown was not seeking to secure the property rights for the public good but to reduce its own costs. In other words, it sought to guarantee the property rights of such organisations and individuals, i.e. merchants that from the point of view of the Crown were capable of exercising them as efficiently as possible. Besides protecting property rights, economic policy was to organise business life such that it enabled efficient control and made it easier for certain payments, such as customs duties and taxes, to be collected (Keskinen 2012, 41–52; see also Carlén 1997).

At the same time, the power and influence of the burgher estate increased in State politics (Melkersson 1997, 215). The new powerful position of the burghers was also reflected at the local level, where the merchant community seeking to protect their own interests caused conflicts among the burghers themselves. Amid this process of forming a political culture, gender once more became a topic of discussion and finally led to restrictions being placed on the political rights of burgher widows (see e.g. Karlsson Sjögren and Lindström 2004, 241–262).

Magnus Eriksson's Town Law had already decreed that the town themselves had the right to choose the officials charged with governing them (MES 1966, Konungabalken I–II). However, this right did not extend to all the burghers, only the mayor and the council, who were thus able to supplement their own ranks as the need arose. In practice, the right only concerned the members of the council, as in the seventeenth century the Crown appointed the majority of town mayors without their consultation. This was to change in the early eighteenth century when the representatives of the burgher estate at the *Riksdag* began to demand that towns be entitled to freely elect their own officials. Swedish King Frederick I finally issued a decree on the matter in 1723, according to which the town council and mayors were thenceforth to be elected in elections organised among the town's burghers and the town council (Mäntylä 1981, 27–31; Halila 1942, 80–90).

As a result of the new decree, all burghers gained the opportunity to influence local politics. In the early eighteenth century, the intention was still that officials were to be selected by unanimous decision and no actual elections needed to be organised. However, the burghers did not form a single homogenous group but were divided by status, rights, and wealth (Keskinen 2012, 47). This being the case, consensus was short-lived, and in the late 1720s the members of the lower ranks of the burgher class began to demand that elections be held. Voting brought a new problem which the official decrees had not taken into account—how were elections to be organised and how were votes to be allocated between the town's burghers? By the start of the next decade, most Finnish towns had made the transition from unanimous decisions to majority voting whereby each burgher with the right to vote had one vote and the election was won by the candidate who received the highest number of votes (Mäntylä 1977, 40–50).

The right to vote was connected to burgher rights. By official decrees, each person who had been granted burgher rights who owned a permanent place of residence in the town and paid annual taxes to the town's coffers had the right to vote in elections organised in the town. However, during the eighteenth century, the prevailing social and economic stratification among the burghers caused conflicts between these groupings and aroused a debate on who was to be counted as a "true burgher". Wealthier burghers in the Swedish towns were dissatisfied with the current practice. There was also a view that the right to vote should not automatically be granted to every member of the burgher class. Both of these issues aroused debate (Karlsson Sjögren and Lindström 2006, 172, 176).

Seen particularly from the viewpoint of the merchants conducting foreign trade, it was unconscionable that the vote of the poorest burgher carried the same weight in elections as their opinions did. Thus the merchants of Vaasa, Kokkola, and Pietarsaari complained to the King at the 1738 *Riksdag* that the towns' burgher classes largely comprised sailors and carpenters whose annual taxes could not be raised higher than two silver thalers because they could not afford more.[3] Despite this, these people wanted the same right to vote as the merchants who bore the greatest tax burden on their shoulders (Mäntylä 1977, 53–54).

Before the appeals, a decree was issued in 1731 stating that the right to vote in elections to the *Riksdag* was only to be afforded to true burghers, in other words merchants and master craftsmen, who paid their taxes to the Crown and the town. In addition to this, the decree offered an alternative to the towns whereby the votes would be distributed among the burghers according to the tax register, in other words by wealth. The towns' merchant community wanted this practice to apply also to elections for the mayor and town councils. To pressurise the government, the town councils of different towns presented to the *Riksdag* illegalities committed during local elections. For example, in a mayoral election in Kokkola, four carpenters, who had been granted the right to vote, were caught because their employer had ordered them to vote for his own favourite threatening them with a cut in their pay if they did not and rewarding them with days off (Mäntylä 1981, 39–40).

Ultimately, the estates gathered at the *Riksdag* decided on the proposal of the burghers. It was agreed that in future town elections for the mayor, town councillors, and town secretaries the number of votes of burghers would be related to the number of öre calculated in the tax registers. In other words, the number of votes would be based not on a head count of burghers but on their personal wealth. The grounds for the decision were formulated knowingly: "because advantage is to be given to those who bear the greater costs of maintaining the town".[4]

The decree linking the number of votes of the burghers to wealth essentially changed the power relations at the local level political arena. In Pori, for example, the lower burgher class was numerically larger than the class of craftsmen and merchants. Hence their collective tax burden was notably higher than that of the merchants, who paid a third of the tax collected for the whole town. However, this tax rate was based on their number, not on their economic wealth or the profits of their business activities. When calculated per person, the rates paid by the merchants were two or three times that of the other burgher groups in Pori. The change in the law notably increased the number of votes available to the merchants and gave them leverage to dictate the end result of elections should they wish to (Keskinen 2012, 161–162).

The background to the change in the law was thus the need of the burghers who held the power in towns to uphold and strengthen their own position in local society and secondly the endeavours of lower social groupings of burghers to obtain new benefits and rights for themselves. Besides social status, the burghers also discussed whether the right to vote should be dependent on gender. Even in the 1730s, the merchant communities in Finnish towns were broadly of the opinion that the widows of wealthy merchants should have the right to vote in elections organised in the towns as "by virtue of their husband's activities they had gained a better view of general matters than some labourer" (Mäntylä 1977, 62).

Widows running large-scale commercial enterprises were common in all towns in the Kingdom of Sweden in the eighteenth century. In Finland's largest town of Turku, burgher widows were encountered in every business sector. Numerically, they accounted for approximately 6–10 per cent of the entire town's burghers. Although widows running businesses naturally tended to be most commonly found among craftsmen and the lower ranks of the burgher class, they could also be found among the town's merchant elite. In debates at the *Riksdag*, the question was indeed about the rights of widows of leading merchant families to vote. The political rights of widows of considerably poorer master craftsmen and members of the lower burgher class did not, however, seem to interest the representatives meeting at the *Riksdag* at all (Vainio-Korhonen 2002b, 35–54; Mäntylä 1977, 62).

According to Åsa Karlsson Sjögren's and Peter Lindström's research on the political culture in Swedish towns in the Age of Liberty, the importance of widowhood was changing in the eighteenth century. Among other things, the town council of Vaasa decided that it was not appropriate for women to meet like the other burghers in the town hall to decide the town's matters and that these weaker and simple women should remain in the circles which God had decreed for them in line with general custom and not seek something to which they were not entitled (Nikula 1978, 18).

Merchants' widows were thus no longer seen as the heirs of their husbands' merchant rights, but as women who merely represented the property of their late spouse. Burgher rights, on the other hand, were personal rights that were based on swearing an oath before God, the King, the Mayor, and the town council. A woman could not make such an oath and, this being the case, she could not be a true burgher. And because only true burghers were allowed to vote, the question arose of whether women could have the right to vote at all. Concern about the voting behaviour of widows grew even more among merchant society after the change in the law in 1743. Varying the number of votes based on wealth and tax fees namely increased the relative weight of widows in elections. After a long debate, the *Riksdag* finally reached a decision in 1758 which banned merchants' widows from voting in elections for town officials (Karlsson Sjögren and Lindström 2006, 143).

From the point of view of widows, the question involved the same kind of double morality as the debate on merchant rights. On the one hand, the law decreed that women were not allowed to vote but on the other the same law obliged them as widows to pay taxes to the town and to fulfil the same other financial obligations as the other burghers did. This being the case, it was no wonder that some of the widowed women refused to submit to the decision. For example, in Turku, Anna Elisabeth Baer, the widow of a merchant, Hedvig Söderman, the widow of a bookbinder, and Helena Ottiliana Richter, the widow of a tanner, requested the right to vote in the 1771 elections for representatives to the *Riksdag* on the basis that they paid considerable amounts of tax to the city. All of their petitions were rejected (Nikula 1978, 18).

Baer was a particularly wealthy widow who continued successfully in business for nine years after the death of her husband (Vainio-Korhonen 2002a). Her late husband had acted among other things as the town's representative to the *Riksdag*. Despite this, the town council would not grant Baer's petition, although she asserted that as a widow she was not under anyone else's guardianship and that she had the right to conduct business in town. The town council justified its decision by the fact that she had not personally been granted burgher rights and that she had not sworn a burgher oath—this being the case, Baer could not be considered as a true burgher despite her wealth or the fact that she ran a business (Karlsson Sjögren and Lindström 2006, 189–190).

From Maiden to Merchant

Merchant's daughter Maria Augustin from Turku is a prime example of how a capable woman, trained by her father, couldn't be granted burgher rights, particularly because she was unmarried and thus fundamentally legally incompetent in society. As a young man, her father, Mathias Augustin the elder, had proven himself to be an energetic master of his own destiny: the son of a farmer from Somero gradually became a wealthy and influential grocer and ship-owner in Turku. Mathias Augustin the younger, who shared his name with his father, also grew up to become a capable businessman. In 1771, he opened his own shop and eventually became a rich mansion owner and patron of a metalworks business. Maria Augustin's entrepreneurial skills were no worse than those of her father or brother. When her brother left home, Maria took the reins.

In 1775, the 26 year-old Maria Augustin took responsibility for her ageing father's extensive business. Miss Augustin's trading skills are probably best demonstrated by the fact that the company did so well under her stewardship that its operating profit was subject to the second highest income tax in Turku.

Maria had learnt from her father. His strong belief in his daughter's skills is evident in the following "reference":

> *That my dear daughter, maiden Maria Augustin, has taken care of my household—not just during the lifetime of her late mother, but also after it—and that for fifteen years she has supervised and looked after my business: let this be certified of her. Turku, 29 September 1790. Math. Augustin*[5]

Men who intended to become merchants of salt and trinkets were called in for questioning by senior, experienced traders in the presence of the mayor and one alderman. Maria Augustin was not able to demonstrate her skills in this way, so she relied on the reference written by her father.

From Father to Daughter

In 1790, Mathias Augustin the elder turned 80. In the economically turbulent times of the Russo-Swedish War, he felt his powers were finally slipping away from him and he wanted to transfer his business into his daughter's name. However, the successor's gender and marital status were problematic. Throughout their lives, unmarried women were under the guardianship of their fathers or other male representatives, and they could not enter into contracts or engage in business in their own names. The guardian also had "matchmaking rights": the maiden could only marry with her matchmaker's permission.

Due to these legal issues, the utmost care was required to plan how the business would be handed down to the next generation. At that point, Maria Augustin was forty, middle-aged and unmarried. Like all other women in her position, she was still subject to guardianship. However, the king had the power to declare maidens fully competent. As her father's strength deteriorated, Maria and Mathias Augustin reached out to the only option open to them—the king's assistance. In the Stockholm Royal Palace on 19 February 1790, King Gustav III declared:

> *Let Maria Augustin be legally competent, and let her henceforth look after and take responsibility for herself and her property without the intervention of a guardian.*[6]

However, the guardian's matchmaking right was not affected. If Maria were to marry, the suitor would have to seek her father's blessing. If Maria were to inherit, she would need to be represented by a man.[7] This polarised decision gave Maria Augustin power over her livelihood but left out the issues of inheritance and marriage, which were highly important in society at that time. Marriages and legacies were tools for wealthy families to govern the transfer of important immovable property from one generation to the next, and there was no desire to entrust women with this decision-making power.

When the king's decision had made Maria Augustin financially independent and, thereby, entitled to engage in business, Mathias Augustin began preparing the transfer of the business to his daughter and his own transition into retirement. In April 1790, he relinquished his burgher rights with the town council's consent. In October of the same year, the elders of Turku received a letter from Maria Augustin stating that the large inventory—iron, salt, and other goods belonging to her father's business—could not all be sold off at once. Maria stated in her letter that she had already been handling her father's business for fifteen years and was legally competent by virtue of the king's decree. To ensure that her father would not have to suffer unreasonable losses in his old age:

> *I am forced [. . .] to humbly plead that I may be allowed, in return for a reasonable annual trading tax, to sell the stock of goods that is left and, in unfortunate circumstances, remains a burden upon my dear father. As this does not infringe upon anyone's interests, I take heart in the hope that, mindful of the substantial sum in burgher taxes paid by my dear father over several years, [. . .] I may receive a favourable decision.*[8]

The entire manoeuvre was extremely skilfully planned and constructed. Although Maria's economic agency had been guaranteed by royal decree, she did not apply for burgher rights because, as a woman, she could not legally have received them. Instead, she sought the right to engage in trade without belonging to the burgher estate. In this case, she would have paid the city treasury a special trading tax (contingent tax). This type of membership of the "contingent burgher" provided an opportunity for those who did not belong to the actual estate—including women—to engage in trade, industry, running restaurants or cafés, or selling garden products within certain limits. Members of the contingent burghers were not required to hold a degree in trading but they did not have any of the political rights and obligations of the burgher estate either.

The reasoning set out in Maria Augustin's application was also compelling. As a member of the burgher estate, her father had for decades paid plenty of burgher tax—often at the highest rate—into the city's coffers and he now needed the help of the burgher community. Otherwise, his shop's unsold inventory would land him in financial difficulty. In order to convince the city elders, Maria's professional skills were proven by her father's letter, in which Mathias Augustin stated that his daughter had run the business for fifteen years. Maria Augustin also tried to pre-empt the most common grounds for refusal by stating in her letter that her application did not "infringe upon anyone's interests". In the class society of the eighteenth century, everyone closely guarded the interests accorded to them by estate privilege. The most important benefit for the burgher estate was the exclusive right to engage in certain types of business or artisanal profession.

Here, Maria Augustin was requesting permission to continue her father's business for two years in return for a contingent tax. However, the town council declined Maria's application on the grounds of her gender. The elders were not even swayed by the fact that the king had declared Maria Augustin to be of age, meaning that she was able to enter into commitments and manage her property without a guardian. The city elders objected to the application on the grounds that the law required burgher to be men. They also considered that the applicant was not living in such destitution that she should be granted a special permit on the grounds of poverty. According to the town council, acceding to the application may even have set a dangerous precedent in favour of women. And after all, this particular woman had a brother, whom the town council considered well equipped to look after his father's business without the daughter needing to get embroiled in the matter in any way.

Appeal to the King

Maria Augustin was not satisfied with the town council's negative decision. She appealed the matter to the Commercial Department of the Board of Trade (Kommerskollegium), which granted her the right in March 1792 to continue her father's business for one year in return for a trading tax.[9] A few months later, Maria Augustin contacted the town council of Turku again, but this time, her letter was not nearly as humble as the previous one:

> It has never been my intention to personally set about becoming a merchant and member of the burgher estate in this city. [. . .] But because my late father took the effort while he was still alive to most humbly petition the most honourable Royal Commercial Department for a decision on this matter, it would be, as I see it, unforgivable if I did nothing to seek benefit for myself in this [decision].

> As I was remembered in the last assessment [for taxation] by means of a substantial contingency charge, although the negligible shares in ships that I inherited do not generate any return in light of the Turkish unrest, and because I have inherited merchandise that cannot be auctioned without great losses and, finally, because I have allowed several months to elapse since the time promised to me by the most honourable Royal Commercial Department, I am very hopeful that the most noble town council and gentlemen elders of the city do not consider me to have done anybody wrong if I offer for sale in my shop a part of the merchandise that has fallen to me to which I have referred.
>
> Most noble town council and gentlemen elders of the city: do not take this to be a new petition of any kind, rather as a proposed means of avoiding an appeal addressed to His Royal Majesty and the Government in this insignificant matter. I would consider this to be a thoughtless [act on the part of the town council] in these otherwise highly miserable and problematic times.[10]

The letter is not a little derisive in tone, as Maria points out the hefty tax that has been levied on her. At least this unmarried woman—one of the wealthiest in Turku—did not allow her gender or marital status to restrict her use of language as she reeled off some home truths about her financial position for the benefit of the town council members. The opening phrase, "It has never been my intention to personally set about becoming a merchant and member of the burgher estate in this city", was almost shameless in its directness and contravened all of the norms of polite writing.

In our opinion, it communicates the intense frustration that the letter's signatory felt with the activities of the city elders. The remark about "substantial contingency charges" makes the elders appear somewhat ridiculous. After all, Maria had petitioned for trading rights (and been declined) in return for precisely this tax a couple of years previously. Now the city was proceeding to tax her with a firm hand even though its top administrators had not granted a business licence. Given the hierarchical letter-writing culture of the time, the final paragraph can be considered directly combative, particularly when written by a woman. Maria threatened the town council with an appeal addressed to the king if the decision was not to her liking. The assertion at the end of the letter that they were living in "miserable and problematic times" probably refers to the shooting of King Gustav III at the opera in Stockholm in March 1792.

This time, the town council gave in to Maria Augustin's request and granted her a year-long business licence. However, this did not satisfy Maria Augustin. She appealed the decision of the Commercial Department and the town council and took it to the king, applying for the life-long right to be able to continue the business she had inherited from her father if she paid a contingent trading tax. Gustav IV Adolf's caretaker government granted her this life-long licence in March 1793.[11] In 1793, the town council of Turku also had to grant Maria Augustin life-long contingent burgher rights, which enabled her—in return for a trading tax—to carry on the business she had inherited from her father, who died in 1791.

In the last years of her life, Maria Augustin successfully engaged in shopkeeping and trade with Stockholm, as her father had done before her. Her probate inventory, prepared in 1804, lists an extensive trade inventory of fabrics, laces, threads, accessories, metal goods, tobacco, spices, groceries and salt. Her success is also borne out by the fact that as a contingent burgher, she was among the most heavily taxed businesspeople in Turku. In addition to her property in the city, she owned a big farm estate, shares in three long-haul vessels and a malt house, two shops, and a windmill. Augustin's business accounts have not survived, but, according to the probate inventory, the income of the shop alone for the last four months of 1803 amounted to 877 Swedish riksdaler pegged to silver.[12]

Conclusions

Business legislation originating from the "Swedish period" was not updated in Finland until the second half of the nineteenth century, such that from 1879 onwards women's business fell within the remit of freedom of trade. The estate-based privileges of the burghers of the towns were abolished at the same time. However, the business activities of burgher widows had flagged prior to this, although no Act or decree had required this. In the family-oriented society of the nineteenth century, women resigned to an ever increasing extent to the private circle of the home and left any businesses they may have inherited to their sons or other males to manage.

These aims were visible as early as the eighteenth century when the rights of burgher women to do business and their political rights began to be placed under scrutiny in a different way than before. Voices began to be raised in the social debate claiming that women should be prohibited from doing business entirely because they were fundamentally gullible and simple due to being of the female sex.

The Civil Code of 1734 unequivocally declared for the first time that only men in the Kingdom of Sweden had the opportunity to be trained in the area of trade and apply for trade rights. At the same time, the business activities of widows started to be viewed from a new angle. They were no longer examined or treated primarily as the heirs to their husbands' businesses but as women who merely represented the property of their late spouse and who were not thus themselves even "true burghers". Although they had the right to carry out business as burghers, they had not sworn the burgher oath in person and they were not registered as burghers in their own names.

The business problems of Maria Augustin from Turku derived from this same source. Although she was able, as a person declared as being fully competent, to independently incur debts and enter into financial undertakings, she was not able to swear the burgher oath and thus gain burgher rights due to her sex. The letter of the law and to an ever increasing extent the spirit of the time also started to see women fundamentally as unsuited for responsible business tasks.

Notes

1 In the fourteenth century the average annual pay for a craftsman was 18–25 marks (Kallioinen 2000, 97–98).
2 In her pioneering study on midwives, Kirsi Vainio-Korhonen (2016) has demonstrated that in eighteenth-century Sweden midwives were educated in Stockholm where the crown established a special school for them.
3 Small towns on the Western coast of Finland.
4 On power struggles between burgher classes in Finnish towns see e.g. Granqvist 2016, 157–168; Keskinen 2012, 157–178; Nikula 1970, 280–292.
5 Turku City Archives. Appendices for the minutes of town council (Allegaatit). Mathias Augustin to the town council of Turku 29.9.1790.
6 Turku City Archives. Appendices for the minutes of town council (Allegaatit). The transricpt of the King's declaration 19.2.1790.
7 Turku City Archives. Appendices for the minutes of town council (Allegaatit). The transricpt of the King's declaration 19.2.1790.
8 Turku City Archives. Appendices for the minutes of town council (Allegaatit). Maria Augustin to the town council of Turku 13.10.1790.
9 Turku City Archives. Appendices for the minutes of town council (Allegaatit). Maria Augustin to the town council of Turku 4.6.1792.
10 Turku City Archives. Appendices for the minutes of town council (Allegaatit). Maria Augustin to the town council of Turku 4.6.1792.
11 Turku City Archives. Appendices for the minutes of town council (Allegaatit). The transricpt of the King's declaration 15.3.1793.
12 Turku City Archives. Maria Augustin's probate inventory 12.1.1804.

References

Ågren, K. 2007. *Köpmannen i Stockholm: Grosshandlares ekonomiska och sociala strategier under 1700-talet*. PhD diss., University of Uppsala.

Ågren, M., and A. L. Erickson, eds. 2005. *The Marital economy in Scandinavia and Britain 1400–1900*. Aldeshot: Ashgate.

Boëthius, B. 1943. *Magistraten och borgerskapet i Stockholm 1719–1815*. Stockholm: P. A. Norstedt & Söners Förlag.

Bull, I. 1998. *De trondhjemske handelshusene på 1700-talet: slekt, hushold og forretning*. Trondheim: Norwegian University of Science and Technology.

Carlén, S. 1997. *Staten som marknadens salt: en studie i institutionsbildning, kollektivt handlande och tidig välfärdspolitik på en strategisk varumarknad i övergången mellan merkantilism och liberalism 1720–1862*. Stockholm: Almqvist & Wiksell international.

Clark, A. 1919. *Working Life of Women in the Seventeenth Century*. London: Routledge.

Crowston, C. 2008. "Women, Gender, and Guilds in Early Modern Europe: An Overview of Recent Research." In *The Return of the Guilds*, edited by J. Lucassen, T. De Moor and J. Luiten van Zanden, 19–44. Cambridge: Cambridge University Press.

Dalhede, C. 2006. *Viner, kvinnor, kapital: En 1600-talshandel med potential? Fjärrhandelsfamiljerna Jeronius Möller i Lübeck och Sibrant Valck i Göteborg: Handelsfamiljer på Stormaktstiders Europamarknad 4*. Partille: Warne förlag.

Davidoff, L., and C. Hall. 1987. *Family Fortunes: Men and Women of the English Middle Class 1750–1850*. London and New York: Routledge.

Edgren, L. 1987. *Lärling—Gesäll—mästare: Hantverk och hantverkare i Malmö 1750–1847*. Lund: Dialogos.

Epstein, S. R. 2000. *Freedom and Growth: The Rise of States and Markets in Europe, 1300–1750*. London and New York: Routledge.

Erickson, A. L. 1995. *Women and Property in Early Modern England*. London: Routledge.

Granqvist, J.-M. 2016. "Helsingin porvaristo Viaporin rakennuskaudella (1748–1808): Sosiaalihistoriallinen perustutkimus". PhD diss., University of Helsinki.

Greif, A. 2006. *Institutions and the Path to the Modern Economy: Lessons from Medieval Trade*. Cambridge: Cambridge University Press.

Halila, A. 1942. *Suomen kaupunkien kunnallishallinto 1600-luvulla*. Helsinki: SHS.

Hardwick, J. 1992. "Widowhood and Patriarchy in Seventeenth Century France." *Journal of Social History* 26 (1) (Autumn): 133–148.

Hietala, M., and L. Nilsson, eds. 1999. *Women in Towns: The Social Position of Urban Women in Historical Context*. Helsinki: SHS.

Kallioinen, M. 2000. *Kauppias, kaupunki, kruunu: Turun porvariyhteisö ja talouden organisaatio varhaiskeskiajalta 1570-luvulle*. Bibliotheca Historica 59. Suomalaisen Kirjallisuuden Seura, Helsinki.

Kallioinen, M. 2001. *Informaatio ja ulkomaiset markkinat Dahlströmin kauppahuoneen liiketoiminnassa 1800-luvulla*. Helsinki: SKS.

Karlsson Sjögren, Å. 1998. *Kvinnors rätt i stormaktstidens Gävle*. Umeå: Umeå Universitet.

Karlsson Sjögren, Å., and P. Lindström. 2004. "Widows, Ownership and Political Culture: Sweden 1650–1800." *Scandinavian Journal of History* 29 (3–4): 241–262.

Karlsson Sjögren, Å., and P. Lindström. 2006. "Oikeita, todellisia porvareita? Luokka, sukupuoli ja kieli vapauden ajan kaupunkien poliittisessa kulttuurissa." In *Kahden puolen Pohjanlahtea I: Ihmisiä, yhteisöjä ja aatteita Ruotsissa ja Suomessa 1500-luvulta 1900-luvulle*, edited by G. Bladh and C. Kuvaja. Helsinki: SKS.

Keskinen, J. 2012. "Oma ja yhteinen etu: Kauppiaiden keskinäinen kilpailu ja yhteistyö Porin paikallisyhteisössä 1765–1845." PhD diss., University of Turku.

Keskinen, J. 2013. "Perinteiden jatkajat: Sukupolvenvaihdos 1800-luvun porilaisissa kauppiasperheissä." *Genos* 84 (4): 207–219.

Korpiola, M. 2009. *Between Bethrothal and Bedding: Marriage Formation in Sweden, 1200–1600*. Leiden: Brill.

Lahtinen, A. 2007. *Sopeutuvat, neuvottelevat, kapinalliset: Naiset toimijoina Flemingin sukupiirissä 1470–1620*. Helsinki: SKS.

Lindberg, E. 2001. *Borgerskap och burskap: Om näringsprivilegier och borgerskapets institutioner i Stockholm 1820–1846*. Uppsala: Uppsala Universitet.

Lindström, D. 1991. *Skrå, stad och stat: Stockholm, Malmö och Bergen ca 1350–1622*. Uppsala: Uppsala Universitet.

Lundblad, S. 2007. *Hedersam handelsman eller verksam företagare: Den ekonomiska kulturens omvandling och de ledande ekonomiska aktorerna i Gävle 1765–1869*. PhD diss. University of Uppsala.

Magnus Erikssons Stadlag (MES). 1966. *I nusvensk tolkning av Åke Holmbäck och Elias Wessén*. Lund: Institut för rättshistorisk forskning.

Mäntylä, I. 1977. *Yksimielisyydestä kauppiaiden valtaan: Raatimiesten vaalit 12 kaupungissa 1722–1808*. Helsinki: SHS.

Mäntylä, I. 1981. *Valitut, ehdollepannut ja nimitetyt: Pormestarien vaalit 20 kaupungissa 1720–1808*. Helsinki: SHS.

Melkersson, M. 1997. *Staten, ordningen och friheten: En studie av den styrande elitens syn på statens roll mellan stormakten och 1800-talet*. Uppsala: Uppsala Universitet.

Möller, S. 1954. *Suomen tapulikaupunkien valtaporvaristo ja sen kaupankäyntimenetelmät 1600-luvun alkupuolella*. Helsinki: SHS.

Nikula, O. 1970. *Turun Kaupungin historia I*. Turku: Turun kaupunki.

Nikula, O. 1978. *Finlandska borgare på 1700-talet*. Helsingfors: SLS.

North, D. C. 1985. "Transaction Costs in History." *Journal of European Economic History* 14 (3): 557–576.

Nurmiainen, J. 2009. *Edistys ja yhteinen hyvä vapaudenajan ruotsalaisessa poliittisessa kielessä*. Helsinki: SKS.

Ogilvie, S. 2003. *A Bitter Living: Women, Markets, and Social Capital in Early Modern Germany*. Oxford: Oxford University Press.

Ogilvie, S. 2011. *Institutions and European Trade: Merchant Guilds, 1000–1800*. Cambridge: Cambridge University Press.

Ojala, J. 1999. *Tehokasta liiketoimintaa Pohjanmaan pikkukaupungeissa: Purjemerenkulun kannattavuus ja tuottavuus 1700–1800-luvulla*. Bibliotheca Historica 40. Helsinki: SHS.

Ojala, M. 2014. *Protection, Continuity and Gender: Craft trade culture in the Baltic Sea Region (14th–16th Centuries)*. PhD diss., University of Tampere.

Pylkkänen, A. 2005. "Forming the Marital Economy in the Early Modern Finnish Countryside." In *The Marital Economy in Scandinavia and Britain 1400–1900: Women and Gender in the Early Modern World*, edited by M. Ågren and A. L. Erickson. Aldershot: Ashgate.

Reynolds, S. 1986. *Kingdoms and Communities in Western Europe*. Oxford: Clarendon.

Samuelsson, K. 1951. *De stora köpmanshusen i Stockholm 1730–1815: En studie i den svenska handelskapitalismens historia*. Stockholm: Ekonomisk-Historiska Institute.

Simonton, D. 2013. "Widows and Wenches: Single Women in Eighteenth-Century Urban Economics." In *Female Agency in the Urban Economy: Gender in European Towns, 1640–1830*, edited by D. Simonton and A. Montenach, 93–115. New York and London: Routledge.

Simonton, D., and A. Montenach, eds. 2013. *Female Agency in the Urban Economy. Gender in European Towns 1640–1830*. New York and London: Routledge.

Stadin, K. 2004. *Stånd och Genus I stormaktstidens Sverige*. Lund: Nordic Academic Press.

Toropainen, V. P. 2016. "Päättäväiset porvarskat: Turun johtavan porvariston naisten toimijuus vuosina 1623–1670." PhD diss., University of Turku.

Vainio-Korhonen, K. 1994. *Kultaa ja hopeaa mestarien työkirjoissa: Suomen kultasepäntyö Ruotsin ajan lopulla valtakunnallista taustaa vasten*. Helsinki: SHS.

Vainio-Korhonen, K. 2002a. "Baer, Anna Elisabeth (1722–1799)." In *Kansallisbiografia*-verkkojulkaisu. Helsinki: Suomalaisen Kirjallisuuden Seura, 1997–. www.kansallisbiografia.fi/kansallisbiografia/henkilo/372.

Vainio-Korhonen, K. 2002b. *Ruokaa, vaatteita, hoivaa: Naiset ja yrittäjyys paikallisena ja yleisenä ilmiönä 1700-luvulta nykypäivään*. Helsinki: SKS.

Vainio-Korhonen, K. 2010. "Kaupan ja käsityön ammattikasvatus." In *Huoneentaulun maailma: Kasvatus ja koulutus Suomessa keskiajalta 1860-luvulle*, edited by J. Hanska and K. Vainio-Korhonen, 221–257. Helsinki: SKS.

Vainio-Korhonen, K. 2016. *De frimodiga: Barnmorskor, födande och kroppslighet på 1700-talet*. Helsinki: SLS.

van den Heuvel, D. 2013. "Guilds, Gender Policies and Economic Opportunities for Women in Early Modern Dutch Towns." In *Female Agency in the Urban Economy: Gender in European Towns 1640–1830*, edited by D. Simonton and A. Montenach, 116–133. New York and London: Routledge.

van der Heijden, M., A. Schmidt, and R. Wall. 2007. "Broken Families: Economic Resources and Social Networks of Women Who Head Families". *History of the Family* 12 (4): 223–232.

Williamson, O. E. 1998. "Transaction Cost Economics: How It Works, Where It Is Headed." *De Economist* 146 (1): 23–58.

Wuorinen, A. 1959. *Turku kauppakaupunkina Ruotsin vallan loppukautena I–II*. Helsinki: SHS.

10 A Lost Opportunity or a Lucky Escape?

Non-Successor Daughters and the Family in Business

Janice Byrne and Salma Fattoum

Introduction

Succession—the crucial handing over of power to the next generation—is a key area of interest in family business. When there are numerous potential successors in line, the succession contest is not always based on business or leadership competence. When questions of how gender is implicated in succession are raised, prior research has emphasised the endurance of patriarchal power and primogeniture in family business (Curimbaba 2002; Haberman and Danes 2007; Mulholland 1996, 2003). Even today, second or later generation daughters are less likely than sons to be selected as successors within the family business (Ahrens, Landmann, and Woywode 2015; Martinez Jimenez 2009; Wang 2010).

However, it is increasingly acknowledged that patriarchy provides us with only a partial understanding of gender relations in family business (Hamilton 2006, 2013). Further study and exploration of gendered practices in family business is required to render subtle acts of power and resistance visible (Hamilton 2013; Bruni, Gherardi, and Poggio 2005). Women may in fact hold considerable power in family business, although it is not be always publically visible or represented in the form of explicit titles (Hamilton 2006, 2013; Cole 1997). Furthermore, we should be wary of viewing women as "victims of the male norm" in management (Billing 2011) and open ourselves up to the variety and complexity of their entrepreneurial experiences (Lewis and Simpson 2015).

Extant research has thus far often focused on the ultimate outcome of succession (successor or not). A recent development in family business research views succession not just about the family business being passed on but about how the different family members (and their respective futures) are considered in the context of business more broadly (Discua Cruz, Howorth, and Hamilton 2012). For the next generation, succession should be considered as just one of many career options. Rather than feeling pressured, the next generation should only pursue the successor role if they are willing and able to do the job (Zellweger and Sieger 2012). Sometimes senior and junior generation family members form and engage in family entrepreneurial teams, setting up additional businesses securing the futures of respective family members and the family wealth (Discua Cruz, Howorth, and Hamilton 2012). Highly confident and entrepreneurial family business members may in fact prefer to found their own business rather than follow someone else's footpath (Zellweger and Sieger 2012).

This interest in "intra-family entrepreneurship" (Discua Cruz, Howorth, and Hamilton 2012) calls on us to examine the "family in business" rather than the continuity of "one family business" (Moores 2009). However, to our knowledge, researchers have not yet fully explored the gendered dimension of intra-family entrepreneurship.

Theoretical Grounding

Research on Women in Family Business

Early researchers looking at women in family business painted a relatively bleak picture (Gupta and Levenburg 2013), lamenting their "invisible" status (Gillis Donovan and Moynihan-Brandt 1990; Martinez Jimenez 2009) and showing how women's roles in family business were either downplayed or ignored. This first generation of studies highlighted the primacy of patriarchal relations and the phenomenon of primogeniture—whereby the first-born son is favoured for succession (Dumas 1992; Keating and Little 1997). Gender relations underlined by patriarchal practices "propel male kin to positions of power and influence" (Mulholland 1996, 78). These studies found that women were overshadowed or marginalised in the family firm, often having their successes appropriated by male siblings (Mulholland 1996, 2003). Women family business members often work in the home: looking after the children, assuming household tasks, caring for ill or elderly relatives, helping the husband in his work, and managing the family finances (Voydanoff 1990). If they actively work in the family business, women are usually concentrated in the more so-called "feminine" areas—such as human resources, customer care, and sales support (Galiano and Vinturella 1995)—leaving the more strategic roles for their male siblings.

A second generation of research explored women's motivations and experience of joining the family business and investigated the factors which helped or hindered their taking on leadership roles (Curimbaba 2002; Gatewood et al. 2003; Vera and Dean 2005; Rowe and Hong 2000; Wang 2010). Researchers pointed to how women often assume marginal roles, with few responsibilities and little decision making power (Constantinidis and Cornet 2008; Barrett and Moores 2009). However, there was a more optimistic tone in this second wave of research addressing gender in family business (Gupta and Levenburg 2013; Martinez Jimenez 2009), with researchers heralding the potential of family business to provide a promising arena for the development of women leaders (Ahrens, Landmann, and Woywode 2015; Martinez Jimenez 2009). Women are seen as "nurturers of the next generation of leaders" (Dugan et al. 2008) and the importance of their "emotional leadership" (Martinez Jimenez 2009) is emphasised. Thus, many studies acknowledged the increasing "visibility" and importance of women in family business.

A recent (third) emerging stream of research takes a broader view and explores gender in family business as opposed to women in family business. Here, gender is not seen as short-hand for biological sex but rather as a socially constructed phenomenon. Such researchers take a "gender as doing" approach to research in family business as opposed to a "gender as being" approach (examples include Byrne and Fattoum 2014; Bruni et al. 2005; Hamilton 2006, 2013; Hytti et al. 2017) and focuses on the gendered nature of family business rather than just the (different) experiences of men and women. To say that an analytical unit is gendered means that advantage and disadvantage, exploitation and control, action and emotion, meaning and identity are patterned through, and in terms of, a distinction between male and female, masculine and feminine (Acker 1990). In this line, Hytti et al. (2017), showed how women in family business engaged a masculine identity in certain contexts in order to increase the sense that they belong.

In line with this third stream of research, we believe that conceptualising succession (and intra-family entrepreneurship) as a gendered process is useful. We proceed by briefly outlining the concept of intra-family entrepreneurship.

Intra-Family Entrepreneurship

Historically, researchers addressing succession in family firms have focused on two types of succession processes: ownership and management (Churchill and Hatten 1987; Hugron 1993; Morris et al. 1997). The first type of process (ownership) describes the firm's evolution in general, whereas the second type (management) focuses more particularly on the evolution and the involvement of the main actors, namely predecessor and successor (Cadieux, Lorrain, and Hugron 2002; Handler 1989). Interestingly, recent studies have shown that family internal (management) succession is losing relevance, especially in developed countries (Zellweger and Sieger 2012).

In recent years, some researchers have shifted focus and examine the family in business rather than the continuity of one family business (Moores 2009). Succession in family business is not just about the family business being passed on but about how the different family members (and their respective futures) are considered in the context of business more broadly. In line with this, groundbreaking work by Discua Cruz, Howorth, and Hamilton (2012) threw the spotlight on intra-family entrepreneurship, showing how senior and junior generation family members formed and engaged in family entrepreneurial teams, with family members acting as entrepreneurial "stewards" intent on growing (as opposed to merely maintaining) family assets within a portfolio of businesses.

Despite a recent rising interest in gender in family business (Al-Dajani et al. 2014; Martinez Jimenez 2009), there is limited empirical work addressing the particular question of gender and CEO succession (Ahrens, Landmann, and Woywode 2015; Brockhaus 2004; Jimenez 2009). While recent research has shown that young family business members succession intentions do not differ by gender (Zellweger and Sieger 2012), the predecessor's gender preference has been found to play a key role in defining the rules and constraints of the leadership "contest" among siblings (Ahrens, Landmann, and Woywode 2015). Strong societal and cultural norms continue to shape family members expectations that the oldest son *should* be the natural successor (primogeniture rule), with alternative successors being presented as exceptions (Constantinidis and Nelson 2009). Deeply ingrained attitudes and beliefs with respect to gender roles—what men and women are and are not capable of—colour family members' expectations of the next generation (Byrne and Fattoum 2014). The choices they make have significant implications for the generations to come. We know that specific actions on the part of the family, particularly the incumbent leader, can greatly impact the succession process (Constantinidis and Nelson 2009).

Much research on management succession in family business focuses on the final outcome—successor or not—and confirms gender inequality (women are overlooked or overshadowed). However, such a focus may be deceptive in terms of the variety of gendered outcomes which can occur as family business (and families in business) transition from one generation to the next. To our knowledge, no research has addressed how gender plays out in intra-family entrepreneurship or looked at non-successors career outcomes from a gender perspective. Thus, we departed from a broad research question: "How are the career outcomes of next generation family business members gendered?"

Method

In our research, we combine a narrative, case study methodology (Hytti et al. 2017; Hamilton 2013). We collected the career narratives of six family business members in two separate family businesses via interview and position these as career narratives (Larty and Hamilton 2009). We focus in particular on the next generation's career outcomes: succession and business startup.

To guide our analysis, we draw on Larty and Hamilton's (2009) three stage framework for analysing narrative material. In stage 1, we pay attention to: the "plot" of the narratives; how events were pieced together; the role of the narrator; the role of other characters and the purpose or "function" of the story. We then (stage 2) consider the (multiple) contexts of narrative production, paying particular attention to their co-construction by various family members as well as any canonical narratives or discourses which are drawn on. Family members' stories are embedded in a particular historical, cultural, and societal setting. Acknowledging this helps us identify areas worthy of further analysis.

We analysed each of our family members' narratives individually in accordance with stage 1 of Larty and Hamilton's framework.[1] In this chapter (for brevity and reader convenience) we present a consolidated summary version of each of the two family businesses in appendix 1. In the findings section below, we zoom in on two main "events" in the narratives—that of "choosing a successor" and "setting up your own business". We then highlight some pertinent aspects of the "context" in which these narratives are situated as well as the "dominant discourses" drawn on (stage 2). We use direct extracts from the narratives as much as possible in order to allow our reader to fully appreciate the contextual and embedded nature of the family business members' stories (see table 10.1 for additional quotations).

Findings

Choice of Successor: Not for Her?

In both family businesses, the second oldest child (and only son) become the ultimate family business successor. In the following paragraphs, we present how family business members narrate the "event" of succession in each case, with a particular focus on their understanding (or their representation) of why the daughter did not succeed the family business.

In Car Parts, Carole (the eldest daughter and non-successor) was never considered for the role of successor. Her brother Philip, who had significant early exposure to the company (summer jobs and college internships), was always the "destined" successor. After an MBA and successful business startup experience in the United States, Philip returned to France around the time that his father Frank had decided to retire. Frank offered Philip the opportunity to take over the family firm, and after a brief period working in the quality control and sales department, Philip took over management of the large majority of the group's affairs at the age of twenty-nine. We met with Frank just after Philip had taken over the family business. He recounted how Philip was "*even doing a better job than I did*" and mentioned that his only concern was the financial crisis. He was adamant that any eventual problems would be due to external forces rather than his son's actions:

> *I know he's made of sturdy stuff. And even now, in the (financial) crisis, he's suffering. But if it doesn't work, it doesn't work. It's not because of incompetence. He will have done everything to make it work.*
>
> (Frank, predecessor, Car Parts)

When prompted about other potential successors, predecessor Frank says his daughters wouldn't have been able to take on the family firm. While he never doubts the competencies of his son, he is reticent about his daughters' ability: "*because girls have a little something which makes them less daring, on average*". He also points out that when he raised the possibility of succession in conversation with his eldest daughter, she did not even consider the proposition ("*she said to me, 'Dad, you must be kidding!'*"). Philip, echoes his father's sentiments, and claimed that his three sister's "*weren't interested*" in the role of successor.

Like her brother, Carole attended a business school, however, as a young girl she was not exposed to the family business to the same extent. Carole's engagement with the family firm was isolated to a brief period after her studies—a kind of "stop gap" measure. Compared to her brother, she describes her (younger) self as being much less sure of her career aspirations. Carole's story also diverges from that of her brother and father with respect to *why* she didn't become successor. For Carole, it was not so much about her lack of interest which accounted for her being passed over but rather her father's clear preference for a male successor. She maintains it was always inevitable that her brother would take on the family firm and speaks about her father's foregone conclusion that it would be her brother as opposed to her or her two sisters, regardless of their '*competencies*' or "*desire*". While her father fully expected his son to play an important role in the family business, he offered his daughter the opportunity to work there just while she was "*waiting to find something else*" after her studies. While Frank talks of his son "*taking his place*", Carole "*never felt comfortable*" in the family firm. In stark contrast, Philip talks of how his father "*not only put me at ease, but he gave me a real boost because he always encouraged me*". Carole tells of how "*it would have been terrible*" for her father if her brother hadn't joined the family business. Carole's tone is "matter of fact" and she appears quite accepting of this:

> *My father had three girls and one boy and it was always the same refrain. It was Philip who was going to (succeed) . . . even if we were capable and we had wanted to. . . . It would have been nice (to be successor) but it was never what he talked about.*

However, while Carole exhibits a certain acceptance of the status quo she also stressed how her "*professional life is not limited to his (her father's) company*". She left the family firm and set up her own recruitment business. Three years after Philip became successor of Car Parts, the family business declared bankruptcy. Philip set up another business in the months following the firm's closure.

In Dairy Inc, Robert (predecessor) wanted both of his children to join the family firm "directly" after their studies. The oldest daughter, Noreen, was his first choice but she renounced the opportunity and her brother Paul became successor. Noreen maintains that she was "convinced" from a young age that the hotel trade was where she wanted to work. Her qualifications and internships were all related to the hotel and tourism industry. Despite this, her sense of duty and a certain amount of social pressure from her father ("*he totally wanted me to come*") and boyfriend ("*he told me I couldn't say no*"), Noreen joined the family business in a management role when she finished her education. However, much to her father's disappointment (and disapproval) she left after the first six months and set up her own hotel business. Throughout her narrative, Noreen cites a number of reasons for not wanting to take over the family business, initially emphasising her love of the hospitality industry as well as her dislike of the northwest region of France. She later evokes a difficult working relationship with her father and the size of the company as other strong determinants of her decision not to take on the successor role. She stresses how her mother encouraged her to have her own independence.

Noreen's brother Paul became the designated family business successor and began running the firm alongside his father (the transition was not yet complete at the time of our research). While Noreen positions herself as the preferred choice and her brother as "default" successor, Paul talks of his joining the family business as an inevitable occurrence. He recounts his early exposure to the family business: remembering visits to the family firm as a small child with his class, as well as accompanying his father to the factory on Sunday afternoons. He describes how all the senior managers had "*seen him in the cradle*" and emphasises his proximity to the workers, having worked alongside them in the factory as a young boy. Following his military service and travels abroad, Paul returned to France and initially joined Noreen in her hotel business, where he worked as a manager at one of her two hotels. His father then called him to tell him about an "*opportunity*" that had come up as export manager in the firm, insisting that Paul's international experience would be a real asset to the family firm. Paul agreed and recounts how he had to "*prove*" his worth on integrating the family firm, using his position as export manager (where he boosted foreign sales significantly) to build his credibility.

Paul recounts how he had always assured his father that he would "*join the business one day*". He emphasises the continuity that succession implies, and affirms his own position as the "*only one*" left to (fully) assure the survival of the family firm. He expresses a sense of duty and obligation to his father and the family business, despite his passion for the racing car industry. Paul refers to his sister Noreen's continued interest and support.

> *She still has shares in the business . . . and, she is also—I didn't mention that—but she is also on the board. She is vice president. . . . So she follows the business from afar. She knows what's happening, we call each other every two weeks and she is interested in what's going on. At the moment she has no desire to come into the business, not in that way anyway . . . she has enough, and well, she is interested from afar and that's it.*

Noreen admits that she still "*likes to know that everything is going ok*". As vice president of the businesses management council, she "*participates in setting strategic objectives and gives opinions on strategy*" as well as "*completing the minutes of what was discussed*". She also regularly acts as a sounding board for both her father and brother about the family business.

There is a continued conflict between Paul and his father. Paul's style of leadership is more collaborative, and he is mildly critical of his father's approach to management which he sees as "*too paternalist*". According to Noreen, her father "*doesn't entirely trust*" Paul and she herself doubts her younger brother's ability. For Noreen, Paul is "*too friendly*" with the managers and "*hasn't had enough hard knocks*" in life (unlike herself, who has experienced her own business struggles). Noreen says: "*Paul . . . is more about feelings . . . he doesn't see the bad in people, he is still young and naive.*" While Noreen is happy to assist in an advisory and support capacity, she clearly states her desire to "*stay away from all that*" (i.e. involvement in the family firm and conflict with her father) and values her own independence.

Starting Your Own Business: With or Without You?

In both family businesses, while neither daughter became the ultimate family business successor, both went on to start their own business with the assistance of their father. In Car Parts, following her brief spell in the family business, Carole worked in an interim recruitment agency for four months. Although she got into the profession "*by chance*", she says she "*fell in love*" with it from the outset and started her own recruitment agency ('RecruitBiz') at the age of 27. After just three months of working in an interim agency, Carole's father Frank asked whether she wanted to start her own business. Carole refers to his role in her business "*at that particular moment*" and also acknowledges the financial support that she received from him, but is keen to attribute her success to her own hard work. She recounts how she worked very hard and long hours at the start (even coming in to clean the agencies at weekends). Carole stresses her enthusiasm and drive, evoking how failure was not an option for her.

In his narrative, Frank (predecessor, Car Parts), asserts a prominent role for himself in Carole's business start-up: "*We set up RecruitBiz for Carole. We try to do something else for those not in mechanics*". All Frank's children were given an early inheritance of 100,000 euros, some of which Carole used as founding capital to start her own business. Car Parts (the original family business) was also one of RecruitBiz's earliest (and bigger) clients—as the firm used the agency to recruit its interim workers. Frank does not however describe the process by which this came about. Carole (and her sister Rachel) narrate a more complex version of events when it comes to the collaboration between RecruitBiz and Car Parts.

The production manager, it was him who decided, he called the agencies. Perhaps my father said to him once, twice or three times "call RecruitBiz as well". At least I think so. I don't know how that worked out. He (the production manager) didn't do that until the day that my father had to impose it on him saying "you have thirty temps planned, now 50 per cent of that has to come from RecruitBiz". Of course that didn't work out well and ended up with the production manager leaving, I don't know if it was at that time or just after. So yes, for a few months we didn't work with them but we were getting on all the same. I was going hell for leather on other things. I was happy.

(Carole, non-successor, Car Parts)

Carole doesn't dwell on how her business, RecruitBiz, became a preferred supplier of the family business—she believes her business would have succeeded with or without the collaboration of Car Parts. Interestingly, Rachel, Carole's youngest sister, tells another side to the story. In Rachel's version of events, it was due to her mother's intervention that her father forced the hand of Car Parts production manager and pressured him to use RecruitBiz. Rachel relates how "*Carole probably doesn't know about all that*".

Prior to the closure of Car Parts, RecruitBiz was no longer supplying a large amount of staff to Car Parts, as with declining orders, the family business stopped recruiting. In light of the subsequent closure of the Car Parts factory, Carole says that she has "*no regrets*" vis-á-vis her own career as she never saw herself "*evolving*" in the family business anyway. She relates how her father has never acknowledged her success as a business woman. For her, now her brother will have to "*show what he is really made of*" now, given that he has since gone into business on his own.

In the case of Dairy Inc, Noreen left the family firm to work in tourism and later set up her own hotel business. She recounts her father's hostility when she announced her departure from the family business. She first worked abroad in a large tourism group but later returned to France to set up "Hotel Paris". Paul appraises Noreen's initial decision to leave the family business, as a choice which made sense in light of her previous education but also because she works in an area that she enjoys and that "*suits her*".

And now she really enjoys being in the hotel industry. It suits her well. She was trained for that too so it was a bit . . . it was to be expected. However she still has shares in the business.

Indeed, Noreen fails to identify with running a business the size of her father's business and appears relieved to be free of that responsibility.

Can you imagine . . . that little company and now it's like that! How do you manage when you have 700 employees? That's huge! Really difficult. I am really happy I didn't go (into the family business).

Despite his previous insistence that he would not help his daughter, Robert (predecessor, Dairy Inc) helped Noreen find her first hotel location and also helped out with acquiring a second location a couple of years later. Noreen describes her father's important role at the outset in finding the initial hotel, as well as her boyfriend's support for her plan. It was Robert who found the "right" location for Noreen's hotel. He then called Noreen who flew back to France directly to view the hotel with him. Before putting in a bid to buy the hotel, Noreen recounts how her father Robert "*sat her down*" to ensure if she was sure about her decision to start her own business:

> *He said to me "My girl, you have a big decision to make. Do you feel up to managing this business, (up to) having a loan on your shoulders?" I said to him "listen Papa, rather than working 24/7, for a miserable salary, I may as well do it for myself. I feel able. It will be hard at the start but I want to do it".*

Robert was also instrumental in ensuring that his daughter got a bank loan. Given her young age (23) and lack of experience, Noreen described how banks were reluctant to lend her money. Her father used his own reputation and custom as leverage, threatening to leave his bank if they did not offer his daughter a loan.

Family Context and Dominant Discourses

In Car Parts, Carole narrates how it was her father who prompted her to consider starting her own recruitment agency but draws on an entrepreneurial discourse of "passion" and determination which also drove her decision. Carole maintains that becoming an entrepreneur was never her ultimate objective, but admits that the fact that her father was one may have had an impact on her. At the same time, Carole is keenly aware that her father did not expect her and her sisters to achieve professional success: "*My Dad even said, 'Girls, if you don't manage, your brother will always be there to provide for you.'*" Carole is openly dismissive of her father's patriarchal discourse. She relates her father's attitude using the word *even* to emphasise the shocking aspect of such a discourse today. She refers to his "*generation*" by way of explaining this and talks about how her father has failed to "*evolve*" with the times. In her father's time, the wives were "*secretaries*" while the men (her father and his "*entrepreneur friends*") did the "*real work*" (and also played golf and tennis together).

Unsurprisingly, both Carole and Philip describe a very traditional family arrangement where their mother looked after the children while their father devoted himself to work. Both Carole and Philip speak of their father's absence at home, although Carole is more critical of this. With respect to her own career, Carole makes a clear distinction between the "before" and "after" of having children, outlining how she had no constraints before.

Being young and without children when she set up RecruitBiz was a definite advantage for her as it meant she could dedicate herself to it fully. She evokes a "*superwoman*"discourse explaining how as a mother, she is "*there*" for her children, whilst also maintaining an active professional (work) life. She recalls how her father "*didn't even know our birthdays*" and asks how somebody could behave like this. She says that paying attention to her children and being there for them is something that comes "*naturally*" to her.

In Dairy Inc, the family on both sides has a long tradition of self-employment. For Noreen, she believes that being your own boss was an inevitable step for both her and her brother, given their family background. She draws on the essentialist "born to be an entrepreneur" aspect of enterprise discourse: "*my father always said that I had the right personality to keep the business going . . . and he still says it*". But while Noreen clearly identifies with entrepreneurship, she affirms that she is "*made*" for small business.

While entrepreneurial souls and spirits might be encouraged and expected in the family, limits were placed on the involvement of women in the Dairy Inc family business. Noreen describes a patriarchal setting where wives are not formally involved in the family business. This is due to a family business "*pact*" which excludes wives from working in the family business, "*otherwise the business is harder to manage*" (Noreen, potential successor Dairy Inc, founder of HotelParis).

Perhaps unsurprisingly then, a stark division of labour and distinction between the private and public was strongly evident in their immediate family. Both Noreen and Paul evoke their father's absence at home during their childhood, and his complete devotion to the family business, which continues: "*For my father the firm is his whole life*" (Noreen, potential successor Dairy Inc, founder of HotelParis). Their home family life was very much a traditional one, with their mother as the primary homemaker. Noreen describes her father Robert as "*a very authoritarian man*" who was "*hard to live with*". She recounts how they were scared of him when they were young, and talks of how that climate of fear extended to the workplace where "*the employees feel the same thing*". Noreen describes her mother as a really "*good wife*" who makes her father's meals every day and how she "*looked after them at home all those years*". Paul emphasises how he himself doesn't "*bring work home*" (like his father did) but rather acts to the contrary and his wife needs to probe him to get him to talk about work in the evening when he gets home.

She describes her mother's "*devotion*" to her father and says how wives like her mother "*don't exist anymore*". Noreen is also very conscious of her mother's dependency on her father. She relates how her mother supported her in her desire to set up her own hotel and not become successor of the family firm. Her mother advised her to "*stay away from all that*"—"all that" being the family firm and the dependency or patriarchal dominance of her father that came with it.

Table 10.1 Choice or exclusion of the successor

	Car Parts	*Dairy Inc*
Choice of successor: not for her?	"I entered the business by doing internships, summer jobs first of all. The first time I went to the company I was 8 years old, and then there were summer jobs to earn a bit of money when I was 15, 16, 17. The business always interested me . . . my father succeeded in making me want to do the same as him from an early age" (Philip, successor, Car Parts). "I was 21 and I didn't feel ready to go working. I came up with various 'strategies' (to not work): a school where you could become bilingual. I didn't have the desire to go working, I wanted to continue to learn. It was more of an escape. In the end, it was my father who said "while waiting to find something, come and work in my business". I went, (working) in a department that didn't really appeal to me, logistics. It was an initial work experience. It's true that it was a little bit different as well because it was also where my father was boss, even if I didn't see him that often. You arrive in a situation or where you are not really at ease. I asked myself why was I there" (Carole, non-successor, Car Parts).	"I graduated from a school specialising in hotel and tourism in 1994 and my father really wanted me to work in the (family) business. And being young, I said that I would work with him. So I finished school . . . at the time when I was a young girl, I really wanted for the (family) business to keep going. But after my hotel school I was so convinced that I wanted to work in the hotel and tourism industry, that to go working—and in the agri-food business—really didn't interest me. . . (and) to go working in Brittany where it rains all the time, didn't really appeal to me at all! So I had an offer of a job in Spain and my father jumped on me saying 'listen, I have just taken over a frozen foods firm in the south and I need a manager. Are you interested?' My boyfriend at the time told me that I couldn't say no, it was about the survival of the (family) business . . . you are lucky to have that, to have this opportunity . . . so I said ok. I started . . . I stayed six months" (Noreen, potential successor, Dairy Inc). "So Dairy Inc originated in 1989. My great-grandfather stated collecting butter from the farms. It was a negotiation exercise, collecting butter from the farms and then selling them in the neighbouring villages . . . after that my grandfather took over from his father. He was called Yves Martin, my grandfather was Yves Martin and my Dad is Yves Martin. And me I am Paul Martin so I am the exception to the rule" (Paul, successor, Dairy Inc).

		"My sister tried out the business, in one of our distribution subsidiaries and . . . she didn't like it at all. She left, she did six months. She left. It was my father who called her, just like he called me incidentally. And she said 'eh . . . ok'. She didn't really know what she wanted to do, she said ok then and then she didn't like it at all . . . and she left" (Paul, successor, Dairy Inc).
Starting your own business: with or without you?	"In September 2002, I opened the door of RecruitBiz. I went knocking on the doors of all those businesses who saw my youth and my enthusiasm and who wanted to give me work. It was up to me to show that I was capable . . . to send workers, to move quickly, to make the right match" (Carole, RecruitBiz founder, Car Parts family business). "I was lucky enough to have a father who gave each of us a donation of almost 100,000 euros each so that enabled me to have a financial guarantee. It's sure that for another person who isn't helped it would be more difficult. To start your own interim agency you need to have finance or be sufficiently sold, at least ten years experience in the domain to go see a bank to get started. Me, for example, with my four years work experience, what would I have done?" (Carole, RecruitBiz founder, Car Parts family business). "I was waiting for a little 'I am proud of you' for a number of years but it never came" (Carole, non-successor, Car Parts).	"I said to him 'listen Dad, I don't like it. I want to return to Switzerland and go back to my boyfriend. I have good experience, I will find work no problem, in the hotel business, or in restauration. He said to me 'if you leave, you'll (have to) look after yourself. I won't help you. You won't get one cent from me. You'll look after yourself. It is out of the question that you leave me if you don't have another proposition'. In fact, I didn't have another offer but my boyfriend came and got me" (Noreen, potential successor, Dairy Inc). "I started looking . . . and at that moment, my father helped me. He said that I couldn't count on him but he helped me find a location in Paris all the same. Because I absolutely wanted to have a hotel, work in the hospitality industry but I didn't want one with a restaurant. And the only city, the only one, where you can succeed without having a restaurant (and hotel) was definitely Paris. So my boyfriend who lived in Zurich was ready to leave his job in Switzerland and come to run the hotel with me. At the same time, we came to Paris a few times to look for hotels and when I went to work for TRAVEL CLUB (abroad) in August, my father continued to look"

(Continued)

Table 10.1 (Continued)

	Car Parts	*Dairy Inc*
		"We signed the sale offer and then I had I find a bank that would lend me money. It was really difficult because at the time I was young, I was 23 and a half and at the start not one bank wanted to support me. My lack of experience and the fact that I had never lived in Paris. So I had a lot of doors closed on me. My father managed to get the loan thanks to his bank, and told them that if the bank didn't lend the money than he would leave them" (Noreen, potential successor, Dairy Inc and founder of HotelParis).
Family context and dominant discourses	"I fell in love with this sector and after three months it was my father who asked what I thought, if I would like to start a business in this area. You could say that at that moment he played a determining role" (Carole, non-successor, Car Parts). "I didn't always have it in my head to start my own business. It's true that with a father who is an entrepreneur you can have that in a corner of your head but I didn't really think about it" (Carole, non-successor, Car Parts).	"I think the fact that all around us we had people with entrepreneurial souls, we couldn't avoid it. It just wasn't possible" (Noreen, potential successor, Dairy Inc and founder of HotelParis). "The work didn't interest me. I am, above all, and I know that now with my experience, I am a saleswoman. I am made for small business and not for big business and I get that from my Mam's side, who is in retail, and my grandfather is in retail. I spent part of my childhood in a store and today I know that I am made for that and not for a business like the (family) business is today . . . much bigger . . . that's how it is" (Noreen, potential successor, Dairy Inc and founder of HotelParis). "Every evening my father talked about work, he never . . . he never know how to separate his professional life from his personal life" (Paul, successor, Dairy Inc). "My mother sacrificed her whole life for us, for her husband. And she continues to sacrifice herself for him, who makes his meal every lunch time, every evening . . . and he doesn't even acknowledge that. He doesn't even realise that he has a wife who is so good because there are not many women like her today! That's finished with! (Noreen, non-successor, Ice and Dairy)

Discussion

In line with stage 3 of Larty and Hamilton's (2009) approach to data analysis, we worked on refining the emergent themes from stages 1 and 2. This involved inter-twining our findings with extant theories and concepts in entrepreneurship and family business research to produce theoretical conclusions and contributions. We now present the output of this third stage—illuminating the implications of our findings relative to the extant literature in this discussion section.

Previously, family business researchers have reported on women's experiences of feeling "invisible" in the family business (Vera and Dean 2005), being "overshadowed" over having their work "appropriated" by male siblings as well as the endurance of primogeniture (Ahrens, Landmann, and Woywode 2015; Mulholland 2003). However, some authors have also revealed the ways in which women resist patriarchal forces (Hamilton 2013) and how their official status was not a necessary reflection of their actual role (Cole 1997; Hamilton 2006). Our study builds on the latter more positive positioning of women in family business, as we demonstrate how both women, while not the ultimate family business successors, built independent entrepreneurial careers as a direct result of their family business background. Hence we identify an interesting (gendered) feature of intra-family entrepreneurship: the endurance of male succession in family business does not preclude daughters' engagement with entrepreneurship outside the family business, but in fact frees them to engage in personal passions, pursue other careers, or escape the constraints that family relations may impose. However, the same cannot be said for their brothers, whose personal interests and life "passions" remain subordinate to the family firm legacy.

In the first instance (Car Parts), Carole was not "chosen" or deemed capable by her father. Her brother dismissed her as uninterested. She herself felt out of place and always knew her father did not consider her (or her sisters) as a potential successor. This is in line with previous research which shows how women are often marginalised in family business and/or not appropriately socialised for the successor role (i.e. Mulholland 2003; Constantinidis and Nelson 2009). Carole set up her own recruitment business while her brother Philip took on the family firm. Three years later, the family firm was declared bankrupt and Philip was left without a job. Meanwhile, Carole had three recruitment agencies, a staff of forty people and employed one of her sisters.

For Philip, by virtue of his gender, his future in the family business was never in question. His early exposure to the family firm, his close relationship with his father, Frank, and his desire to follow in Frank's footsteps—coupled with Frank's admiration for his son—meant that joining the family business was a foregone conclusion. Often, cohesive family relations—where members are close and supportive—can leave next generation family members feeling "locked in" out of familial obligation and left with feelings of standing in the family's shadow, rather than being empowered to strike his or her own path to success (Zellweger and Sieger 2012). This may be detrimental to the firm's future.

In the case of Dairy Inc, Noreen was the preferred successor but after a six-month trial in the family business, she decided it was not for her and left. Indeed it is not a given that the next generation (female) members will actually want to take over the business (Zellweger and Sieger 2012). Noreen's brother Paul became successor. His father was reluctant to let go of the business and retained most of the control. Noreen set up her own hotel business and was happy in her independence. Highly confident and entrepreneurial family business members are often the ones who prefer to found their own business rather than follow in someone else's path (Zellweger and Sieger 2012). Noreen has shares in the family business and retained a role on the board, giving input and advice on financial and strategic issues from afar. Paul experiences conflict with his father and is impatient for his father to step down. At the time of our interviews no date had been set. In both instances, rather than viewing the women as "victims" of a patriarchal system in family business, we can view the women as "victors" given that they start independent entities in areas which are coherent with their interests and are free of the "control" of their fathers. Gender patterns the experience of succession with sons being subject to stronger expectations and pressures to continue the family firm (Constantinidis and Nelson 2009). While Noreen—given her passion for the hotel industry—was effectively allowed "off the hook", her brother Paul (despite his passion for the race car industry) was not. Our findings thus question the "woman as victims of the male norm" portrayal which gender (and management or entrepreneurship) research sometimes implies (Billing 2011; Lewis 2014).

Secondly, our cases could also add to Hamilton's (2013) contestation of women's role in family business. We add to her argument that women in family business may sometimes act to subvert patriarchy. In our two cases, the daughters were aided or counselled by their mothers and furthered their careers in line with their personal preferences and interests. In Dairy Inc, Noreen's mother advised her to stay away from the family business in order to avoid the stress and conflictual relations with her father. In Car Parts, Carole's mother pressured her father to do business with Carole's new firm. Furthermore, while neither daughter was the ultimate successor of the family firm, they both benefited from their father's financial, social, and human capital. In this way they could be said to be benefiting from paternal relations in a different way to their brothers. Women often face barriers related to their gender when seeking finance (Marlow and Patton 2005) and with little work experience and her young age, Carole had limited means to raise external capital but used the money her father had given her to start her business. Carole also benefited from her father's social capital and network. One of RecruitBiz's early clients was Car Parts—due to an enforced contracting agreement which was arranged by her father (at the insistence of her mother). In the case of Dairy Inc, Robert not only helped his daughter locate the hotel site and negotiate the sale, he also secured a loan for her.

Prior research has shown how gender patterns the experience of family business succession, with sons being subject to stronger expectations and pressures to continue the family firm (Constantinidis and Nelson 2009). Our study lends interesting insights into how gender patterns intra-family entrepreneurship more broadly, but also how class is an important consideration here too. We pinpoint how daughters in family business have the opportunity to pursue entrepreneurial careers. We thus highlight the intersectional nature of (dis)advantage that emerges from membership of two "privileged" social categories: gender and class. Despite their gender, but because of their class privileges, intra-family entrepreneurship has enabled Carole and Noreen with the autonomy, flexibility, and quality of life they desire. By virtue of their "daughter of family business owner" status, both women received significant financial aid which they may not have been able to receive otherwise. Both daughters benefited from a class privilege which enabled them access to financial, social, and human capital which enabled them to start their own business. Both daughters' narratives fail to fully acknowledge this "privileged" status.

Thirdly, all next generation respondents' narratives draw on popular entrepreneurial discourses to present themselves as legitimate entrepreneurs and/or successors—doing long hours, taking risks, surmounting obstacles, passion, hard work, and determination. While neither daughter became the family business successors, both strongly emphasise their own self-reliance in setting up their own business. This discourse of self-reliance, typical of enterprise discourse, means that they do not fully acknowledge their father's role in helping secure finance or gaining market access. While Carole did not feel welcome in the family business, she knew from the outset that it was not her destiny. She "fell in love" with the recruitment industry, worked hard, did long hours, and "knocked on all the doors" to prove herself. She downplays her father's role of financial assistance. She also fails to fully acknowledge the advantage her business had in having the family firm as a "guaranteed" client. Noreen stresses how she has self-employment in her blood "on both sides" and talks about her hard work and long days at the outset. She presents herself as a driven and risk-taking individual as she turns down the option of security and financial stability as the family business successor in preference for her hotel business "dream". She too claims significant agency here, and depicts her father's (and brother's) involvement in setting up her business—searching (and finding) her first hotel location, securing the loan, operations etc.—as additional incidents along the way in her career trajectory. Effectively both Noreen and Carole acknowledge the influence of their entrepreneurial backgrounds but fail to give significant credit to the resources (financial support, trade, network) that their position as daughter of a family business owner afforded them. Perhaps admitting a more dominant role for their father in business start-up conflicts with their desire to identify as independent entrepreneurial women.

Conclusion

In this chapter, we chart the story of two family business, tracing the narratives of two sons (successors) and two daughters (non-successors), alongside accompanying interview data from other members of their family business. Given that our study focuses on family firms in France, we answer the call to consider family business and succession in different cultural contexts (Gupta and Levenburg 2013)—as a large majority of prior research draws on North American samples.

We adopt a combined narrative, case study approach (Hamilton 2006, 2013; Hytti et al. 2017) to pursue our research. Our methodological approach enabled us to bring the voice of the family business member to the fore, showing how they construct and (re)construct their (gendered) experience of family business, succession, and intra-family entrepreneurship. Previous research has shown how interiorised cultural beliefs about gender and leadership may skew family members' perceptions of next generation members' competence as successors—meaning daughters are not considered (or may not consider themselves) as viable successors. Such research tends to present women as disadvantaged victims of the male nom. In both of our cases, neither daughter is revealed as a *victim* of a patriarchal system but rather as a *victor*. Both daughters identify as entrepreneurs, launch their own business venture in areas more closely aligned with their interests than the family firm, take advantage of their father's human, financial, and social capital and succeed—free of the controlling influence and presence of their father. Their brothers meanwhile are left to burden the responsibility of the family firm alone (in one case, having to deal with bankruptcy and firm closure). Furthermore, our findings show how privilege arising from the daughters' class status allows both third generation daughters to launch their own businesses, securing them professions which were highly personally fulfilling. Hence, our findings illuminate the importance of considering inter-sectionality when considering entrepreneurial outcomes.

The findings from our research contribute to a growing body of research documenting the sociological importance of attitudes about gender to women (and men)'s professional (work-based) outcomes (Cunningham 2008), but in the family business context. Our social constructionist perspective reveals how succession and intra-family entrepreneurship processes, practices and outcomes are themselves "gendered". We also contribute to the emerging studies in family business research which focus on the "family in business" as opposed to the "family business" (Moores 2009), highlighting how gender effects manifest in "intra-family entrepreneurship" (Discua Cruz, Howorth, and Hamilton 2012), revealing the positive implications for daughters who manage to "side step" the poisoned chalice that their brothers are given.

Our findings paint a more positive picture for next generation women while hinting at negative normative pressures for male offspring.

Note

1 Plot; sequence of events; narrator role; other characters' roles; story purpose or "function"

References

Acker, J. 1990. "Hierarchies, Jobs, Bodies: A Theory of Gendered Organizations." *Gender and Society* 4 (2): 139–158.

Ahrens, J.-P., A. Landmann, and M. Woywode. 2015. "Gender Preferences in the CEO Successions of Family Firms: Family Characteristics and Human Capital of the Successor." *Journal of Family Business Strategy* 6: 86–103.

Al-Dajani, H., Z. Bika, L. Collins, and J. Swail. 2014. "Gender and Family Business: New Theoretical Directions." *International Journal of Gender and Entrepreneurship* 6 (3): 218–230.

Barrett, M., and K. Moores. 2009. *Women in Family Business Leadership Roles: Daughters on Stage*. Cheltenham, UK and Northampton: Edward Elgar.

Billing, Y. D. 2011. "Are Women in Management Victims of the Phantom of the Male Norm?" *Gender, Work & Organization* 18 (3): 298–317.

Brockhaus, R. 2004. "Family Business Succession: Suggestions for Future Research." *Family Business Review* 17: 165–177.

Bruni, A., S. Gherardi, and B. Poggio. 2005. *Gender and Entrepreneurship: An Ethnographic Approach*. London and New York: Routledge.

Byrne, J., and S. Fattoum. 2014. "A Gender Perspective on Family Business Succession: Case Studies from France." In *Women's Entrepreneurship in the 21st Century*, edited by K. V. Lewis, C. Henry, E. J. Gatewood, and J. Watson. Cheltenham, UK and Northampton: Edward Elgar Publishing.

Cadieux, L., J. Lorrain, and P. Hugron. 2002. "Succession in Women-Owned Family Businesses: A Case Study." *Family Business Review* 15 (1): 17–30.

Churchill, N., and K. Hatten. 1987. "Non-Marketbased Transfers of Wealth and Power: A Research Framework for Small Businesses." *American Journal of Small Business* 11 (3): 51–67.

Cole, P. 1997. "Women in Family Business." *Family Business Review* 10 (4): 353–372.

Constantinidis, C., and A. Cornet. 2008. "Daughters Taking Over the Family Business: A Gender Analysis." 31st Institute for Small Business and Entrepreneurship Conference: International Entrepreneurship, 5th–7th November, Belfast, Ireland.

Constantinidis, C., and T. Nelson. 2009. "Intégrer les problématiques de la succession et du genre selon la perspective de la fille dans l'entreprise familiale: Une enquête transnationale." *Management International* 14 (1): 43–54.

Cunningham, M. 2008. "Influence of Gender Ideology and Housework Allocation on Women's Employment Over the Life Course." *Social Science Research* 37 (1): 254–267. www.ncbi.nlm.nih.gov/pmc/articles/PMC2396342/#R9.

Curimbaba, F. 2002. "The Dynamics of Women's Roles as Family Business Managers." *Family Business Review* 15 (3): 239–252.

Discua Cruz, A., C. Howorth, and E. Hamilton. 2012. "Intrafamily Entrepreneurship: The Formation and Membership of Family Entrepreneurial Teams." *Entrepreneurship Theory and Practice* 37 (1): 17–46.

Dugan, A., S. Krone, K. LeCouvie, J. Pendergast, D. Kenyon-Rouvinez, and A. Schuman. 2008. *A Woman's Place: The Crucial Roles of Women in Family Business*. London: Palgrave Macmillan.

Dumas, C. 1992. "Integrating the Daughter into Family Business Management." *Entrepreneurship Theory & Practice* 16 (4): 41–55.

Galiano, A., and J. Vinturella. 1995. "Implications of Gender Bias in the Family Business." *Family Business Review* 8 (3): 177–188.

Gatewood, E., N. Carter, C. Brush, P. Greene, and M. Hart. 2003. *Women Entrepreneurs, Their Ventures, and the Venture Capital Industry: An Annotated Bibliography*. Stockholm: ESBRI.

Gillis Donovan, J., and C. Moynihan-Brandt. 1990. "The Power of Invisible Women in the Family Business." *Family Business Review* 3 (2): 153–167.

Gupta, V., and N. Levenburg. 2013. "Women in Family Business: Three Generations of Research." In *Handbook of Research on Family Business*, edited by K. X. Smyrnios, P. Z. Poutziouris, and S. Goel. Cheltenham, UK and Northampton: Edward Elgar Publishing.

Haberman, H., and S. Danes. 2007. "Father-Daughter and Father-Son Family Business Management Transfer Comparison: Family FIRO Model Application." *Family Business Review* 20 (2): 163–184.

Hamilton, E. 2006. "Whose Story Is It Anyway? Narrative Accounts of the Role of Women in Founding and Establishing Family Businesses." *International Small Business Journal* 24 (3): 253–271.

Hamilton, E. 2013. "The Discourse of Entrepreneurial Masculinities (and Femininities)." *Entrepreneurship and Regional Development* 25 (1–2): 90–99.

Handler, W. 1989. "Managing the Family Firm Succession Process: The Next Generation Family Member's Experience." Doctoral diss., School of Management, Boston University.

Hugron, P. 1993. "L'entrepreneur et la succession d'entreprise: analyse de 12 processus." Cahier de recherche CREF 93–03, Ecole des Hautes Etudes Commerciales.

Hytti, U., G. A. Alsos, J. Heinonen, and E. Ljunggren. 2017. "Navigating the Family Business: A Gendered Analysis of Identity Constructionof Daughters." *International Small Business Journal* 35 (6): 665–686.

Keating, N., and H. Little. 1997. "Choosing the Successor in New Zealand Family Farms." *Family Business Review* 10 (2): 157–171.

Larty, J., and E. Hamilton. 2009. "The Gendered Discourses of Entrepreneurship." Institute of Small Business and Entrepreneurship (ISBE) 32nd Annual Conference (Liverpool).

Lewis, P. 2014. "Postfeminism, Femininities and Organization Studies: Exploring a New Agenda." *Organization Studies* 35: 1845–1866.

Lewis, P., and R. Simpson. 2015. "Understanding and Researching 'choice' in Women's Career Trajectories." *In Handbook of Gendered Careers in Management: Getting In, Getting On, Getting Out*, edited by A. M. Broadbridge and S. L. Fielden. Cheltenham: Edward Elgar Publishing.

Marlow, S., and D. Patton. 2005. "All Credit to Men? Entrepreneurship, Finance and Gender." *Entrepreneurship Theory and Practice* 29 (6): 717–735.

Martinez Jimenez, R. 2009. "Research on Women on Family Firms: Status and Future Directions." *Family Business Review* 22 (1): 53–64.

Moores, K. 2009. "Paradigms and Theory Building in the Domain of Business Families." *Family Business Review* 22 (2): 167–180.

Morris, M., R. Williams, J. Allen, and R. Avila. 1997. "Correlates of Success in Family Business Transitions." *Journal of Business Venturing* 12: 385–401.

Mulholland, K. 1996. "Gender and Property Relations Within Entrepreneurial Wealthy Families." *Gender, Work and Organisation* 3 (2): 78–102.

Mulholland, K. 2003. *Class, Gender, and the Family Business*. Basingstoke: Palgrave Macmillan.

Rowe, B., and G.-S. Hong. 2000. "The Role of Wives in Family Businesses: The Paid and Unpaid Work of Women." *Family Business Review* 13 (1): 1–13.

Vera, C., and M. Dean. 2005. "An Examination of the Challenges Daughters Face in Family Business Succession." *Family Business Review* 18 (4): 321–345.

Voydanoff, P. 1990. "Economic Distress and Family Relations: A Review of the Eighties." *Journal of Marriage and the Family* 52: 1099–1115.

Wang, C. 2010. "Daughter Exclusion in Family Business Succession: A Review of the Literature." *Journal of Family and Economics Issues* 31 (4): 475–484.

Zellweger, T., and P. Sieger. 2012. *Coming Home or Breaking Free? Career Choice Intentions of the Next Generation in Family Businesses*. Work Report. Ernst & Young, University of St.Gallen.

Appendix 1

	Car Parts	*Dairy Inc*
Founded	– In 1948; in Northern France	– In 1898; in Northern France
Nature of business	– Spare parts firm – 100% family owned – 400+ employees – Revenues approx. 48 million euros annually	– Dairy, later ice-cream production – 100% family owned – 500+ employees – Revenues approx. 95 million euros annually
Generation	– Passing from second to third generation	– Passing from second to third generation
Family	– Frank (predecessor) and his wife Jessica (second generation) – Four children: Carole (oldest sibling, non-successor), Philip (successor), Veronique, and Rachel (non-successor daughters)	– Robert (predecessor) and wife Martine (second generation) Two children: Noreen (non-successor) and Paul (successor)
Narratives collected from	– Predecessor Frank (second generation), – Successor Philip (third generation) – Two non-successor daughters, Carole and Rachel (third generation)	– Non-successor (third generation): Noreen – Successor Philip (third generation)
Main actors in narratives	– Original founder, the predecessor (Frank) and his wife (Jessica) as well as their four children: Philip (successor), Veronique, Carole and Rachel (all non-successors). Carole's husband and the production manager also feature.	– Original founder, Robert (predecessor) and Martine (mother, wife, "daughter of entrepreneurs") as well as Paul and Noreen. Pierre (Robert's brother, assistant family firm director) features briefly as does Noreen's husband and some Dairy Inc managers.
Focus	– Career narratives of two members of the third generation: Carole and Philip	– Career narratives of two members of third generation: Noreen and Paul

	Car Parts	*Dairy Inc*
Family business successor	Philip: – only son, third eldest sibling – maximum exposure to family firm (summer jobs; college internships) – studied engineering, later went on to complete an MBA in the US – While there, he set up a wine selling business	Paul: – second oldest sibling – strong interest in racing cars and a flair for writing; initially dreamed of becoming a sports car journalist – after high school, completed two years obligatory military service – spent a period of time helping Noreen (sister) in her hotel business before joining the family business
Intra-family entrepreneur	Carole – Frank's second oldest daughter – She was less exposed to family firm than her brother – She holds a business degree and worked for a short time in the family business after her studies – She worked in interim recruitment and discovered a real passion for the industry, before launching her own firm with the financial assistance of her father – she set up her own recruitment business at the age of 27 – Today she manages and runs three recruitment agencies employing over forty employees and has no involvement in the family firm (which went bankrupt within three years of her brother taking over)	Noreen – oldest of the two siblings – strong interest in the hospitality sector; studied hotel and tourism – she was her father's original "preferred choice" for successor – she joined the family business after her primary degree, but left within six months – she set up her own hotel business (Hotel Paris) at the age of 27, with the financial support of her father – she currently owns and manages two hotels in the Paris region – she is not involved in the day to day running of Dairy Inc but participates in quarterly board meetings

Section III

Women in Business Succession

11 The Leaders, the Outcasts, and the Others

Which Role for Daughters in Family Businesses?

Francesca Maria Cesaroni and Annalisa Sentuti

Introduction

Succession has been one of the main research topics in family business (hereafter FB) studies in last few decades (Sharma 2004). So far, most of the research on this topic has focused on the traditional succession process from father to son. The main reason is that, until some years ago, daughters' exclusion from succession was one of the main strongholds in FB continuity. The rule of transmission—not written, but among the most sacred and respectfully observed—always dictated that a business be transmitted from the father to the first-born male child, or at least to another male family member. Daughters were not considered potential successors, were often oriented towards other jobs and/or recompensed with other financial benefits from family assets.

In the last few decades, women's involvement in FB ownership, governance, and management has been slowly but gradually increasing (Vera and Dean 2005; EY 2015), and the binomial "daughters and succession" has become extremely relevant. This evolution is changing the physiognomy of the succession process, resulting in new scenarios for FBs and new perspectives of research and analysis. However, only some scholars have focused their attention on daughters' role in the succession process (Martinez Jimenez 2009; Wang 2010), so this topic continues to be only partially explored and further research is necessary. As a matter of fact, despite the increasing interest in the theme of daughters' involvement in FB succession, existing studies are still fragmented and sporadic. Three main research areas have received particular attention: 1) daughters' reasons why they choose (or not) to join the FB and to realise a career from within; 2) daughters' roles; 3) conditions that facilitate (or hinder) the daughters' ability to take on the leadership.

Existing studies generally focus on a single research area. They do not offer an integrated perspective and fail to systematically consider all aspects of daughters' experience in the succession process. Moreover, most studies do not adopt the daughters' perspective. They focus on the context (family and/or family business) where the succession process takes place, or they analyse women by comparing them with men. As a consequence, research that offers a broad and integrated perspective is still missing and the daughters' point of view often remains overlooked.

This chapter adopts an integrated perspective as it analyses different aspects of female experience in FBs centred on the daughters' role and position, in order to understand how they live their experience in the FB, why they decide to enter the FB, what their personal and professional goals and ambitions are, what the training paths they follow are, what role they play and how they are satisfied/dissatisfied about their role in the FB. For this purpose, based on a multiple case study, we describe possible profiles daughters can assume nowadays in the succession process, as well as considering their motivations, ambitions, effective role and satisfaction.

The rest of the chapter is structured as follows. First, we present a literature overview on daughters' role in FB succession. Subsequently, the methodology is described, followed by a description of each profile. The chapter ends with our conclusions.

Daughters and Family Business Succession

Daughters' involvement in FB ownership, management, and leadership is a continuously increasing phenomenon. Until the end of the eighties, studies concerning succession showed a strong "androcentric" standpoint. The succession process was mainly conceived as a traditional passage "from father to son". Only since the end of the eighties and the early nineties (with Dumas' first contributions in 1989 and 1990) has FB research been dealing with the growing participation of daughters in FBs in many Western countries, including Italy, and a new research topic has been developed. Based on the main contributions in the literature, an evolutionary trend can be drawn up. This evolution determined the transition from a phase of "daughters' exclusion" to a phase of "daughters' consideration".

In the first phase, research on FB succession did not consider daughters or their potential role. Only a few authors have explicitly mentioned daughters in their studies on FB (Abbott and Meredith 1984) and most of them mainly seek to emphasise limitations, difficulties, and obstacles that daughters were forced to face instead of the opportunities of their involvement in the succession process (Barnes 1988; Piantoni 1990; Kets de Vries 1993). In this first phase, a negative approach emerged. A sceptical attitude towards daughters' involvement in FB succession prevailed, based upon the stereotype of the weak, helpless, naïve, and easily influenced woman (e.g. by her husband). Daughters were mainly considered as a problem to solve and their exclusion from succession was considered a good solution. Daughters did not have—and it was better that way—a role in the succession process.

Since the end of the eighties and the early nineties, scholars' interest in the role of daughters in FB has been increasing and they have profoundly changed their perspective. The phase of "daughters' consideration" moved its first steps in that period, and today the binomial "daughters and FB succession" represents a prosperous area of research. Daughters are no longer considered as a problem to be solved but a resource to value, a potential to exploit, and an opportunity to be seized. As Griffeth, Allen, and Barrett (2006) suggested, many FBs face the succession process and have a small pool of talented family members interested in the business. In this perspective, the daughters' exclusion can represent a wasted resource and a lost opportunity (Le Breton-Miller, Miller, and Steier 2004). Many authors have called for further research on this topic and several studies have been conducted in order to better understand daughters' experience in FBs (Martinez Jimenez 2009, Wang 2010).

A first strand of research has focused on daughters' ambitions and motivations why they choose (or not) to join the FB. Early studies pointed out that several daughters do not aspire to plan a career in the FB but join the business to help their family in a time of crisis, or to fill a position that no other relative wants or because other options are less attractive (Dumas 1989, 1992; Salganicoff 1990). Vera and Dean (2005) noticed an attitude of "detachment" from the FB, which could be due to daughters' awareness of still not being appropriately considered. Gatewood et al. (2003) maintained that daughters are driven by "pull" or "push" motivations for engagement within the FB. Daughters who have grown up to perceive the FB as their own, with a desire to play an active role and to contribute to the continuity of the FB, exhibit "pull motivations". Daughters with more difficult contexts can form a "reactive vision" of the FB, not considering themselves as "true" potential successors (Dumas 1998), and they demonstrate "push motivations" because they are often constrained by situations of necessity to work in the company.

The issue of daughters' role in the FB succession process represents another important area of research. Several scholars analysed daughters' involvement in FB ownership, leadership, and management, and some of them proposed useful typologies. Curimbaba (2002) maintained that family dimension and composition (order of birth, number of brothers and other men from the same generation) can affect daughters' roles in the FB. She described three daughters' experiences—professional heiresses, invisible heiresses, and anchors. Cesaroni and Sentuti (2014) focused on roles that women (mostly daughters but not only) can play within their FBs when the leader is a man. They established three profiles for women: completely invisible women, figurehead women, and manager women. Other research has extensively shown that daughters are often involved in FBs with marginal roles, few responsibilities, and little decision power. In addition, they face greater difficulties in being chosen as successors and in being involved in FBs with a leadership role (Martinez Jimenez 2009; Wang 2010).

A third research area analyses factors and conditions that affect daughters' ability to take over the leadership role. According to some authors, FBs offer more career opportunities to daughters (Salganicoff 1990; Cole 1997; Gnan and Montemerlo 2008).

However, it is widely recognised that the successor's gender is the main factor that hinders the daughters' path towards a leadership role today (Martinez Jimenez 2009), as predecessors still rarely consider their daughter as a real potential successor (Francis 1999; Martin 2001; Lee, Lim, and Lim 2003; Martinez Jimenez 2009; Wang 2010). Some authors (Aronoff 1998; Gersick et al. 1999) noticed that many families choose to create a team of siblings—sons and daughters—to share leadership and ownership in the future so that all descendants are potential successors, regardless of gender. But even in these cases, the effective leader is very often the eldest son (García-Álvarez, López-Sintas, and Saldaña Gonzalvo 2002). In other cases, daughters' roles are the result of a "forced" involvement, a consequence of "mere equilibrium in the ownership", or they only play a formal role without any real responsibilities or decision power (Gnan and Montemerlo 2008). At the same time, some research has demonstrated that often daughters do not consider themselves as potential successors, seeing their involvement in the FB as simply a job opportunity, without leadership ambition (Vera and Dean 2005). Daughters can assume the leadership of the FB only in "special circumstances" (Wang 2010) such as when: all siblings are female and the family has no male heirs (Dumas 1998; Curimbaba 2002; Garcia-Alvarez, López-Sintas, and Saldaña Gonzalvo 2002; Haberman and Danes 2007); no male family members are interested in running the business (Dumas 1998; Vera and Dean 2005); the family or the business is going through a tough time (e.g. a predecessor's sudden illness, a risk of failure for the business) (Dumas 1998; Curimbaba 2002); there are conflicts between family members (Barrett and Moores 2011); the daughter has a close relationship with the predecessor (Curimbaba 2002). Concerning the latter point, Smythe and Sardeshmukh (2013) found that early socialisation within the FB, better communication between father-daughter and a deeper understanding of the "father's shadow", favoured the negotiation of the leadership role for the daughter. More recently, Hytti et al. (2017) conducted a gendered analysis of how daughters construct their identities as FB leaders. Their findings suggest that daughters construct and negotiate their leadership identities "in their interactions with others by opposing, expanding and making use of the gendered scripts available to them. They move between concealing their leader identity and producing a masculinised identity as a strong owner" (Hytti et al. 2017, 17).

To sum up, during the last decades scholars have shifted their attention from problems caused by daughters' involvement in the FB, to their motivations/ambitions to join the firm, roles within the FB, and the possibility to take over the leadership role. Even if these studies are very useful for understanding daughters' experiences in their FB, they are mainly focused on a single aspect and hence a fragmented perspective emerges. We are of the opinion that an integrated investigation, centred on daughters' perspective, can offer a more comprehensive knowledge of the phenomenon, as it can consider both daughters' motivations, the role actually held within the FB, and satisfaction received from their role.

Methodology

Research Method

To achieve our goal, we adopted a qualitative research based on a multiple case study (Eisenhardt and Graebner 2007; Miles, Huberman, and Saldana 2014).

A wide consensus exists in FB literature on the usefulness and effectiveness of case studies to advance research on this topic (De Massis and Kotlar 2014). This method enables researchers to investigate complex phenomena, to examine in-depth real-life current events and to observe the meaning of people's experiences. Therefore, it is particularly useful in studying the succession process, in which a number of variables such as the main actors' goals, preferences, and personal choices, family relationships, and family and business members' behaviours, can greatly affect the process and its final outcome (Nordqvist, Hall, and Melin 2009).

Case Selection

The research involved five Italian women, daughters of FB owners. Italy presents a wide gender gap (WEF 2016) and women's involvement in FB has been slow and limited (Corbetta, Minichilli, and Quarato 2015). Some research conducted in Italy has underlined that FBs favour women's participation (Gnan and Montemerlo 2008). However, evidence showed that there are some "off limits" areas, where women are absent or very few in number. Women are mainly involved as shareholders, co-owners, or members of the board of directors and often hold managerial roles with functional responsibilities, but they very rarely take part in top management roles and entrepreneurial leadership (Gnan and Montemerlo 2008). This is why we think that Italy is a particularly suitable context for our research.

Interviewed daughters were identified through a purposeful case selection (Patton 2002), based on the authors' personal knowledge, contacts from previous studies, and information provided by business associations. In line with our research questions, we looked for FBs that had recently undergone, or were currently undergoing, a succession process, in which at least one daughter was somehow involved. Analysed daughters, their family businesses and family composition are briefly described in Table 11.1.

Table 11.1 Overview of analysed daughters, their family businesses, and family composition

*Name**	*Age*	*Role in the FB*	*Firm size*	*Industry*	*Generation in control*	*Family composition*
Vanessa	46	Chief legal officer	Small	Engineering	2nd	Father (founder): founded another business Mother: chief administrative office An elder sister: CEO
Stephanie	43	Head of HR and accounting office	Small	Chemical industry	3rd	Father: CEO Mother: no role in the FB A younger brother: marketing and sales manager
Catherine	53	CEO	Large	Manufacturing	2nd	Father (founder): dead Over ten family members actively involved in the FB
Marilyn	48	CEO	Medium	Office furniture	2nd	Father (founder): retired Mother: no role in the FB A younger sister: member of the board and employee in the administrative office
Rebecca	45	None	Small	Thermal baths	1st	Father (founder): CEO A younger daughter: employee in the administrative office

* All names of interviewees have been changed to ensure the confidentiality of the informants.

Data Collection

Data was collected through in-depth, face-to-face, semi-structured interviews (Qu and Dumay 2011). Respondents were initially asked to introduce themselves and were permitted to talk freely about their experience in the FB and their relationship with their predecessor (father or mother) and other family and business members (especially other relatives and siblings). Then special emphasis was placed on daughters' formal position in their FB and on their motivation, personal goals, and satisfaction/dissatisfaction about this position.

Interviews took place between autumn 2011 and spring 2015 and varied in length from two to four hours; they were recorded and transcribed verbatim.

Data Analysis

Available data was initially analysed in order to build individual case study summaries (Miles and Huberman 1994). Subsequently, authors cycled through multiple readings of the data and carried out a cross-case analysis in order to compare daughters' experiences and identify differences and similarities. This analysis helped us to outline five daughters' profiles (Table 11.2), each characterised by distinctive features with regard to: 1) personal goals before entering the FB; 2) push/pull reasons for joining the FB; 3) daughters' role and position in the FB; 4) motives that brought daughters to play a particular role in the FB; 5) training and skills; 6) satisfaction/dissatisfaction of their role in the FB.

Each profile is the final result of daughters' personal and professional goals and expectations, their will to play a specific role in the FB and the possibility to indeed realise their intentions. In the next section, daughters' profiles are outlined and discussed in depth with a descriptive approach, in order to define a comprehensive framework of the context in which daughters' experience in the FB took place (e.g. family composition; FB features; daughter's experience and characteristics; how succession unfolded; consistency between the daughter's role and her motivations and preferences).

Daughters' Profiles

1. *Marilyn: Leader by Choice*

After graduating from high school, Marilyn spent a year in the UK in order to learn English and "*to face difficulties*" in life. She then got a degree in political science and finally joined the FB. Founded in 1963 by Marilyn's father and his brother, the firm produces Made in Italy office furniture and has eighty employees. Marilyn joined the business in 2000 and, after a period of training in different departments, she began working with increasing

Table 11.2 Daughters' profiles

	Leader by choice	*Leader because "she has to"*	*Manager by choice*	*Invisible co-leader*	*Outcast*
Role in the FB	Leadership of the FB.	Leadership of the FB.	Functional /Managerial role (Chief Legal Officer).	Functional / Managerial role (Chief HR and Accounting Office).	No role and detachment from the FB.
Personal goals before entering the FB	She wanted to be the FB leader.	She wanted to realise her career outside the FB.	She wanted to have a satisfactory job, with low-ranking power.	She would have taken over the helm of the FB.	She wanted to have an important role in the FB.
Push/pull reasons for joining the FB	She has always been strongly "attracted" to the FB.	She was "pushed" towards the firm due to a crisis (illness of the predecessor) and need to ensure FB continuity (no one was interested in the FB).	She was "attracted" to the FB. FB is intended as a professional opportunity to do a job consistent with her professional skills and interests.	She was "attracted" to the FB.	She was "attracted" to the FB.
Motives for their role in the FB	Her leadership role is the ultimate goal of a process that she has tenaciously pursued, attracted by the desire to follow in her father footsteps and lead the FB.	She decided to run the FB because of moral obligation, a feeling of loyalty towards family and gratitude towards her parents.	Working in the FB with a minor position is considered an optimal solution as it allows a smooth handling of the work-life balance.	She accepted this role because of a strong attachment to her family and FB, coupled with the desire to personally contribute to the continuity of the FB.	Her predecessor believes that women are not able or suited to running a business.

Training and skills	She tenaciously prepared herself to gain skills consistent with the leadership role.	She followed a training and educational pathway not at all consistent with the leadership role.	Her training and skills are consistent with the professional role.	Her training and skills are consistent with the leadership role.	Her training and skills are consistent with the leadership role.
Satisfaction/ dissatisfaction about their role in the FB	She is very satisfied with her role in the FB, as she has fulfilled her dream.	Now she is devoted to the FB, but at the beginning she felt forced to accept the leadership role.	She is satisfied with her position and reassured by the fact that another family member is running the FB.	She is not completely satisfied, because she had ambitions to be the leader of the FB and now she must be content with a minor role.	She is disappointed and hurt by her experience with the FB.

power and responsibility: "*My first steps in the business were very singular. I was at the same time a member of the board of directors and 'the last of employees'. Starting at the bottom was very important in order to understand our employees' work and how to improve the business. Meanwhile, I was on the board. I didn't understand almost anything at the beginning! However, I started familiarising myself with several issues concerning the business. My main goal was to run the firm, so I needed a broader view of it*". These words clearly reveal her desire to join and develop the FB: "*At age six I already had clear ideas: I wanted a family and to be an entrepreneur, I already wanted it! So what did I do? I started with determination and went on with conviction. And the succession was well managed at 100 per cent. [. . .] My goal has always been to be at the head of this company and to develop the business. Because a second generation cannot only maintain it, it must necessarily develop the business. And I'm doing it*". With humility but also great tenacity and resourcefulness, Marilyn tried to learn from everyone in the firm and then demonstrate her skills as a potential leader, able to run the business. In this perspective, mindful of her previous experience abroad, Marilyn decided to internationalise the business, increasing export sales from 4 per cent to 35 per cent in just a few years. She also encouraged teamwork and decided to involve employees in decision-making, favouring a climate of cohesion and harmony. Her approach led her to successfully gain trust in the firm. But her father's support was also a determining role in Marilyn's training and affirmation: "*My father was great, because even if he saw some mistake or something he would have done differently (having more than 25 years of experience), he let me do it my way. He slowly gave me directions; I personalised his recommendations and then I began to experiment and carry out my tasks. Even when he saw that I was making little mistakes, he let me go on. This is critical! It is a psychological game. The predecessor should know how to leave and the successor should have the ability to understand and learn with humility. [. . .] He understood my thought process and took confidence from this, always giving me support, and his support was my energy, it was my charge.*" In 2006, Marilyn's father passed down the helm to her, and she became the company's CEO. She is very fulfilled: "*My father slowly detached himself from the business and became a consultant. Nowadays I am happy, the company is fine, my father calls me and asks me if it's all right. I'm satisfied because I'm getting what I set out for myself when I was young. I'm reaching my personal and professional goals with success*".

Marilyn's experience clearly shows that, for her, leading the FB is a goal that she has pursued with tenacity and perseverance. She is a leader by choice: Marilyn was able to take over the FB leadership and fulfil her dreams. Since she was young, Marilyn has desired to succeed her father and lead the company. And with this goal in mind, she prepared herself as much as possible to gain the necessary skills. Her solid preparation and qualification was relevant, but two other factors allowed her to achieve her ambitions: 1) her deep bond with her father and the FB, that created a strong motivation to join the business; 2) the support and esteem from her parents, who strongly believed in her ability and promoted her involvement and legitimacy in the company.

However, it should be noted that there were not any males present in the younger generation. Marilyn only has a sister, who joined the company but preferred a minor role without entrepreneurial responsibilities: "*I have a sister who is six years younger and she is a member of the board. However, she works as an employee in the administrative office and has never had the ambition to be in a leadership role. Therefore she has never been an obstacle*". Hence, Marilyn did not have to compete with anyone.

2. *Catherine: Leader Because "She Has to"*

"*I wanted to be an archaeologist . . . exactly, a different story!*" Catherine stated at the beginning of our interview. Today she is the CEO of her FB, founded by her father and his three brothers in 1977. Currently the company is a big manufacturing firm with 500 employees. It is owned by four families with over ten family members actively involved in the business. Catherine's father forced her to attend an accounting high school and to get a degree in economics in order to push her towards the business. "*I was very conditioned by my father*"—Catherine affirmed—"*Abandoning my dream of becoming an archaeologist, I'd have liked to get a second degree in law with the aim to practice as a certificated accountant or lawyer. It wasn't possible. My father forced me to join the business. The company was in trouble and there were important decisions to be made. My father was 70 years old. He was ill and no longer had the strength to deal with difficulties. The others were completely absent; they did not have the will or the skills to manage the situation. My father knew I had a strong character and asked me to handle the situation. I did it, with the spirit to defend my family and our company.*" After she successfully resolved the situation, her father drove her to assume an increasingly important role in the company. She became a member of the board some years later: "*I was careful at the beginning, in silence, listening to people more capable than me. I felt like a sponge, I learned. Then there were several occasions in which it was necessary for me to put forward out what I had learned and I did, contrary to others who had neither the ability, nor the desire or the skills to do so.*" Therefore, despite herself, in 1999 Catherine was nominated CEO. Even though other family members aspired to that role, the board chose her: "*Everyone wanted to do it. No one was able to do it. It came naturally.*" She is aware that no one else could have assumed her role. However, she increasingly feels the weight of such a great and undesired responsibility: "*Right now, no one in my family is able to do what I do because it is very arduous. It takes character, not preparation or capacity, only character. It's in my DNA; you can't learn this at school. I'm facing unimaginable things. I'm enduring it and this takes character. I will pay on a physical level, I'm sure. However, I became CEO . . . I don't know . . . in the end, it was inevitable.*" Catherine's experience has profoundly influenced her approach towards her two children: "*My parents imposed me to join the family business. I will not do that with my children. I won't let them do my work as an inheritance, it is the last thing I would do. I have a son who would like to be involved in the family business, but I'm trying to keep him away because it is a sacrifice and is genuinely burdensome.*"

Catherine's story recounts the forced choice made under conditions of highly emotional involvement, which forced her to give up her own ambitions and career aspirations in order to replace the predecessor, who was seriously ill. Her choice was mainly caused by her sense of responsibility towards her family and her desire not to disappoint her parents. She is a leader because "she has to", as she became an entrepreneur not out of ambition, but due to the need to ensure FB continuity, since no other family member was concerned or likely to lead the company. She was forced by events, which 'pushed' her to take on the leadership, despite her desire to have a different professional career.

3. *Vanessa: Manager by Choice*

After graduating in law in 2000, Vanessa decided to practice as a lawyer. In that period, she had rejected the idea of joining the FB. Vanessa had no particular interest in it because, she said, "*it did not really match with my aspirations*". Her FB is a small construction engineering company, founded by her father in the seventies. Some years later, Vanessa's mother decided to join the business as chief in the administrative office. In 1998, Vanessa's older sister, Edith, decided to join the business. Edith clearly had always been very interested in the company and tried to prepare as much as possible to gain the necessary skills to keep up with the business. On the contrary Vanessa aspired to a different career. Her ambition was to practice as a lawyer. But two years after graduation, her family situation changed radically when she married and had a son, and she reconsidered her career choices. She revalued the chance to work in the FB, in order to have greater freedom and more free time for her child and her husband. Now she is in charge of the FB's legal office. Vanessa explained her decision to work in the company: "*When I was younger, I didn't think about working in the firm. Then I got married, had a child, and said to myself: "Let's try it". I was happy. I carved out my own space. Now I'm satisfied with my work. I have time for my family and also some free time. I don't care about leading the company. Doing my job is enough for me.*"

Her father recently passed down the leadership to Vanessa's sister. Vanessa and Edith have been living under the same roof, in a family with an intense entrepreneurial atmosphere. Nevertheless, their ambitions and their life projects have always been very different. Edith has been very attracted to her father's work since childhood and she never missed an opportunity to spend time with him at the company. On the contrary, the FB has never been attractive to Vanessa. A rewarding profession has always been one of her purposes, but she also wanted to have time for her family and her children, since she has always considered them a priority. Thus, when her father passed down the leadership to Edith, Vanessa was pleased because she never cared about leading the FB.

Vanessa is a manager by choice. She works in the FB with a task role, without leadership responsibilities, but she does not see her position as a waiver or as exclusion. On the contrary, she has purposefully left the helm of the business to her sister, and has preferred a role with less power, that leaves her enough time and energy to devote herself to her private life. Behind Vanessa's decision to enter the FB is the awareness that working in an FB can represent an optimal solution for a woman, as it allows for the smooth handling of the work-life balance. Thanks to her job in her FB, Vanessa is satisfied as a woman, as a mother/wife, and as a daughter. As a woman, because she has a job consonant to her studies and professional interests and can satisfy her career ambitions; as a mother/wife because she is flexible in organising her working hours and has enough free time for her family and private life; as a daughter because she knows that the continuity of the FB is ensured by her sister at the helm of the company.

4. *Stephanie: Invisible Co-Leader*

Stephanie is currently in charge of HR and the accounting office in her FB, an ink producer with fifty employees. Stephanie's great-grandfather founded the firm in 1929. At that time, the family consisted of four children: three daughters and a son. In 1932, even if it was unusual for that period, the older daughter—Stephanie's grandmother—began working in the administrative office. However, all of the founder's expectations fell on his only son who, though still young, started to follow his father's footsteps. Unfortunately, the founder's son died in the Second World War and with him the conditions of continuity dictated by the culture of the time. The founder's daughter started to manage the business with her father. However, she never became the successor simply because she was a woman. In 1972, the baton was directly passed down to her son, the founder's nephew—Stephanie's father. Two years later Stephanie was born. And in 1981 her brother arrived. Stephanie joined the FB in 2007, after graduating in foreign languages and cultures and having several years of experience as an accountant in another firm. She worked very hard: "*I spent most of my time in the business. The firm became my first and true family*". Her brother joined the FB in 2008, after graduating in economics. Both siblings were involved in the business respecting a gradual path, based on their specific attitude. Their father decided that each one had to be familiar with the production process and market conditions of all types of ink they produced, and finally, with the numbers of the business, the accounting. At the same time, the siblings equally shared the ownership and began moving towards a shared leadership role. However, the father is still the CEO and it is clear to everyone that the real successor will be his son. "*In my father's eyes, I'm still his little girl. He is overprotective with me because I'm a woman*"—Stephanie said—"*For instance, when we need to visit a client off-site or abroad, my father prefers delegating my brother. If I must go because my brother can't, my father always wants to come with me because 'it is better for a woman not to travel alone'*". Stephanie also declared that compared to her brother, she has to work twice as hard in order to demonstrate her ability to her father and that it is not easy to accept her father's dual approach. However, she accepted the co-leader role, although she is subordinate to her brother, because of her strong desire to personally contribute to the FB continuity. Moreover, Stephanie is aware of the traditional women's role in her family: "*My father's attitude is based on a gender issue. In our culture and tradition, women take care of the family and their presence in the family business remains invisible even if it's crucial. This conception has been passed down from the founder to his nephew, my father. Although today this attitude is strongly attenuated, the roots of the male approach continue on. I know that my brother will be the future leader of the company. It will be so and it is natural*".

Stephanie is an invisible co-leader. She is involved in the ownership of the business and is a member of the entrepreneurial team. But she is currently in the shadow of her father and in the future, she will be in the shadow of her brother, who will become the official leader. Even if she desired to take on the leadership of the FB, Stephanie was forced to give up her ambitions and to accept a minor role, leaving the company's leadership to a male family member. She considers her secondary role in the FB as a waiver, because she knows that her dreams will never come true. However, she is aware that her brother's leadership cannot be avoided nor criticised. Stephanie knows that this division of roles between brother and sister is an unavoidable solution. She accepts this role because of her strong attachment to her family and her FB. The latter is considered a family asset, not only from a financial point of view, but also as a legacy of culture, traditions, and values and is considered as an integral part of family identity. In the name of this objective, considered a priority, she has accepted her father's choice, and in the end she really thinks that it is a natural solution.

5. *Rebecca: Outcast*

Rebecca is the eldest of two daughters and since she was a teenager, she went to great lengths for the firm, pulled in by her desire to work with her father. He founded two thermal spas in the seventies, and the businesses grew especially throughout the nineties. Rebecca joined the business after high school and gained a lot of experience in the firm: "*I started working for the firm during school holidays when I was 14, and when I finished school, I dedicated all of my time to my job. I always wanted to be part of the firm and I gradually became my father's assistant, his deputy.*" All went well until Rebecca made it clear that she wanted to take on more responsibility: "*After a few years, I started to understand the business's possible points of weakness, the areas to revise or to improve. So, I began talking with my father about possible changes.*" However, her father blocked all of her initiatives, and Rebecca believes that he was unable to accept that a woman could have increasing power in the business, even if she was his daughter. "*The problem was that my father never accepted my ideas for change: if the same suggestions came from a man, even if he wasn't an employee, he would listen and approve of them; however, not when they came from me. The fact that I was a woman, when he always wanted a son—who was never born—meant my ideas weren't worthy of consideration.*" Exasperated by non-stop obstruction, Rebecca finally decided to quit the firm: "*I always gave it my best shot, but this competition with my father led me to make a radical decision: I left the company and went to university.*" Some years later, Rebecca got a degree in psychology and never returned to the FB.

Despite a strong desire to assume a managerial role in her FB, Rebecca failed to meet her goal and decided to leave the firm due to extreme conflicts with her father. In her story is clear that she suffered from a lack of moral support and solidarity from her father, who did not believe in her potential, mainly because she is a woman. Instead of dialogue, sharing, and mutual trust, the attitude of Rebecca's father was one of closure, no sharing of knowledge, and hostility. This caused the daughter's detachment and exclusion from the FB.

Discussion and Conclusions

This chapter has investigated daughters' experiences within the FB in order to describe possible profiles that they may assume nowadays in the succession process. Each profile considers not only the daughters' effective role in their FB but also the motivations, ambitions and satisfaction they receive from their work. Five profiles have been identified and described, also highlighting limitations that still remain, despite the greater openness of FBs towards daughters.

In this perspective, three important empirical findings have emerged, providing an important contribution to the theory discussion on these topics. First, evidence shows that not all daughters with a leadership role show similar motivations and ambitions. Some daughters have desired to take on a leadership role since childhood and strongly pursued their goals with success. Conversely, other daughters become leaders "despite themselves", because "they have to", since no other family members have been concerned or likely to lead the FB (Wang 2010). In such situations, daughters can accept a role inconsistent with their previous goals because they are pressured by a feeling of moral obligation towards their family. In the words of Sharma and Irving (2005) and Dawson et al. (2015), their decision can be the result of a high normative commitment. These authors define normative commitment as "feelings of obligation to pursue a career in the family business" in order to "maintain good relationships with the senior generation". Our results highlight that daughters can show a strong normative commitment, which "forces" them to give up their dreams and accept a role inconsistent with their previous goals. This attitude can be the result of the education received since childhood, if this education has been oriented towards a high sense of duty, loyalty to the family, duty not to disregard parents' expectations. From this point of view, our results are in line with Dawson et al. (2015)'s statement about the importance of family expectations and family orientation as antecedents of the normative commitment. These authors also claim that gender is significantly related to normative commitment, as women show a "feeling of higher obligation" (Dawson et al. 2015, 562). According to the authors this result can be due to a prevailing traditional cultural model, in which women are expected to play caring roles not only in the family realm, but also in the business realm of the family business system. Our analysis does not allow the confirmation that women are moved by a higher feeling of obligation than men. However, in line with Nelson and Constantinidis (2017), who have further developed the model of Dawson et al. (2015) by including gender as an antecedent of normative commitment, we are convinced that this topic deserves further insights. In fact, including the gender variable in the analysis is important not only to understand if women really present a higher normative commitment, but also to understand the reasons behind it. In fact, being equal the level of normative commitment, men and women could be moved by very different reasons and factors, which should be thoroughly investigated. So this topic could be a research strand to be developed in future studies, also based on the comparison of the experiences of daughters and sons who have been socialised into the company and have had no choice but to accept the FB leadership.

Second, based on our results, daughters' exclusion from FB succession still persists. Although it is no longer "the rule", even today some FB owners deny their daughters' access to leadership. Daughters who aspire to leadership have sometimes to accept a minor role, mainly because, according to Ahrens, Landmann, and Woywode (2015), gender preferences in favour of male family heirs still persist. Growing up with this awareness seems to persuade daughters to accept their subordinate role with conscious resignation. In other cases, daughters are not willing to accept a minor role and decide to leave the firm because of the predecessor's closure and hostility based on the gender issue.

Third, our analysis shows that the marginal role of daughters in FBs is not always the result of gender discrimination, as some daughters can be satisfied with their secondary position.

This result gives rise to conflicting reflections. On one hand, this result could be the effect of a difference between the socialisation of sons and daughters in the FB. When both genders are represented among younger generations, daughters are very often socialised differently and this is a key factor to daughters' exclusion from leadership roles (Dumas 1998; Constantinidis 2010; Byrne and Fattoum 2015). Their desire to join (or not) the FB, as well as to play (or not) a leadership role, in fact, could have been formed in a completely non-deliberate and spontaneous way. They may have been influenced by the time they spent in the company during their childhood and by the encouragement, stimuli, and suggestions they received from family concerning their future career. These aspects could have indeed been key contributors to the daughters' career choices, and even what seems to be a free choice could be affected by gender differences in socialisation. Contrastingly, sometimes women can voluntarily and deliberately choose a secondary position, without leadership responsibilities and with a limited involvement. In fact, rather than being a waiver, or a second-best choice, such a position could be something to aspire to, since there are numerous advantages associated with it. As a matter of fact, a secondary position in an FB could turn out to be an optimal work/career solution for a woman, better than working with the same role in a different business (non-FB) or being the leader of the FB. From this point of view, FBs can represent a more favourable work environment for women, and working in an FB with a secondary position can represent a victory for women, as they can find a good balance between family commitments, personal ambitions, and professional satisfactions. In fact, an FB can offer women a professional opportunity to do a job consistent with their skills and interests. At the same time, FB can allow women to be flexible in organising their working hours and their private and family life. Since this is a central issue in women's studies, understanding if and under what conditions FBs can actually help women in managing work-life balance is of crucial importance. It is also important to further investigate what may influence a woman's ability to appreciate the benefits associated with such a position in a FB.

On a practical level, these results draw FB owners' attention to provide more support for daughter succession, in order to avoid "sub-optimal choices of successors" (Wang 2010) or lose talented family members only because of a gender issue. A greater awareness of these issues could help predecessors better plan the career of younger generations, helping daughters to use their talent. Our findings suggest that it is also crucial to sensitise predecessors to consider daughters as potential successors and rethink socialisation and the leadership selection processes as a means to favouring a change within FBs towards gender equality. At the same time, according to Dawson et al. (2015), "it may be wise for FB owners to proceed cautiously before attempting to create a sense of obligation in family members that [. . .] may inadvertently make them feel trapped in the firm".

While this research has analysed daughters' experience in the succession process with regard to a single country, we would encourage future studies to compare daughters' experiences across countries and investigate how cultural factors may affect daughters' ambitions and roles in FBs. In addition, a comparison between sons and daughters is suggested in order to understand if some profiles (e.g. leader because "she has to" or "manager by choice") might also characterise male experiences and in which way.

In conclusion, the issue of daughters in FB succession has received increasing attention in the last few decades (Martinez Jimenez 2009; Wang 2010; Gupta and Levenburg 2013). However, this is a partially unknown and not completely explored topic, and it offers many opportunities for further investigations in this regard. We, therefore, look forward to other researchers in the family business studies gaining deeper knowledge on this subject.

References

Abbott, B., and G. G. Meredith. 1984. *Family Business Management in Australia*. Sydney: McGraw-Hill.

Ahrens, J.-P., A. Landmann, and M. Woywode. 2015. "Gender Preferences in the CEO Successions of Family Firms: Family Characteristics and Human Capital of the Successor." *Journal of Family Business Strategy* 6 (2): 86–103.

Aronoff, C. E. 1998. "Megatrends in Family Business." *Family Business Review* 11 (3): 181–185.

Barnes, L. B. 1988. "Incongruent Hierarchies: Daughters and Younger Sons as Company CEOs." *Family Business Review*, 1 (1): 9–21.

Barrett, M., and K. Moores. 2011. "Australia: The Challenge of Father-Daughter Succession in Family Business: A Case Study from the Land Down Under." In *Father Daughter Succession in Family Business: A Cross-Cultural Perspective*, edited by D. Halkias, P. W. Thurman, C. Smith, and R. S. Nason, 285–293. Farnham, UK: Gower Publishing.

Byrne, J., and S. Fattoum. 2015. "The Gendered Nature of Family Business Succession: Case Studies from France." In *Context, Process and Gender in Entrepreneurship: Frontiers in European Entrepreneurship Research*, edited by R. Blackburn, U. Hytti and F. Welter, 127–152. Cheltenham: Edward Elgar Publishing.

Cesaroni, F. M., and A. Sentuti. 2014. "Women and Family Businesses: When Women Are Left Only Minor Roles." *The History of the Family* 19 (3): 358–379.

Cole, P. M. 1997. "Women in Family Business." *Family Business Review* 10 (4): 353–371.

Constantinidis, C. 2010. "Entreprise familiale et genre." *Revue Française de Gestion* 1: 143–159.

Corbetta, G., A. Minichilli, and F. Quarato. 2015. *Osservatorio AUB. VII Rapporto Aidaf-Unicredit-Bocconi*. www.aidaf.it/wp-content/uploads/2014/08/FOCUS-VII-OSSERVATORIO.pdf.

Curimbaba, F. 2002. "The Dynamics of Women's Roles as Family Business Managers." *Family Business Review* 15 (3): 239–252.

Dawson, A., P. Sharma, P. G. Irving, J. Marcus, and F. Chirico. 2015. "Predictors of Later Generation Family Members' Commitment to Family Enterprises." *Entrepreneurship Theory and Practice* 39 (3): 545–569.

De Massis, A., and J. Kotlar. 2014. "The Case Study Method in Family Business Research: Guidelines for Qualitative Scholarship." *Journal of Family Business Strategy* 5 (1): 15–29.

Dumas, C. 1989. "Understanding of Father-Daughter and Father-Son Dyads in Family-Owned Businesses." *Family Business Review* 2 (1): 31–46.

Dumas, C. 1990. "Preparing the New CEO: Managing the Father-Daughter Succession Process in Family Businesses." *Family Business Review* 3 (2): 169–181.

Dumas, C. 1992. "Integrating the Daughter into Family Business Management." *Entrepreneurship: Theory and Practice* 16 (4): 41–56.

Dumas, C. 1998. "Women's Pathways to Participation and Leadership in the Family-Owned Firm." *Family Business Review* 11 (3): 219–228.

Eisenhardt, K. M., and M. E. Graebner. 2007. "Theory Building from Cases: Opportunities and Challenges." *Academy of Management Journal* 50 (1), 25–32.

EY—Family Business Center of Excellence. 2015. *Women in Leadership: The Family Business Advantage*. EYGM. https://familybusiness.ey-vx.com/pdfs/ey-women-in-leadership-the-family-business-advantage.pdf.

Francis, A. E. 1999. *The Daughter Also Rises: How Women Overcome Obstacles and Advance in the Family-Owned Business*. Rudi: San Francisco.

García-Álvarez, E., J. López-Sintas, and P. Saldaña Gonzalvo. 2002. "Socialization Patterns of Successor in First- to Second-Generation Family Businesses." *Family Business Review* 15 (3): 189–204.

Gatewood, E., N. M. Carter, C. G. Brush, P. G. Greene, and M. M. Hart 2003. *Women Entrepreneurs, Their Ventures, and the Venture Capital Industry: An Annotated Bibliography*. Stockholm: Esbri.

Gersick, K. E., I. Lansberg, M. Desjardins, and B. Dunn. 1999. "Stages and Transitions: Managing Change in the Family Business." *Family Business Review* 12 (4): 287–297.

Gnan, L., and D. Montemerlo. 2008. *Le PMI familiari in Italia tra tradizione e novità*. Milano: Egea.

Griffeth, R. W., D. G. Allen, and R. Barrett. 2006. "Integration of Family-Owned Business Succession with Turnover and Life Cycle Models: Development of a Successor Retention Process Model." *Human Resource Management Review* 16 (4): 490–507.

Gupta, V., and N. M. Levenburg. 2013. "Women in Family Business: Three Generations of Research." In *Handbook of Research on Family Business*, edited by K. X. Smyrnios, P. Z. Poutziouris, and S. Goel, 346–367. Cheltenham: Edward Elgar.

Haberman, H., and S. M. Danes. 2007. "Father-Daughter and Father-Son Family Business Management Transfer Comparison: Family FIRO Model Application." *Family Business Review* 20 (2): 163–184.

Hytti, U., G. A. Alsos, J. Heinonen, and E. Ljunggren. 2017. "Navigating the Family Business: A Gendered Analysis of Identity Construction of Daughters." *International Small Business Journal* 35 (6): 665–686.

Kets de Vries, M. F. R. 1993. "The Dynamics of Family Controlled Firms: The Good and the Bad News." *Organizational Dynamics* 21 (3): 59–71.

Le Breton-Miller, I., D. Miller, and L. P. Steier. 2004. "Toward an Integrative Model of Effective FOB Succession." *Entrepreneurship Theory and Practice* 28 (4): 305–328.

Lee, K. S., G. H. Lim, and W. S. Lim. 2003. "Family Business Succession: Appropriation Risk and Choice of Successor." *Academy of Management Review* 28 (4): 657–666.

Martin, L. 2001. "More Jobs for the Boys? Succession Planning in SMEs." *Women in Management Review* 16 (5): 222–231.

Martinez Jimenez, R. 2009. "Research on Women in Family Firms: Current Status and Future Directions." *Family Business Review* 22 (1) (March): 53–64.

Miles, M. B., and A. M. Huberman. 1994. *Qualitative Data Analysis: An Expanded Sourcebook*. London: Sage.

Miles, M. B., A. M. Huberman, and J. Saldana. 2014. *Qualitative Data Analysis: A Methods Sourcebook*. 3rd ed. London: Sage.

Nelson, T., and C. Constantinidis. 2017. "Sex and Gender in Family Business Succession Research: A Review and Forward Agenda from a Social Construction Perspective." *Family Business Review* 30 (3): 219–241.

Nordqvist, M., A. Hall, and L. Melin. 2009. "Qualitative Research on Family Businesses: The Relevance and Usefulness of the Interpretive Approach." *Journal of Management and Organization* 15 (3): 294–308.

Patton, M. Q. 2002. *Qualitative Research & Evaluation Methods*. Thousand Oaks: Sage.

Piantoni, G. 1990. *La successione familiare in azienda*. Milano: Etas.

Qu, S. D., and J. Dumay. 2011. "The Qualitative Research Interview." *Qualitative Research in Accounting & Management* 8 (3): 238–264.

Salganicoff, M. 1990. "Women in Family Business: Challenges and Opportunities." *Family Business Review* 3 (2): 125–137.

Sharma, P. 2004. "An Overview of the Field of Family Business Studies: Current Status and Directions for the Future." *Family Business Review* 17 (1): 1–36.

Sharma, P., and P. G. Irving. 2005. "Four Bases of Family Business Successor Commitment: Antecedents and Consequences." *Entrepreneurship Theory and Practice* 29 (1): 13–33.

Smythe, J., and S. R. Sardeshmukh. 2013. "Fathers and Daughters in Family Business." *Small Enterprise Research* 20 (2): 98–109.

Vera, C. F., and M. A. Dean. 2005. "An Examination of the Challenges Daughters Face in Family Business Succession." *Family Business Review* 18 (4): 321–345.

Wang, C. 2010. "Daughter Exclusion in Family Business Succession: A Review of the Literature." *Journal of Family and Economic Issues* 31 (4): 475–484.

WEF. 2016. *Global Gender Gap Report 2016*. http://www3.weforum.org/docs/GGGR16/WEF_Global_Gender_Gap_Report_2016.pdf.

12 Enterprising Widows

Family, Business, and the Succession Process

Catriona M. Macleod

What can the experiences of widowed businesswomen in Scotland reveal about the nature of business families and the succession process? Taking Glasgow as a case study, this chapter will investigate the fortunes of urban businesswomen, examining their roles in business succession, the relationships involved, and their agency within the wider community. Glasgow in the eighteenth and nineteenth centuries was rapidly expanding and fast establishing itself as an international trading centre and an important industrial region. The population grew from c.31,700 in 1755 to c.200,000 by 1830, which established Glasgow as the largest city in Scotland (Devine 1995, 6–10; Nenadic 1994, 126). Newspapers, trade directories, and tax records pay testament to the bustling urban enterprise that filled the city's streets, both feeding off and supporting its growing population, burgeoning trans-Atlantic trade, and developing industry. The advent of widowhood offers an opportunity to examine business families and their strategies for survival in this dynamic urban context. Widowhood is a point at which women's roles in family concerns often become visible in the historical record, and concurrently a moment when businesses can be identified as family concerns. Marrying contemporary understandings of business succession with a historical perspective offers a way of discussing family business with potential to make comparisons over the *longue durée* easier. Recent work on modern-day family firm succession has explored life-story approaches and advocated a social exchange perspective as a means to unify research findings (Daspit et al. 2015; Hamilton 2006). This chapter will consider the value of these approaches when applied in a historical context and offer a historical perspective on succession in family business.

Contemporary research on business families suggests that male founders and business owners have often been conceptualised as the primary entrepreneurial figure within a family, with women's roles less recognised (Hamilton 2006, 253). This is not dissimilar is some respects from the ways that past business families have been imagined by historians. Entrepreneurial widows were once habitually explained in the historiography as caretakers of family businesses, temporarily looking after a concern until they could pass it on to an appropriate male heir (e.g. Whatley 1994, 35). These narratives stemmed from assumptions about the workings of patriarchal and patrilineal social structures. While patriarchal social and economic structures certainly did place boundaries around women's economic activities, it is now very clear that there was considerable diversity in the range of roles that they could occupy in the early modern past (Simonton 2013; Cavallo and Warner 1999; Moring 2007; Barker 2006; Erickson 2008). In her research on modern businesses, Eleanor Hamilton (2006) has similarly demonstrated that life-history accounts of family business reveal diverse models of entrepreneurship and relationships between members of family businesses. The narrative accounts that she utilised are harder to access in a historical context, but other sources highlight the range of strategies that female entrepreneurs utilised as widows, and the variety of business relationships they developed with business partners and/or with the next generation. Considering a social exchange perspective as a broad umbrella approach to analysing succession processes also offers a way of looking at family businesses and their integration into networks of kin, friends, and trading partners. Exploring succession processes provides another approach for assessing and explaining the variety of options for widowed businesswomen in the past. The evidence from the sample of widowed businesswomen examined here suggests various strategies and succession models including: ceasing to trade; continuing the business until their own death; continuing the business and overseeing succession to the next generation; and continuing or establishing a separate enterprise. Those who remarried are harder to see in this sample, because the sources used here tend to obscure married women's contributions. Some shared management roles with children or other business partners. Some restructured businesses to fit with their skills, capacities, or ambitions. Widowed businesswomen often managed succession to another generation, but parent to child succession was not indiscriminate. Not all children were necessarily trained for or intended to take up the reigns although they might be supported to set up in another trade. Considering these strategies can help unpick some of the contexts in which these various strategies arose, including widows' potential bargaining power within their families and extended business and kin networks.

Historians have investigated the legal, financial, and social implications of widowhood, which has often been characterised as either a phase of relative independence in comparison with marriage, or as a very precarious period when women could experience extreme poverty (for a review see van der Heijden, Schmidt, and Wall 2007). The work of historians like Deborah Simonton (2013, 93), Beatrice Moring (2007, 245), and Penelope Lane has shown that urban widows with businesses could be in a position to increase their assets. This chapter suggests that a social exchange perspective can provide a helpful perspective in a historical context, and may add to our understandings of the variety of widow's experiences as heads of businesses and households by offering explanations of why some women were able to establish themselves as successful businesspeople.

Social Exchange Perspective

Social exchange perspectives provide a way to examine the social structures that define and delimit succession processes, as well as leaving space to incorporate individual motives and agency (Daspit et al. 2015, 2). It prioritises the relationships between interconnected parties, which can be individuals such as members of a family business, or "collective actors". In contemporary research, this framework has proved useful in linking up understandings of the individual motives and skills required for successful transfer of a business from one leader to another; the group relationships that affect the succession process; and the macro-level planning and structuring of succession (Long and Chrisman 2014).

Social exchange theory focuses on relationships and reciprocity, and sets of rules that govern how people conceive of and react to exchange as key to determining how individuals and businesses act (Long and Chrisman 2014, 264). The theory posits two main forms of exchange: restricted and generalised. The former refers to exchanges where a direct form of short term reciprocity is expected by all parties. Usually subject to contractual obligations, all expect to benefit with a specific end in view. On the other hand, in generalised forms of exchange the parties do not expect any immediate return on their actions. In these cases, reciprocity is indirect, and the relationships between participants are often based on friendship or kinship. The value may be in the benefit to a group, rather than individual gain (Long and Chrisman 2014, 263). The resources exchanged in either case may be of economic or socioeconomic value, and the participants in the exchange expect mutually beneficial behaviour. Repeated interactions of this sort create social systems of obligation and expectations (Daspit et al. 2015, 3). This approach seems commensurate with the workings of the early modern society, especially in a context where personal and interpersonal credit relations were an essential part of local, urban economies (Muldrew 1998; Spence 2016).

Gender Perspective

Gender is an important element here, and historical as well as contemporary research has highlighted the exclusion that social exchange can create. Sheilagh Ogilvie's (2004) work, for instance, on gender, work, and social capital has demonstrated the ways that women were marginalised and excluded from social capital in early modern Europe. The social glue that held society together was structured along patriarchal lines, and the institutions such as guilds and town councils, in which such capital was created and stored were often male-only. In Glasgow crafts, trades, and merchants were organised into incorporations which, although diminishing in power during this period, were a prominent feature of municipal government and excluded women. This is important, because social exchange in this context may have served to simultaneously exclude women from positions of institutional power, *and* allow them in some circumstances considerable agency within local kin and business networks.

Focusing on women's roles in family business and in succession offers a gendered perspective that serves to highlight some of the gender dynamics in small businesses, but also offers a fresh way of thinking about how to conceptualise family business. This is clear in both contemporary and historical perspectives. Taking women's roles into account affords a new perspective on the character and structure of family business. Eleanor Hamilton's (2006, 258) work highlights this feature in the contemporary literature. She demonstrates that paying attention to women's roles informs how businesses were established and maintained, and challenges the notion that a male founder or owner is the main protagonist in family business narratives. Hamilton (2006, 253), however, has argued that contemporary work on women's roles in family business has focused too much on the marginalisation of women, and that turning the focus to the family rather than individual owner-managers suggests other ways of conceptualising women's roles, and highlights the ways that hierarchical structures can be undermined. She demonstrates that power relations between men and women and within families and family businesses are shifting and unstable rather than static (Hamilton 2006, 268). Her central contestation is that putting family at the centre of family business research allows a greater understanding of how businesses are established and maintained in practice than would be possible if the business was placed at the centre of analysis (Hamilton 2006, 267). In other words, when the business itself is the main focus of analysis, entrepreneurship can be inaccurately characterised as "individualistic" (Hamilton 2006, 254). Similarly, turning our attention to widows' activities in the past refocuses attention on the family which the business existed to support. It additionally serves to highlight the roles that women were likely to have played as wives before taking over as named business proprietors. As historians have noted, the term "wife" did not simply denote marital status in the early modern period, but is thought to have held occupational connotations (Shepard 2015, 273). Thinking about women's roles, then, helps us to understand both families and businesses from different angles.

Family Business and Demographic Context

The evidence presented here focuses on retail, trade, and service enterprises performed by a household. In this context, family business was often conducted within the home and might involve some or all members of a household, including servants and apprentices. Family businesses in this period had to contend with precarious demographic circumstances: in many cases death and succession were probably synonymous. They also operated in an insecure economic environment, and as such the environment of succession contained several wildcards that families and households had various strategies for dealing with. Widows might carry on a business in the same way as it had been conducted before the death of their spouse, but some made changes, specialising or diversifying the services they offered. Some trained children to take on the business, while others supported the next generation by establishing their new concerns. Some women may have acted as "caretakers" of a business concern, "retiring" from trade in older age if they could, but many worked until their own death.

Historical Context

Although research into modern business succession can be useful for historians, there are important differences between research on modern and historical family businesses, not least in the understandings of terminology. Some key terms can differ significantly in their usage when applied in either historical or contemporary settings. This has important implications for the understanding of succession in family business in the past. Terms such as incumbent and successor can be misleading or inappropriate when applied to family businesses in the past which in some circumstances were structured differently from the family firms under scrutiny in contemporary studies. As noted above, the family businesses that are the focus of this research were often smaller enterprises, and the available data does not always make it possible to clearly identify the roles of different family members or other non-family employees of the business. By identifying widows carrying on a family business, this chapter does not assume that widows were necessarily the successors of their husband-incumbents, even if their late husband may have held an occupational title that suggested they were head of the business. It is now clearly established that men's occupational titles are not a reliable indicator of who performed which tasks, and that women's activities could be subsumed within the marital household, becoming visible only upon widowhood (Fiebranz et al. 2011). As Jane Whittle (2014, 295) found in her study of widows in early modern England, it can be impossible to tell whether widows' activities represent a continuation of their husband's trade or a continuation of their own occupation, which went unrecorded during marriage. In some instances, it may be more accurate to describe widows as succeeding to the role of head of *household*, with the implication that they may have previously been acting as a joint head of the business of the household, that could include a shared enterprise or an independently run enterprise of her own.

This also points to the change in the definition of family over time. Naomi Tadmor (1996, 111) has described the "family" of the eighteenth century and earlier as the "household-family": all the members of a household including servants and apprentices not directly related to the head of household. These household-family members often had roles in family businesses. The dynamics of the household-family and their relation to a business enterprise may have been conceived rather differently to relationships between modern employers and employees.

Finally, family business itself might be viewed as a different entity in a historical context, particularly in relation to smaller enterprises that were often household-based. In many cases, the enterprises under discussion here were very closely inter-related with households, and they were often one part of a broader survival strategy within a household economy that encompassed multiple activities. Richard Wall's (1986, 294) concept of the "adaptive family economy" is useful here in highlighting how early modern households could diversify work activities to protect themselves in difficult periods and make the most of profitable times. A household might have supported itself by a variety of means, and a variety of enterprises. In some instances, there is clear evidence of discrete businesses run by family members and passed through generations, but in other cases, household enterprises were more varied and ostensibly different activities might be undertaken within the same business. Several enterprises may have been continued simultaneously to support a household, or businesses might diversify and change with succession and transfer of management. This means that many small family businesses of the eighteenth and early nineteenth century were positioned within the context of the household, and were a part of the household economy, in ways that required different adaption strategies in the face of change.

The main evidence for this chapter is drawn from a qualitative sample of widowed businesswomen in Glasgow, identified by record linkage across a number of sources. Tracing widows' activities through trade directories, newspaper adverts, wills and testaments, tax records, bank account ledgers, and in debt litigation provides information about the duration of their time as independent businesswomen, as well as the size and value of their businesses. The extended family, community, and business networks of these widows illustrate the symbiotic relationships between business families and networks of kith and kin. Despite the fragmented nature of the source material, in some cases the relationships between family members of a household enterprise can be at least partially established, allowing some comment on the creation of trust between incumbent and successor that contemporary research has identified as so important to successful transitions in business leadership. This research will also identify the skill set and resources possessed by widows, reflecting on possible succession strategies between husbands and wives, as well as passing on status, knowledge, tools, training, and resources to the next generation to set them up in the same or an alternative trade.

Identifying widows is not straightforward in the historical record because marital status is difficult to assess in some sources. Entries in trade directories, for example, are often ambiguous. Of women listed in a sample of directories from 1783–1823, 83 per cent used the title 'Mrs', and only a very few were labelled as 'Widow'.[1] This makes it hard to distinguish between women on the basis of marital status. Further, Amy Erickson's (2014, 53) work on the history of the word Mistress and its abbreviation Mrs has convincingly shown that it had been a title signifying ownership of capital rather than marital status, and that the former meaning was still in use in this period. More information is always required to determine whether a woman identified as 'Mrs' was a widow, a wife, or simply a woman with capital and status. Fortunately, other sources can be more specific, and record-linkage can identify which women were widows by cross-referencing trade directory entries, newspapers, tax records, and current account ledgers in Glasgow's banks with wills and testaments. These sources have been used to profile forty-eight women who are clearly identifiable in more than one source, where that information confirmed their status as widowed businesswomen and recorded the minimum length of time that they were in trade. The women that formed this sample were a varied group, but most worked in urban trades and services including the sale of drink or food as grocers, bakers and spirit dealers, in the sale of textile goods and clothes as stocking shop owners and shoe sellers, in the sale of books but also as coppersmiths, tinsmiths and fish hook makers. This is reasonably typical of urban women's work across the British Isles (Barker 2006; Erickson 2008).

The evidence allows us to consider women as "successors" to a family business, but also as "incumbents" who had to deal with future succession and these two aspects will structure the discussion that follows. Widows' ties to extended family provided mutually beneficial outcomes that prompt speculation about the broader functions of family business, and it is possible that one element of the motivation for entrepreneurial activity was the need to support wider kin networks beyond immediate family and household needs. As such, both "restricted" and "generalised" forms of exchange involving household enterprises can be examined, as well as the creation of systems of obligation that may have influenced how successfully widows were able to establish themselves as the heads of families and businesses.

Widows as "Successors"

There may have been a number of motives for women to assume the title of leader of a family business, but it is apparent that family businesses required the skills and experience of widows for the continuing subsistence or prosperity of the household and business. The women in this sample were largely the widows of tradesmen, and most often continued in the same trade, although a few had a separate enterprise. Some continued to trade as a means of subsistence until their own death, some faced difficulties and potential bankruptcy, while others were profitable notwithstanding depleted material resources and others turned to property letting or otherwise living on their assets in old age. These women were not dependent figures, but tended to have dependents to provide for and ensure the future security of their family. They did, however, often rely upon networks of extended family, colleagues, and friends for support—probably the same networks that would have supported them during marriage.

Due to the nature of the sources, the widows in this sample tend not to have been amongst the poorest in society. Beatrice Moring (2007, 245) and Deborah Simonton (2013, 93) have both found that widows with businesses were in a position to increase their assets. But some *were* left with few resources in widowhood, and could be in precarious circumstances. Mrs Janet Henderson was a vintner in Candleriggs in Glasgow, who was rumoured to be near financial collapse in the 1820s and died in debt in 1830.[2] Small enterprise was an uncertain business, and women like Janet Henderson may have trod a fine line between solvency and bankruptcy. Yet widows who found themselves left with few resources could sometimes reverse their fortunes when they had sole control of the purse strings and the business decisions. The vintner Catherine Nottman or Knox, who ran a prosperous business for around twenty years as a widow, berated her late husband in her will for having left her with debts to pay and no funds with which to answer them, and contrasted that with her own financial success and her ability to bequeath her wealth on to her relatives.[3]

Often, widows took over in households that had just enough resources to support itself. For example, when the tobacconist John Meikle died in 1784 or 1785 without a will, his moveable property amounted to a little over £30 sterling largely consisting of household furniture and a few book debts. His wife Elizabeth Gardner filed a petition along with his inventory, requesting that £27 9s 6d be deducted from the total amount "for the Defuncts (sic) funeral expenses, for House rents, Servants, wages, maintenance of his family and other articles paid by her".[4] They were an average-sized business: Elizabeth Gardner was recorded that year renting a shop worth £7 annually, which was what the majority of shopkeepers with taxable premises paid in the city.[5] The submission of a petition to deduct the money for household purposes may have been a tactic that allowed her to continue life with as little disruption as possible. In the event, she continued in business for at least six years. The tobacconist business did not make her a large fortune, but it brought in enough to rent a decent shop and maintain the household, though there was probably little choice but to carry it on in her widowhood.

Wealthier widows, however, still took over family business concerns. Christian Hamilton or Gowdilock ran her family stocking shop for sixteen years after her spouses' decease, and had a moveable estate worth over £1,000, on her own death. She still had stock in her shop when she died, but she she also had a small amount of income from interest on money lent in bills and promissory notes.[6] While some of the widows in the sample made a sufficient livelihood, others like Christian were able to accumulate resources which they could use to diversify their income.

Planning for Succession

Rates of widowhood were relatively high in this period, and wives were probably expected to take on the roles we see here in the event of a decease. Although death usually appears to have been the point at which widows became the named proprietors of a business, sometimes illness could prompt an earlier transfer of title. Mary Fleming and her husband David Muir were umbrella makers in Glasgow. When David became ill, Mary took a course of action that would set her up to continue their umbrella making business for twenty-five years. Some six months before her husband's death in December 1813, their listing in the trade directory was changed so that it carried her own name. By taking the helm during her husband's illness and publicly announcing her actions and plans for the future of the business in this way, she demonstrated her capability, knowledge, and skilfulness in her trade. At her much later death she still had "stock in shop".[7]

Some families made more formal provisions for the decease of a partner, setting up wives as heads of families and businesses, and demonstrating the nature of the trust that could exist between spouses in business families. James Galbraith, a coppersmith, stipulated in his will that his wife Mary Smith would have liferent use of all his property, including tools and utensils of trade at his death. The tools would eventually go to their son, but not until Mary's death or remarriage, and she continued to trade for at least ten years after her husband's death in 1813. The business was to be kept within the Galbraith family, so while Mary was entrusted with the business herself until the end of her life, a future spouse would not be, because of the legal rights concerning marital property.[8]

Wives were also sometimes named as the executrix on their husband's estate or if, like the bookseller Margaret Sandeman, their husband died intestate, they could claim their right as his widow to act as executrix.[9] Amy Erickson (1999) has found that there were declining numbers of widows named as executrix from the eighteenth century in England, and others have also noted the growing preference for men to appoint trustees to oversee their estate on death. The appointment of trustees must, by necessity, have limited widow's ability to control the family's financial affairs. But in some cases their ability to continue in trade does not appear to have been adversely affected by the appointment of trustees. Robina Simpson, or Lyon, was a widowed tinsmith who took over from her husband in 1816. Her husband John Lyon made a will in which he appointed three trustees to carry out the instructions he left for the disposal of his property: Alexander Panton, a physician, James Lyon, a brush maker and perhaps a relative, and William Sealer, a writer. Robina's choices may have been limited by the trustees' role as executors, but she continued to operate as a tinsmith for over ten years in her widowhood and it is possible that it was helpful to have a group of people to share the job of dealing with her husband's effects and to deliberate with over decisions regarding the estate and her future. Her husband's estate was relatively large when he died, worth £1479 1d 4 ½d. Hers was smaller at £984 8s 5d, but considering that her husband's will had allotted her the interest of his estate only with the rest to pass to his children when they were "able to do for themselves", it is substantial.[10]

Other widows were included in lists of executors with groups of men, and sometimes outlived them all, ending up as sole executrix. In 1808, James Galbraith, a coppersmith in Glasgow, made a will stipulating that his wife Mary Smith was to be executor, along with James Hamilton, Robert Jamieson, baker in Glasgow, William Menzies, manufacturer, and James Wylie coppersmith. Mary was always to be "one of the quorum". When James died in 1817, the other named executors refused the role, or had died, leaving Mary as sole executrix.[11] She continued his business and advertised as a coppersmith until at least 1823. The appointment of trustees may have restricted widow's individual agency, but it did not necessarily prevent them from continuing to trade or making a good living. Though there is little evidence of their interactions and negotiations, the success of these widows suggests that there could have been advantages to having a group of trustees to deliberate with in some circumstances.

Networks

The appointment of executors points to the networks that business families maintained, which they may have hoped would help to smooth over the process of business succession. In some cases, wives were numbered amongst a group of relations as executors for their husbands. Margaret Todd, for instance, was listed amongst a group of relations from both her own and her husband's family to administer his estate on their children's behalf, and Margaret was to have liferent use of it. She continued the family bakery business, under the name of Mrs James Ure.[12] There were several bakers from the Ure family in Glasgow, including one of the other trustees, John Ure, based in Bridgegate.[13] Margaret drew up the inventory of her husband's moveable estate listing bolls of wheat that were worth far more than the household furniture and baking utensils put together, at £294, as well as £60 worth of fine flour, £10 worth of course flour and £5 worth of butter. It is possible that John and other members of the Ure family supported her endeavours to continue as a sole business proprietor and to manage these goods. There's no evidence of the dynamics between Margaret and her trustees, but they may have been intended to help her manage the family's quite extensive property across Glasgow as well as the bakery business.

Cases like those above suggest that women were active in family businesses long before widowhood; as wives they developed the skills required, and also built networks of family, friends, and tradespeople. Since succession appears often to have been synonymous with the death of a spouse, households and businesses, whether run by a widow or a widower, faced depleted human resources rather than just a change of management and these networks may have been relied on to get through a difficult transition. "Generalised" forms of social exchange practiced in business and social life could set up bonds of reciprocity and obligation that widows (and presumably widowers) could draw on in crisis. Social and familial networks could be key for women carrying on trade after their husbands had died (Collinge 2013, 110–132). It has been shown elsewhere that endogamous marriage patterns were prominent in many urban trades, including very clearly for Scotland in the print trade (Houston 1983; Mann 1999). Deborah Simonton (2013, 102) has also found that endogamous trade patterns could provide important safety-nets for widows. Husbands and wives brought skill or knowledge of a trade to their marriage, but they also brought links to important occupational networks. This meant that at widowhood, women had recourse to extended webs of family in the same or related trades, as well as friends and colleagues who could supply business advice, raw materials, or a market for their goods. These were relationships built upon during marriage, but often pre-dated it. Women often entered marriage with skills in trade, shopkeeping, and accounting and during marriage could build upon these skills, allowing them to continue in trade as widows. During marriage, they might make new links with their husband's kin and business networks, but they also relied on connections that pre-dated marriage. One indicator of the importance of these shared marital networks was that widows in Glasgow tended to adopt their husbands' names, like Mrs James Ure above, even though this wasn't the general practise for married women in Scotland. They did so to retain the identity of their business, which was common practice across Scotland (Simonton 2013, 105). But in many cases, they also relied on the connections with their natal families. Jean Smith, for example, was a shoe seller in the early nineteenth century. Her husband David Law had been a shoemaker. She acted as his executrix when he died in 1809, and she herself carried on in the same industry with a shoe shop under the name of Mrs Law. She died much later in 1842, and was still trading at that point.[14] Some ten years before she died, she had a will drawn up in which she named four men as trustees of her estate, which was all to pass to her five children. Of these men, two were shoemakers and one of those shoemakers was a relative of hers, David Smith. It is likely that she entered marriage with knowledge of or perhaps training in the shoemaking trade. Her own skill allowed her to continue to trade after the death of her spouse, and she was also able to rely on her kin as well as business connections made when her husband was still alive. This seems to have been effective, since her moveable estate was valued at £1347 10s 5d. Her husband's had been worth £327 4s 11d.[15]

It seems apparent that these networks were reciprocal, and widows contributed back into local and familial communities in various ways. Widowed businesswomen also appointed groups of male executors to manage their affairs in the event of their deaths, and these can tell us more about their interlinked occupational and familial networks. The changekeeper Christian Whitson stipulated that her bequests were to be managed by six men whose trades may have been linked to hers: John Boyd, junior merchant in Glasgow, Alexander Forrester, grain merchant in Glasgow, Alexander Forrester, grain merchant in Alloa, John Whytlaw, merchant in Glasgow, Robert Hannan, brewer in Anderston, and Robert McKilliken clerk in Anderston Brewery. Some of Christian's bequests were to the wives and children of these men. One of her relatives, Marion Whitson, was the widow of a brewer in Anderston, so she clearly had strong links within that trade through family and marital connections. Her links with grain merchants may have been made through the brewing and malting trade contacts that she had. She continued in business for at least twelve years after her husband's death, and appears to have been very prosperous—perhaps in part because of her connections in related trades.[16]

Christian Whitson also tried to ensure that the profits of her business activity would feed back to support extended kin and friends, of older as well as younger generations. In her will, the first bequest that she stipulated was for the sum of £400 to be paid to Robert Hannan of the Anderston Brewery on the condition that he paid his father, James Hannan £10 sterling yearly for life. Similarly, she left the sum of £50 to John Whitson, mariner in Leith, on the condition that he pay his mother Margaret Windlay £2 10s a year.[17] She arranged an annuity of £10 to Marion Whitson, the widow of a brewer and a relative of Christian's who resided with her.[18] Christian Whitson was acutely aware of her own position and her ability to provide a safety net to others in terms of small retirement funds or gifts of capital and she was not atypical in her actions. Many businesswomen made similar bequests in their wills if they had been able to acquire sufficient capital. This suggests that widowed women in business played important social and economic roles that oiled the wheels of commerce as well as supporting extended kin. It suggests that focusing more on the family side of family business adds an important dimension to business histories (Popp 2012, 4). As well as managing the transmission of a business to their immediate family, widows were deeply embedded in extended networks of kin and friends. Their relationship to these networks was symbiotic: widows at the helm of a household and a business could call on the support of extended kin who were often in related trades, but in turn, they also often supported multiple generations of families with assets they were able to accumulate over many years of independent trade. This is similar in many ways to the strong social bonds forged between merchant families through the naming of godparents in eighteenth- and nineteenth-century Finland (Keskinen 2013).

Widows as Incumbents

Wealthier widows like the vintner Catherine Nottman were sometimes able to retire from active trade in their latter years. Catherine's inventory suggests she did so, since there were no tools, shop furniture, or stock in trade listed, but she had a respectable estate largely made up of bank deposits.[19] Beatrice Moring (2007, 242) has found that in urban Sweden and Finland, townspeople who were able to create profit from craft shops and trading tended to invest it in property that could support them in old age. Jane Humphries (1998, 39) also describes a link between age and the taking in of lodgers by women in early industrial Britain. If they had the resources, older women used property as an income stream in their old age, supporting themselves on the rental income it produced. For example, Janet Fyfe, a stabler, appeared to have given up her trade by the time she was approaching the end of her life. She had a small income from her right by ground annual (a form of property ownership) to land in Portugal Street in Laurieston, near Glasgow from which she made about £20 a year. She bequeathed this money to her sister Margaret Fyfe, who had moved in with her in the 1830s. Perhaps the sisters supported each other in old age.[20] Similarly, when Robina Simson or Lyon, a tinsmith, died many years after her husband she also left a will and testament that suggested she had retired from trade and subsisted on rental income. It details a number of land acquisitions, mostly made in the 1830s, which supports the impression that property investment and subsequent rental income could be a strategy for "retirement".[21] As has been noted above, however, many other women never did stop trading and even after a long widowhood still had stock in trade and book debts listed in their inventories.

Succession

In some cases, widows who ceased trading oversaw the succession of a family business to their children. In 1783, for example, Mrs Aird placed an advert in the *Glasgow Mercury* notifying customers that she was retiring from business, but that her daughters would continue giving sewing lessons and making grave clothes as she had formerly done.[22] The issue of appointing trustees to wills points to another feature of widowed businesswomen's lives: their children. Where a husband appointed a group of executors, whether or not his wife was included among them, the reason was usually to ensure the transmission of his property to his children when they came of age. Simonton (2013, 98) points out that Daniel Defoe saw the tradesman's wife as an important part of the business, who should be able to manage it for their children's sake if he died, but only in the sense of "holding the business in trust". It has already become clear that the women in this study frequently continued in trade for long periods of time, or until their own death, rather than until their children were able to step into the role. Sometimes, of course, widows had no children to support and worked for their own livelihood. In other cases, their children followed a different route, and the family business was wound up whenever the mother stopped trading. When children did intend to succeed their mothers, widows managed the transition to the next generation and they were pivotal figures in that process, not simply temporary stand-ins.

It's also clear that widows at the helm of a family business did not pass the responsibility for its future success indiscriminately on to their children. In some cases particular family members were singled out for succession. Jean Smith, or Law, the shoe shop proprietor had two sons, but they do not appear to have been involved in the family trade. Instead, one of her daughters is mentioned as her primary assistant. Jean made a special bequest to her daughter Janet: over and above the equal share of the estate that each sibling would receive, Janet was to have a further £400 sterling:

> In respect of the attention and Constant attendance given by her to the business conducted by me in Saltmarket Glasgow and as a remuneration to her for such services.[23]

There's no evidence that her other children were involved in the business, and she certainly did not intend passing it on to her sons.

Moreover, when family enterprises were retained for another generation, the widow's time in trade meant that it was beneficial for her children to be associated with her name, for the legitimacy and credibility it carried. Jean Mackenzie advertised her retirement from her upholstery, oil, colours, and painting business in 1784, and announced publicly that she had passed on the reins to her son.[24] Newspaper adverts like this show that widowed business women who worked in partnership with their children had an important role as named proprietors of family enterprises (Simonton 2013, 109).

Additionally, although there is a large literature that has established that widows were seen as the "deserving poor", widows with successful business concerns were usually supporters of dependents (Sharpe 1999, 220–239). Elizabeth Irvine or McIntyre traded as an umbrella maker for twenty-four years from 1823 to 1857 after her husband James Irvine died. She left all her estate to her three unmarried daughters, claiming to have provided for the rest of her family at the time of their marriages and in other ways. This underlines that widows' responsibility was to manage the family property for their own livelihood as well as to provide for future generations. The inventory accompanying her will suggests that Elizabeth Irvine was operating as an umbrella maker until her decease. Her stock in trade was her largest asset, worth over half of her total moveable estate when she died. She was aware of this, since it was the first item that she listed for her daughters to inherit.[25]

Some widows had to set up several of their offspring in trade. Lillias Semple, or Gibb, was a baker in Glasgow who presided over the Gibb baking business for twelve years before her death. She took over from her husband Archibald Gibb when he died around 1815 or 1816. She retained the same premises until her own death in 1829. During that time, the business was run under her name, but two of her younger sons took on the trade and worked with her. The first to do so died, and then her younger son took over. Her eldest son, John Gibb, was also a baker, but had his own separate bakery at 170 Gallowgate, not far from his mother and brothers.[26] It appears that he had been set up with his own baking equipment at an earlier point, leaving Lillias to carry on her own activities and pass her business down to the younger sons. She ensured that all her sons were well set up to make their own living, but her example demonstrates that there was no certainty that children would survive to carry on a family concern. So while she facilitated the start of her sons' careers at the end of hers, she was certainly not a stand-in figure until her sons were able to manage by themselves. She managed the family estate and set out clearly how it was to be divided in her will—presumably her husband Archibald had not done so, or else she had inherited his property outright at his death. Her oldest living son, John, was to inherit all her heritable property, as well as her household furniture. He was obliged to pay her funeral and sickbed expenses from this estate. She lived in a house directly above a house and shop used for the baking business and also had use of the bakehouse. Those latter business premises however, were to pass Gabriel Gibb, her youngest son. He was to inherit all the moveable property contained in those business premises to allow him to continue as a baker.[27]

Widows also set up new businesses with their children rather than passing down the skills or tools of their husband's work. Agnes Fleming, for one, was the widow of William McCallum, and worked as a milliner and latterly as a silk mercer. William McCallum was listed in the trade directories as a haberdasher, and after he died around 1810, Agnes started advertising her millinery business at their address on Hutcheson Street. By 1819 she was running a "silk lace and muslin warehouse" from the same address, and in 1820 went into partnership with her son under the name of "A. McCallum & Son". The firm went into administration before her death, and in her will she stated that she had been a sleeping partner in the business. Yet her name was above the door, she continued to hire milliners to work for her, and left one of them a large bequest in her will, and she had interests in the stock and profits of that business amounting to £1020 4s.[28] She clearly provided capital, knowledge of the textile trades, and her own reputation to launch her son's business. Widows frequently provided important start-up capital for their children's independent enterprises, such as Janet Fyfe, a stabler who lent her son who was a butcher £350.[29]

When widows had no surviving children of their own to support, they often provided for nieces and nephews. Minny Waugh, or Munn, the widow of Neil Munn, traded as a vintner and stabler in widowhood. Minny made her niece, Alison Wilson, sole executrix and the main beneficiary of her will. Alison Wilson was also a widow at the time that Minny made her will; her husband had been a mason in Glasgow.[30] Catherine Nottman, a wealthy vintner, had her niece Catherine McKenzie living with her at the time that she wrote her will. They were clearly close at that point: her bequest to her niece was the first of those listed in the will, in which she bestowed on her niece personal items including her silver plate, her copy of Broun's Bible, and all her clothes. She later recanted and left her nothing—a reminder that family networks were not always reliable or uncomplicated and that all forms of exchange were subject to human emotion.[31]

Conclusions

The experiences of widowed businesswomen operating under the demographic and economic uncertainties of the eighteenth and early nineteenth centuries demonstrates that family businesses relied on kin, social, and business networks to ease the succession process when the head of a household died. Succession was usually prompted by a death, but family businesses had various strategies for dealing with the changes in household structure and resources that came as a result. Widows had the experience, skill, and networked connections to assume the role of the named head of a family business, and often did so not to maintain a business for the next generation but to support a household. Analysing succession from the perspective of widows reveals the important roles that women played in family businesses and confirms that they were far more than caretakers, and were very likely to have played key business roles as wives, establishing themselves as skilled and competent candidates to maintain family concerns. Business families also fostered kin and business network, and mutual reciprocity within wider communities. Widows might rely on the support of relatives and business connections, or the executors of their husbands' estates, but they also used their own resources to provide support to the elderly and younger members of their communities through bequests or loans of capital, and presumably by passing on skills. This chapter has addressed two aspects of modern family business research namely: Eleanor Hamilton's point that scholars gain a more accurate picture of family business if they prioritise the family rather than the business in their research questions; secondly that a social exchange perspective provides a useful over-arching concept for family business research. Although there are differences in context and terminology in historical case studies, these can provide useful approaches with which to discuss the workings of eighteenth- and early-nineteenth-century family firms, and allow us to potentially trace continuities in family business dynamics. In turn, a historical perspective might offer an opportunity for studies of the family firm over the *longue duree* and suggest the varied roles that women have long played in the family, local, and national economies.

Notes

1 A sample of Glasgow's trade directories has been examined, beginning with the first published directory of the city: *John Tait's Glasgow Directory* (Glasgow, 1783); taking in the second edition of Nathaniel Jones, *Jones' Glasgow Directory* (Glasgow 1789); finally William McFeat's *The Glasgow Directory* of 1803, 1813, and 1823.

2 NRS, Glasgow Sheriff Court Inventories SC36/48/22/401, 23 March 1831; GCL, *Glasgow Herald*, issue 2111, 21 March, 1823.
3 NRS, Glasgow Sheriff Court Register of Testaments, SC36/51/18/457; NRS, Glasgow Sheriff Court, Register of Inventories and Settlements, SC36/48/29.
4 NRS, Glasgow Commissary Court Register of Testaments, CC9/7/72.
5 NRS, King's Remembrancer Office: Assessed Tax Schedules, Shop Tax E326/4/2.
6 McFeat, *Glasgow Directory,* (1814). In 1785, William Gowdilock, merchant, had a shop on King Street worth £10; NRS Glasgow Sheriff Court, Register of Inventories and Settlements, 23 November 1820 SC36/48.16.
7 Mrs David Muir, umbrella maker, 86 Glassford Street, McFeat, *Glasgow Directory* (1813 & 1823); NRS Commissary Court Register of Testaments, CC10/7/2/173, and SC36/48/27/245.
8 NRS, Glasgow Sheriff Court, Register of Settlements, SC36/51/6; Register of Inventories and Settlements SC36/48/20/823; McFeat, *Glasgow Directory* (1823).
9 NRS, Glasgow Sheriff Court Register of Inventories and Settlements, SC36/48/9.
10 NRS, Glasgow Sheriff Court Register of Inventories and Settlements, SC36/51/27.
11 NRS, Glasgow Sheriff Court, Register of Inventories and Settlements, SC36/51/6; SC36/48/20/823.
12 Other Ure bakers are listed in: McFeat, *Glasgow Directory* (1814).
13 Tait, *John Tait's Directory* (1783).
14 Her inventory lists the value of her stock in trade and also the amount of money in her house and shop. NRS Glasgow Sheriff Court Register of Inventories and Settlements, SC36/48/29.
15 NRS, Glasgow Sheriff Court Register of Inventories and Settlements, SC36/48/29.
16 NRS, Glasgow Sheriff Court Register of Settlements, SC36/51/5.
17 NRS, Glasgow Sheriff Court, Register of Inventories SC36/51/5.
18 NRS, Glasgow Sheriff Court Register of Settlements, SC36/51/5.
19 NRS Glasgow Sheriff Court Register of Inventories and Settlements, SC36/48/29, Register of Settlements SC36/51/18; McFeat, *Glasgow Directory* (1823).
20 NRS, Glasgow Sheriff Court, Register of Settlements, SC36/51/24; Register of Inventories, SC36/48/33; McFeat, *Glasgow Directory* (1823).
21 NRS, Glasgow Sheriff Court, Register of Settlements, SC36/51/27/788.
22 GCL *Glasgow Mercury*, issue 263, 9 January, 1783.
23 NRS, Glasgow Sheriff Court Register of Settlements, SC36/51/18.
24 GCL, *Glasgow Mercury,* issue 365, 23 December 1784.
25 NRS Glasgow Sheriff Court Register of Inventories SC36/48/43/529; Glasgow Sheriff Court Register of Settlements, SC36/51/37/253; McFeat, *Glasgow Directory* (1823).
26 NRS, Glasgow Sheriff Court Register of Inventories and Settlements, SC36/48/21; NRS, Glasgow Sheriff Court Register of Settlements, SC36/51/7.
27 NRS, Glasgow Sheriff Court Register of Settlements, SC36/51/7.
28 McFeat, *Glasgow Directory*, (1813); NRS Glasgow Sheriff Court Register of Inventories and Settlements, SC36/51/12/363.
29 NRS, Glasgow Sheriff Court Register of Settlements, SC36/51/24; Register of Inventories, SC36/48/33; McFeat, *Glasgow Directory* (1823).
30 NRS Glasgow Sheriff Court, Register of Inventories and Settlements, SC36/48/46; Register of Settlements, SC36/51/40, Glasgow Directory 1823.
31 NRS Glasgow Sheriff Court Register of Settlements, SC36/51/18/457.

References

Barker, H. 2006. *The Business of Women: Female Enterprise and Urban Development in Northern England 1760–1830*. Oxford: Oxford University Press.

Cavallo, S., and L. Warner, eds. 1999. *Widowhood in Medieval and Early Modern Europe*. London: Routledge.

Collinge, P. 2013. "A Genteel Hand in the Malt Business: Barbara Ford (1755–1840) of Ashbourne." *Midland History* 39 (1): 110–132.

Daspit, J. J., D. T. Holt, J. J. Chrisman, and R. G. Long. 2015. "Examining Family Firm Succession from a Social Exchange Perspective: A Multiphase, Multistakeholder Review." *Family Business Review* 29 (1): 44–64.

Devine, T. 1995. "Introduction." In *Glasgow Vol 1: Beginnings to 1830*, edited by T. Devine and Gordon Jackson, 6–10. Manchester: Manchester University Press.

Erickson, A. L. 1999. "Property and Widowhood in England 1660–1840." In *Widowhood in Medieval and Early Modern Europe*, edited by S. Cavallo and L. Warner, 145–163. London: Routledge.

Erickson, A. L. 2008. "Married Women's Occupations in Eighteenth-Century London." *Continuity and Change* 23 (2): 267–307.

Erickson, A. L. 2014. "Mistresses and Marriage, or a Short History of the Mrs." *History Workshop Journal* 78 (1): 39–57.

Fiebranz, R., E. Lindberg, J. Lindström, and M. Ågren. 2011. "Making Verbs Count: The Research Project 'Gender and Work' and Its Methodology." *Scandinavian Economic History Review* 59 (3): 273–293.

Hamilton, E. 2006. "Whose Story Is It Anyway? Narrative Accounts of the Role of Women in Founding and Establishing Family Businesses." *International Small Business Journal* 24 (3) (June): 253–271.

Houston, R. A. 1983. "Marriage Formation and Domestic Industry: Occupational Endogamy in Kilmarnock, Ayrshire, 1697–1764." *Journal of Family History* 8: 215–229.

Humphries, J. 1998. "Female-Headed Households in Early Industrial Britain: The Vanguard of the Proletariat?" *Labour History Review* 63 (1): 31–65.

Keskinen, J. 2013. "The Chosen Ones: Godmotherhood as a Networking Strategy in the Merchant Community of Pori, 1765–1820." In *Female Agency in the Urban Economy: Gender in European Towns, 1640–1830*, edited by D. Simonton and A. Montenach, 224–243. London: Routledge.

Long, R. G., and J. J. Chrisman. 2014. "Management Succession in Family Business." In *Sage Handbook of Family Business*, edited by L. Melin, M. Nordqvist, and P. Sharma, 249–268. Thousand Oaks, CA: Sage.

Mann, A. J. 1999. "Embroidery to Enterprise: The Role of Women in the Book Trade of Early Modern Scotland." In *Women in Scotland, c. 1100–c. 1750*, edited by E. Ewan and M. Meikle, 137–151. East Linton, Scotland: Tuckwell.

Moring, B. 2007. "The Standard of Living of Widows: Inventories as an Indicator of the Economic Situation of Widows." *The History of the Family* 12 (4): 233–249.

Muldrew, C. 1998. *The Economy of Obligation: The Culture of Credit and Social Relations in Early Modern England*. Basingstoke: Palgrave Macmillan.

Nenadic, S. 1994. "Middle Rank Consumers and Domestic Culture in Edinburgh and Glasgow 1720–1840." *Past and Present*, no. 145, 122–156.

Ogilvie, S. 2004. "How Does Social Capital Affect Women? Guilds and Communities in Early Modern Germany." *American Historical Review* 109 (2): 325–359.

Popp, A. 2012. *Entrepreneurial Families: Business, Marriage and Life in the Early Nineteenth Century*. London: Pickering and Chatto.

Sharpe, P. 1999. "Survival Strategies and Stories: Poor Widows and Widowers in Early Industrial England." In *Widowhood in Medieval and Early Modern Europe*, edited by S. Cavallo and L. Warner, 220–239. London: Routledge.

Shepard, A. 2015. *Accounting for Oneself: Worth, Status and the Social Order in Early Modern England*. Oxford: Oxford University Press.

Simonton, D. 2013. "Widows and Wenches: Single Women in Eighteenth-Century Urban Economics." In *Female Agency in the Urban Economy: Gender in European Towns, 1640–1830*, edited by D. Simonton and A. Montenach, 93–115. New York and London: Routledge.

Spence, C. 2016. *Women, Credit, and Debt in Early Modern Scotland*. Manchester: Manchester University Press.

Tadmor, N. 1996. "The Concept of the Household Family." *Past and Present*, no. 151, 111–140.

van der Heijden, M., A. Schmidt, and R. Wall. 2007. "Broken Families: Economic Resources and Social Networks of Women Who Head Families." *History of the Family* 12 (4): 223–232.

Wall, R. 1986. "Work, Welfare and the Family: An Illustration of the Adaptive Family." In *The World We Have Gained: Histories of Population and Social Structure*, edited by L. Bonfield, R. M. Smith, and K. Wrightson. Oxford: Blackwell.

Whatley, C. 1994. "Women and the Economic Transformation of Scotland." *Scottish Economic and Social History* 14 (1): 19–40.

Whittle, J. 2014. "Enteprising Widows and Active Wives: Women's Unpaid Work in the Household Economy of Early Modern England." *History of the Family* 19 (3): 283–300.

Published Primary Sources

Jones, Nathaniel, Jones's Glasgow Directory, (Glasgow, 1789)
McFeat, William, The Glasgow Directory, (Glasgow, 1801)
McFeat, William, The Glasgow Directory, (Glasgow, 1803)
McFeat, William, The Glasgow Directory, (Glasgow, 1814)
McFeat, William, The Glasgow Directory, (Glasgow, 1823)
Tait, John, John Tait's Glasgow Directory, (Glasgow, 1783)

13 He Suddenly Died

Unplanned Succession in Family Firms

Jarna Heinonen and Elisabet Ljunggren

Introduction

The family business literature conceptualises family business systems as comprising of the family, the business and the ownership sub-system (Tagiuri and Davis 1996). These sub-systems interconnect in different ways; for instance, decisions in the business may be influenced by the owners' preferences. In the same way, decisions on ownership or business strategy are influenced, for example, by the needs of the family (see e.g. Alsos, Carter, and Ljunggren 2014). However, research has pointed at a lack of knowledge about the interplay of the family sub-system with the two other sub-systems (Zachary 2011; Basco and Rodriguez 2009). In addition, the business and ownership sub-systems are often perceived to be (economic) rational, while the family sub-system to a larger degree is perceived as governed by emotions, or as Murray (2002, 76) says, in these systems the emotional and rational are united in "an uneasy marriage".

We know that succession is regarded as one of the most crucial events in the life of a family business (Ahrens, Landmann, and Woywode 2015) where all three sub-systems are affected, e.g. the issues who should have ownership, who should be in charge of the business and of family decisions, and who is the most suitable successor are part of both rational and emotional assessments. The continuity of the business is important for the family (e.g. livelihood and capital/ownership maintenance) and the business' employees (e.g. job security). Therefore, in studying family–business interconnectedness (i.e. where the three sub-systems meet), the succession process can be perceived as a phase or an event where emotionality and rationality come to the surface.

A large bulk of the family business literature focuses on planned succession, that is, succession planned and prepared in advance in collaboration with the predecessor and the next generation to take over the firm. However, this does not always occur because unexpected things happen, such as illness and sudden deaths. Therefore, family businesses sometimes face premature succession, and the business needs to be transferred to the next generation without thorough planning and the presence of the predecessor.

The research on such premature and unplanned successions is scare. For this chapter, we have conducted case studies of three family businesses in Finland that experienced premature and unplanned succession due to the unexpected death of the owner, CEO, father, and husband. The research question addressed is: how do families and family firms cope with unplanned succession due to the sudden loss of a family member who is the CEO and owner?

The study contributes to the family business literature both theoretically and empirically. Empirically, we provide unique data on unplanned succession as a consequence of a sudden death. Such situations are seldom studied due to their delicate nature and the consequent inaccessibility of data. Theoretically, we contribute by bringing to light new insights about decision making during a critical incident—premature and unplanned succession—and argue, in line with Shepherd (2009), that emotions can be a resource in the interconnectedness between the family and the business, particularly when coinciding with pragmatic decisions. Finally, we suggest further research on effectuation as a decision-making logic and on grief recovery processes to gain a better understanding of how to cope with premature succession after the loss of a CEO and family member.

Next, we present the theoretical grounds of the study. We then explain the methodological approach applied and present the cases and analyses. Finally, we discuss our findings and present the conclusions.

Sub-systems' Interconnectedness, the Succession Process, and Emotions

The chapter takes as its theoretical point of departure the heterogeneous family business literature and primarily draws on research on the interconnectedness of family and business and on the succession process and emotions. The family embeddedness perspective (Aldrich and Cliff 2003) views the business and family sub-systems as intertwined. However, looking at the literature on family–business interconnectedness, researchers point at the lack of knowledge on how the family sub-system shapes and is visible in the business and ownership sub-systems (Zachary 2011; Basco and Rodriguez 2009). Despite the family being introduced as a crucial part of the "Sustainable Family Business Theory" (see e.g. Stafford et al. 1999), little seems to be known about how dynamics in the family subsystem affect both ownership and the business. In short, the family's needs and the businesses' needs can be both overlapping and contradictory; the big question is how this is balanced. We claim that the succession process is a phase in the life of a family business where the interconnectedness between the firm and the family, the rational and the emotional, becomes more exposed and thus easier to study. Succession has been a focal point in much of the family business literature (see e.g. Chrisman, Chua, and Sharma 1998; Sharma, Chrisman, and Chua 2003; Zahra and Sharma 2004; De Massis, Chua, and Chrisman 2008; Basco and Rodriguez 2009;

Lam 2011; Litz, Pearson, and Litchfield 2012; Gilding, Gregory, and Cosson 2013; Helin and Jabri 2015), and this stream of research has dealt with both rational and emotional issues.

One could claim that issues such as taxes, law, and financing represent the rational sides of the succession process. Here, the advantages of planned succession processes are dealt with (Handler and Kram 2004; Dyck et al. 2002), as a longer time span reserved for planning makes it possible to conduct needed operational and ownership arrangements. This implies understanding the succession in economic terms, that is, avoiding loss due to the taxation of property or inheritance tax. However, Hytti, Stenholm, and Peura (2011) suggest that goal-oriented planning is not a sufficient prerequisite for a successful business transfer, as original conditions are likely to change and cause delays in the succession process. Therefore, the plan needs to be adjusted accordingly.

Among the emotional issues the succession literature deals with are, for instance, the exchanges between incumbents and successors (Daspit et al. 2016), the role and motives of the incumbent and the problems the incumbent may have in letting the business go (Gilding, Gregory, and Cosson 2013), and the incumbents' role in preparing their children to become owner-managers. We know that creating an identity as a business manager and owner is one part of this (Hytti et al. 2017). Often, the incumbent has an idea of which of the children is the most suitable successor. Research has shown that sons are usually both preferred and expected successors, as documented in the United States and Korea (Kuratko, Hornsby, and Montagno 1993), Germany (Schröder, Schmitt-Rodermund, and Arnaud 2011), New Zealand (Keating and Little 1997), Denmark (Bennedsen et al. 2007), and the United Kingdom and France (Bloom and Van Reenen 2007); therefore, treating the siblings differently may be a source of negative emotions and disagreement. Furthermore, previous family firm studies suggest that although women may be considered inferior to men in economic terms, they are often perceived as superior in emotional terms. Therefore, women (daughters) are perceived as disadvantaged as potential successors but still impactful in succession as emotional buffers (Heinonen and Hytti 2012).

It is only recently that the need to understand successions as interactive, dynamic, and often lengthy social processes involving multiple stakeholders has been identified (Lam 2011; Salvato and Corbetta 2013; Daspit et al. 2016). It is argued that a business succession processes might take ten to fifteen years. Therefore, it is advised to start planning the succession in good time to make sure that the incumbent manages to step down and that the successor(s) gets the chance to create their new identity and role in the family business. Nevertheless, a succession is not always planned. When the succession happens suddenly due to, for instance, the sudden death or illnesses of a family member who also holds an important position in the family firm, how is it dealt with? The existing literature does not address unplanned or sudden and premature succession, particularly when the incumbent is not available to negotiate with and to make needed preparations with the other parties involved.

In addition to this, we know that the succession process can be emotional and might reveal or spawn conflicts among the new generation taking over the firm or between the incumbent and the successor(s). For example, Hytti, Stenholm, and Peura (2011) suggest that a fusion of rational and emotional aspects in business transfers may explain the reason for delayed transfers. High emotions are likely to be even more emphasised when the incumbent dies unexpectedly, as such unplanned events obviously stir up strong feelings in the family sphere on one hand and call for immediate decisions and action in the firm on the other. Indeed, a number of scholars have called for more research on emotions in family business (e.g. Astrachan and Jaskiewicz 2008; Brundin and Languilaire 2012), as this aspect has been understudied (Berrone, Cruz, and Gomez-Mejia 2012). The existing studies mainly focus on emotions in the family sphere (Carlock and Ward 2001), ignoring the equally emotional business sphere. However, there is evidence that emotions shape, for example, the cognition, decision making, behaviour, and strategy formulation involved in family businesses (Berrone, Cruz, and Gomez-Mejia 2012; Astrachan and Jaskiewicz 2008; Baron 2008). The critical incident of a death makes it possible to study the interconnectedness of family and business spheres and particularly the ways in which emotions shape family business related decisions.

Methodology

We have conducted case studies of three at least second-generation family firms that have recently undergone a premature and unplanned succession process and therefore needed to decide how to continue with the firm. Therefore, the family members were able to reflect on how they struggled with the loss and coped with it both family- and business-wise. The cases are unique, but all have in common that a family member who was the CEO/owner died suddenly. These data give us the chance to study hitherto unexplored parts of the interconnectedness of family and family business and thereby contribute to the literature. All firms had employees drawn from outside the family, and two were large firms with more than 250 employees. We used an event-based sample criterion (Neergaard 2007) for purposeful case selection (Patton 1990, 2005) and sought firms where women became successors after the death, as we were also interested in women's roles in succession. Because different stakeholders have different perspectives, it was important to obtain information from several family members for each case (De Massis, Chua, and Chrisman 2008). Our empirical material consists of between one and three interviews per firm conducted in summer 2012 (Table 13.1), and each interview lasted one to two hours.

The interviews were open-ended, and the participants were invited to talk freely on the themes of the family and company history, the death of the

Table 13.1 Interview participants

Case A (three participants)	Two successors/owners (daughters Clare and Cecilia) working in the company and an owner (Mary, mother and widow of the deceased owner) not working in the company
Case B (three participants)	Successor/owner/current CEO (widow Laura), brother of the late CEO (Robert), mother of the late CEO (Rose)
Case C (one participant)	Current CEO (daughter Barbara)

CEO or owner of the company, and the subsequent succession process, as well as the emotions, particularly grief, related to the unplanned incident. The methodological approach is inductive, that is, the data is analysed with the intent of teasing out important themes addressed by the respondents.

All interviews were transcribed verbatim. In the initial step of the analysis, all interviews were read, and sections dealing with the death of the CEO and/or the owner and the related coping processes were noted. The analysis focused on how the participants themselves made sense of the event and how they managed and coped with the unexpected situation within the family and the firm. The case descriptions combining and triangulating information from the different interviews were constructed to create an overview of each case company and their "survival game". Basic information and key events are summarised in Table 13.2 in the appendix. The analysis is based on the accounts of the key people in the family and the business from the perspective of getting through the death of the CEO or the owner.

Findings

CASE A: "Engineering" refers to an engineering firm acquired in 2001 by the late husband/father, George. He died suddenly in 2007 and his daughters, Clare and Cecilia, who were in their 20s, and his wife, Mary, decided to continue the business despite bids to buy it—mainly for tax reasons but also for emotional reasons (to keep it as a legacy) and to secure the employees' jobs. Clare was still at school at the time and Cecilia, who is four years older, was happy working as an employee elsewhere and had no plans to work for the family firm. After her father's death, she started there immediately. As soon as possible, they hired a male CEO who took charge of all firm operations. Mother Mary owns 50 per cent of the firm, but the daughters plan to buy her shares. According to the sisters, the mother has never been involved in the company. Mary is ready to sell the firm to her daughters, provided that the ownership is kept in the family and the firm remains a family business. Although Clare and Cecilia now profess to love their jobs, they dream of being entrepreneurs together in another setting, such as a coffee shop. During their ownership, both sisters have become mothers, and this has shaped their work in the family business.

Clare, Cecilia, and Mary's Accounts of Case A: Engineering

The sisters and their mother were all interviewed separately, but the accounts of the sisters in particular resonate with each other. Clare describes the death of her father and their decision to continue running the firm: "*When our father died, it was awful. The newspapers wrote about it, and people started calling asking us if we wanted to sell. And we weren't even sure if we had inherited the business or if there were large debts—we had no idea of the business. . . . We contacted the lawyer, who explained that we indeed owned the firm. . . . It was chaotic . . . . I thought from the very beginning that we should not sell it . . . I had always thought that I would go and work there*". Cecilia's account confirms Clare's description: "*I do not remember anything . . . but we did not talk about selling—it was no option . . . the business had to live on so that the guys could continue to work*", suggesting that although everything was unclear selling the firm was not a real option.

For mother Mary it was too painful to even visit the factory, as it reminded her of her late husband. Mary tells how they were not at all welcomed by the employees: "*They just said 'What are you doing here?' . . . It was shocking when we realised that we were not accepted and they did not want us there at all*". However, Cecilia started working at the firm immediately and Clare joined her later after finishing school. "*We didn't do anything meaningful there . . . we just sat in our dad's room and went through the papers and responded to dad's emails*", Clare says. They relied on their father's business networks and friends. "*Two girls in their 20s sitting on the other side of the table and big men telling us what entrepreneurship is all about and we just nod and say yes, yes, let us go forward*". Both sisters stated how important it was that they had people to trust. They had their father's key people to support them. As Clare says: "*Everything went nicely . . . we got a lot of support . . . and I think that the firm really helped us at the most difficult time. We had something to do and could not stay at home*". The sisters both acknowledge the support received from different people and realise how they had no time to grieve as the firm kept them occupied. The way in which the family and the firm survived the death of the father is confirmed by the mother: "*We were asked how we knew what to do. We did not really know. It was as if we had had robots inside ourselves*". It was obvious to all of them that they wanted to continue the father's legacy but had no plan about how to do this. They just went on day by day. Later, the sisters realised how lucky they were that no one cheated them.

The employees became more relaxed when the family announced that the company was not for sale and that they were searching for a new CEO. Clare recalls: "*We both understood that we couldn't run the company and therefore the first thing to do was to hire a CEO and we contacted a recruiting company to take care of it*". Clare recalls how her mother "*searched for someone like our dad*", and even the mother admits that their new CEO is calm and somewhat similar to her late husband. Finding a reliable CEO who was easy to work with was crucial for the company and the family. "*Mark was really a find*", says Cecilia. "*We offered him [the CEO] the whole package, gave him the keys*". The CEO got full authority over the operational issues immediately. The daughters continued to work at the firm as secretaries and did their best to support the CEO. Cecilia describes their clear division of work and states that "*Our employees really don't consider us like bosses . . . it is really Mark who is the boss there*". She further tells how important it is to share issues other than firm-related ones with their CEO: "*I cannot say that he acts as if he were our dad but, for example, when I changed my apartment and bank, he told his opinion . . . so we do not only share work-related concerns*". The CEO was crucial for the firm's survival but he was equally an asset for the family. His calmness and trustworthiness created a good working climate in the company and within the family—a kind of "restoration" of the late father and CEO.

Both for Clare and Cecilia it is important to be able to share firm-related concerns together, but they still want to protect their mother: "*Everything worked well with Clare and we wanted to keep our mother out—not to cause her any stress*", Cecilia says, and Clare confirms by stating "*We do and decide everything together . . . I like working with my sister. We are very close. This is not my dream job. But we have decided that if we sell the firm, we sell it together*". Cecilia concurs: "*If I was left here alone, it would be an insane (burden). Now you have somebody who agrees with you or is on the same side with you . . . But it's good that we don't get these feelings of insecurity at the same time*". An important part of Clare and Cecilia feeling capable of continuing with the business is the ability to share the responsibility and burden with each other. This is also confirmed by their mother: "*Clare and Cecilia are so different and they balance each other*". The need for sharing goes back to their father's incapability of discussing the firm with others. As Cecilia puts it: "*Our dad took care of everything alone . . . he had no one to share with and therefore we are so lucky that we have people to trust in, and I can just concentrate on my kids; not very many have such a possibility*". Both sisters and mother particularly recalled how the family had no time for joint family holidays because the father was always at work. Cecilia says that "*One summer, our dad tried to have some days off as a holiday and then two employees called him and handed him notice and he then got a heart attack . . . we have discussed with Clare that we shall not find ourselves in a similar situation*". In practice, the sisters share everything in the firm and consider it as a joint venture and something they are committed to do together.

Mary genuinely appreciates the work done by the CEO and her daughters: "*It [the firm] has developed all the time . . . it tells something of the daughters and the CEO*". She also recalls that after the CEO started, her husband came to her in her dreams: "*He said to me that you will survive and he was so real*", suggesting that coping with a business and a family touches her strongly and goes hand in hand for her. For her, the firm only reminds her of her late husband and therefore she is willing to sell her shares to her daughters, provided the firm continues as a family firm for the future generations. Mary wants to start anew: "*Nothing changes if I sell and then I can start living my own life . . . there is nothing else in my life than my daughters and the grandchildren*". Mary finally admits how George's death united the family but feels sorry that her daughters needed to give up their youth earlier than expected.

CASE B: 'Retail and wholesale' refers to a growing family firm acting as a retailer and wholesaler. The firm was founded in 1925 and the third-generation CEO, Richard, took it over after his father's death in the early 1980s when the firm was close to bankruptcy. A few years later, when the firm had survived the crisis, Richard insisted on buying the relatives out, as none of them were working in the firm. After the management buy-out (MBO), Richard and his wife Laura fully owned the firm. Ever since, Laura has sat on the board of the firm, although she never actually worked full time at the firm while her husband was alive. At Richard's request, she managed some projects for the company and participated in firm events, implying that she knew the firm and its staff. After the MBO, the firm grew rapidly and aggressively both nationally and internationally due to Richard's visionary thinking and his good networks and contacts. During his leadership, the firm grew from a small firm of less than 50 employees to a much larger firm of 1,100 employees located in several countries, with a turnover almost 10 times higher than at the start. In the mid-2000s, Richard suddenly died in an accident and the widow Laura and her children became the owners of the firm. Encouraged by the members of the board, the widow immediately decided to keep the firm in operation and took over the CEO position. This was possible because the firm was run by the managers of the subsidiaries. Laura took charge of the parent firm in particular.

Laura and Rose's Accounts of Case B: Retail and Wholesale

After the tragic accident, Laura immediately negotiated with the board members and organised a briefing for the whole staff the following morning. Laura recalls: "*It was so chaotic . . . crisis communication . . . I will always be grateful to the managers, that our staff heard it [about the accident] from us and not from the competitors*". Laura was encouraged by the board members to step forward and take over: "*Laura you are the one from the family who needs to take over*", she recalls them saying. Laura then quickly decided to continue with the business, and she visited all the sites to demonstrate the family's commitment to continue the business as usual despite the death of her husband, the well-liked CEO. "*And I started circulating around and communicate to the staff that the family wants to continue and I shall start working here*". Laura further says that in his will, Richard had given four options to the family in case of his death. Laura did not even remember all the options but clearly states how they chose the fourth one: to continue 100 per cent and wholeheartedly. "*It was important to calm down the situation and continue . . . there was no other choice as there were 1,100 employees' job at stake and all the work done*". Laura was able to trust the key personnel and clearly felt the responsibility of securing the employees' jobs and continuing Richard's legacy.

Laura was familiar with the business due to her work on the board and the joint discussions with her husband. "*As we did not have any children yet we talked about the firm and it was incredibly fun*", Laura says emotionally regarding the early days of the firm. Interestingly, although she was not working at the firm in the early days, she still refers to "*us*" making the decisions and planning future actions. However, she clearly states that her husband created all the major ideas: "*They were all his ideas and visions which he explained to me*". Laura was clearly knowledgeable about the firm activities, although she was not the one influencing the firm's development. This helped Laura in the takeover, as she had known most of the staff for years. Furthermore, the subsidiary managers ran their operational businesses as if they were their own, and Laura, supported by the board, concentrated on the parent firm. As Laura describes it: "*I have received enormous support from the board and each manager takes care of their own unit . . . so we continue with the existing setting with operative managers. Otherwise, I could not have stepped in based on my experience*". Laura's role was different from that of her late husband, who was running a one-man-show. Richard used to suggest new and bold ideas to the board for discussion, and the board made the decisions usually based on his suggestions. Laura, however, needed to rely on subsidiary managers to make suggestions, and the board then jointly discussed them and made consensus decisions. Laura relies even more on outside board members but still emphasises Richard's principles: "*He always based his decisions on facts and analyses . . . this is how we continued*". Furthermore, she became empowered by the support and loyalty of the staff, who did their best in the new situation: "*The best part of this is the competent employees*", whom Laura could trust. "*I enthusiastically go forward with the firm . . . we have great brands and remarkably wonderful people here*". Laura emphasises the motives behind her efforts and acknowledges that the ideas become one's own only when one is truly involved with the firm. This is something that had happened to her after Richard's death.

Laura also feels relieved that she was able to continue discussing Richard at work: "*What would Richard think about this and how would he act? And we always find an answer what he would do*". The way Laura continued his legacy happened in a very concrete manner every day in decision making. Laura was also permitted and even encouraged to share a memory of Richard at work, and she felt it helped her cope with the loss: "*The firm makes me go forward despite my huge sorrow*". Richard's mother Rose, who was also devastated by his death, further conveys this: "*If Laura hadn't had so much work, she would not have survived. But the work and the colleagues there helped her . . . Laura told me that they laughed at Richard's doings there all the time . . . work has really been everything to her then . . . a kind of therapy*". Laura indeed confirms how the firm helped her to grieve after Richard's death: "*When I get to the firm it is like being in a tram which trembles terribly but I just keep hold of it . . . I got new meaning to my life*". The company became her new project to which she was highly committed and attached and which she was able to influence: "*This is now my big baby. As children get older they start living their own lives . . . this [firm] also lives its own life, but as I am now involved it is a big part of my life and I feel I can also influence*". The attachment to and work at the firm clearly helped in Laura's grieving as she feels it is possible to cherish Richard's memory and continue his legacy. Laura hopes that one day one of their children will be eager to take over the firm.

CASE C: 'Conglomerate' refers to a large conglomerate in technical material sales. In the past, the firm was owned by women but was managed by their husbands, and it is now the fourth generation that is in charge. Currently, Barbara and her children own the firm with Barbara's half-sister. Barbara is the first female member of the family to have worked at the firm. She was never coached to take over the firm or socialised into the firm as a future leader—only as an owner. Nevertheless, she worked in different units of the firm and gradually gained a comprehensive knowledge of its operations. After her father died in 2000, she fought for her position at the company. Barbara's path to becoming CEO was to take over after two unsuccessful (male) managers. It was only after the death of her mother that Barbara was able to take over the whole conglomerate, as her mother chaired the board until her death. As a consequence of the unfinished takeovers, severe inheritance fights over the family summer residence started with the half-sister. Eventually, Barbara's husband was also able to join the firm and work on the management team.

Barbara's Account of Case C: Conglomerate

Barbara's journey to the leading position of the family firm took place after two deaths, those of her father and mother. The succession was never openly discussed within the family, and even in the past it took place only after deaths and usually with some fighting afterwards. "*It [succession] has always happened via death, which is the worst way*". Barbara had never discussed the succession with her father. Barbara believes that "*If my father had had a son, he would have been trained into the firm, and the succession would have been made*", indicating that she as a daughter was not considered a possible successor.

Because Barbara had been working in the firm in various departments as requested by her father, she knew most of the staff, although did not feel she belonged to the work community as an employee. "*The owner's daughter comes here—how should we take it?*" Barbara says about how the staff treated her. She further emphasises how she did not have the choice to work elsewhere: "*I have been pushed to work here . . . I cannot tell anyone that I would like to change my job*", indicating that her life at work was somewhat lonely and not easy.

Before his death, her father had appointed a male CEO for the parent firm. He was the second external CEO in the parent firm during a short period of time. After the father's death, the company managers started to "mark their positions", and Barbara needed to fight to fill the power vacuum left by her father. "*It was a rough school for me, the staff shamelessly tried to take benefit of the situation*", she recalls. After a while, they (the owners) noticed that the new CEO was unsuccessful (even a criminal) and they let him go. "*At this point, I luckily got help from a consultant, who said that there is no other choice than you becoming the CEO. Otherwise, the media will have a field day with this women-owned company. If I, as a woman owner, fire a CEO, the problem is not the CEO but me, that I don't get along with others*". According to Barbara, the trusted consultant was important in pushing her to take leadership. Furthermore, Barbara faced the situation where she had no other choice than stepping in and taking over the firm.

Barbara does not problematise the death of her father and the subsequent succession. "*Every summer, father said that he should tell me more about the firm but he never did . . . he was a product of his era*". Barbara understands and accepts her father's opinion and talks warmly of him. Not only did she need to fight for her position with the male managers in the firm, but she also needed to balance with her mother who was basically in charge as the chair of the board but not accustomed to or capable of making any business decisions. For example, Barbara persuaded her mother to appoint her to the board of the parent firm to "*interpret for you [mother] something you would not understand or hear*", as she would not otherwise be informed of what was going on with the board. After her father's death, Barbara made some changes to the boards of the subsidiary firms but not to the board of the parent firm, as it was chaired by her mother. "*Mother couldn't make any changes as the members had been selected by father*", Barbara states in explaining her mother's attachment to the board and its members. In practice, however, Barbara was the one who was in charge and running the family firm. "*When father died, this really became my life*", says Barbara, demonstrating her extremely strong attachment to and responsibility for the firm.

More painful and distressing was the death of Barbara's mother, the main owner, whose unhealthy behaviour had caused trouble in the family. "*My mother was really strong but not perhaps always in a healthy manner. My mother was never allowed to work. So she couldn't channel her energy into constructive work*". Although Barbara was already firmly managing the firm, she realised that the succession remained unfinalised after her mother's death. "*Although mother had made her will, it is only a suggestion how something is divided. Then an extreme fight started and still continues . . . my [half-]sister still fights with my mother who had made the will, not me*". The firm-related issues were not explicitly touched upon when Barbara referred to her fight with her half-sister regarding the mother's will, but the fight was over the family's prized summer residence. As the half-sister owned minority shares in the firm, the fight also influenced the firm management, as Barbara describes: "*I consider it mentally very stressful . . . I prepared a paper that she does not participate in to the board . . . she can nominate a member, but I do not want it to be her or her daughter . . . only when we have divided everything . . . then we can start talking . . . otherwise I do not bother discussing with her—even on the phone*". Barbara feels deeply sorry about the fight, as she has few relatives. The fight over family property inflamed Barbara's feelings and even disturbed the family firm leadership and board activities. After the death of her mother, Barbara became the chair of the parent company board and oversees the whole conglomerate by herself. She says that the parent firm board needed to have "*old wise experience . . . as there you need to think of the larger whole and the future*", whereas the subsidiary boards were of a more operative nature. This suggests that a clear division of responsibilities made it possible for her to run such a huge entity in a traditional technical field. However, Barbara suffered from not being able to share the business-related issues with anyone within the family due to the unhealthy family relations, and her mother never allowed Barbara's husband to work in the firm. "*Earlier, I had no one to discuss with. I have been very lonely . . . but now we can discuss, we are enthusiastic and interested in the same issues*", Barbara says, referring to her husband who started to work on her management team after her mother's death. This suggests how running a firm also involves sharing ideas with those closest to.

In her account, Barbara repeatedly refers to her personal attachment to the firm. She also critically reflects on her feelings: "*You should never fall in love with property or stocks . . . even if my father built this building, we shall move if it would benefit the firm*". She also attempts to objectively consider the future of the firm: "*so that you could accept yourself that if it is not good for the firm to be a part of our portfolio but to let it develop elsewhere*". In a way, Barbara had already started to consider the future of the firm and whether it would be more suitable for her children to own something else than a fully operative family firm.

Cross-case Analysis

In the three cases, the loss is two-fold: It is both the loss of a family member and at the same time the loss of the CEO/owner. The cases reveal the different ways that families and family businesses cope with the loss of the CEO and owner. In all the cases, the business was continued either by the daughter(s) or the wife of the deceased. The main motivation for not selling the firm was the women's willingness to *continue the family legacy*, that of the late father's or husband's. Clearly, there was no exact plan to begin with about how to manage the firm, but the women pragmatically just *went forward* with the firm day by day, regardless of the hurdles. For Barbara in case C, the main challenge was to take over after unsuccessful CEOs and fight for her position, first with the male managers and later with her mother. In case A, Clare and Cecilia and their mother Mary needed to win the trust of the anxious employees by announcing that the firm was not for sale. They started looking for a new CEO, as they did not want to sell at that point for taxation reasons. Similarly, in case B the widow Laura stepped in as the new CEO immediately to calm the anxiety in the firm. For the women, it was a clear decision to step in as successors. None of them perceived there was any *other choice*, as there was *no* one else to take responsibility in the new situation. Although a death is an emotionally devastating experience for the family members, firms do not wait but require immediate action. Our cases demonstrate how the women, supported by people they trust, made crucial decisions to continue the family firm with the available resources without any preparations or further planning.

The loss of a husband/father and CEO/owner is difficult. In such a situation, occupying oneself with continuing the business is pragmatic behaviour. It helps the business to survive, but being busy also helps in the *grief* process because it offers a distraction from thoughts related to the loss (see restoration-oriented grief dynamics by Shepherd 2009). Continuing the family firm implies *being* heavily *occupied* with something the women were not familiar with. The family members make sense of the loss by feeling that keeping the business running keeps the person alive, that is, continuing the legacy. This was evident in Laura's case, as it was possible for her to cherish the memories of her husband by discussing the business with the managers and by pondering how he would solve the situation at hand. Laura shared the memory of him with the employees, "talked through" her grief with those closest to her in the firm (see loss-oriented grief dynamics by Shepherd 2009) and at the same time took the lead and kept up his work. In case A, the sisters just went through their father's papers at work without actually contributing to firm activities, but this helped them go forward with their lives and understand what the firm was all about. Interestingly, the sisters and mother ended up hiring a CEO with characteristics similar to those of the late CEO in order to make it comfortable for them to work with him. In our data, we see that the pragmatic and perhaps rational decision of keeping the business keeps the family members occupied as part of their emotional grief dynamics.

Our cases also demonstrate that a *clear division of work* made it possible for the women to take over the family businesses in relatively male-dominated and technically oriented businesses. They did not even try to take a similar position in the family firms as the late CEOs had but divided the work load between the managerial team. The women seemed more comfortable as owners and having the ultimate responsibility over the firm and its ownership rather than over the operational issues. As suggested by Hytti et al. (2017), taking over a family business implies identity work, and for women particularly it may mean concealing the leadership identity and creating an ownership identity instead. Furthermore, our cases demonstrate that division of work is made possible by being able or even forced to *trust* key people, such as the consultant in Barbara's case, the father's business networks and friends in case A, or the subsidiary managers and board members in Laura's case. Given the women's prior position, competence, and experience in the family business, trusting someone seems rational. However, it is also emotional and intuitive, as they had no other choice. It seems evident that the women would not have coped alone; some external (male) support was needed, as suggested by Hytti et al. (2017), for the women to step in and take over the family business.

Similarly, it was important for the women to be able to *share* their ideas with those closest to them. This was highlighted in case A, as the sisters jointly made all the major decisions, such as not selling, continuing, hiring, and investing, and shared the worries and joys both of the family and the business. In case C, lacking this possibility to share business issues stressed Barbara, as she had no one to discuss the family business with before her husband joined the firm after the death of her mother. Sharing and trusting not only make it possible to rationally divide the workload but also facilitate the grieving process, as there is someone else who understands the situation. This was evident in case A, particularly as the father's death clearly united the family and made the family stronger to face the forthcoming challenges.

Finally, the interconnectedness of family and business spheres is evident in all our cases, and it is hard to disassociate the spheres. We also see how emotional and rational coping with the loss go hand in hand. Our cases demonstrate how pragmatic decisions, such as keeping and continuing the business and securing the employees' jobs, bridge the emotional and rational, emphasising their interconnectedness. Family members and even firm staff grieve for the loss at work, but for family members being occupied with the firm is a means to "do grieving" and continue with life and the firm. Emotional and even painful grieving can therefore be considered a business asset. However, Case C particularly demonstrates how deeply family-rooted issues may carry over into family business. The unsettled will of Barbara's late mother in relation to the family's summer cottage continues to disrupt not only the sisters' social interaction but also the work of the board. In such a case, grieving and fighting over property is more of a hindrance than a help for the family business.

Figure 13.1 illustrates the interconnectedness of the rational and the emotional in coping with the loss of a family member and a CEO/owner. In all

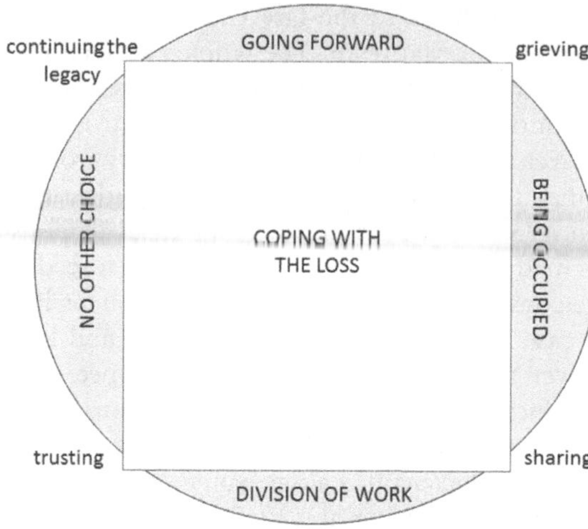

Figure 13.1 Coping with the loss of a family member and a CEO

cases, rational behaviour meets emotions, resulting in actions that take care of both the emotional needs of the family members and the firms' needs. Pragmatic decisions bridge rational and emotional coping. For example, being occupied and going forward with the business is rational behaviour after the death of the CEO but are also clearly part of the grieving process of the family members. From both the rational and emotional perspectives, it is also very practical to be occupied and to move forward in the unexpected situation. Similarly, sharing family business concerns with someone and trusting in those who are closest are laden with emotion but also formed a basis for a division of work in a situation where the women themselves did not have enough experience in running the daily operations of the family firm. These examples clearly demonstrate the interconnectedness of family and business systems, the blurred boundaries of emotionality and rationality and the ways in which pragmatism shapes decisions in a given context. Here, pragmatism is understood as an idea that proves to have value for concrete life and as such is true in the sense of being wholly true as long as it does not conflict with other vital benefits. For how much it is true depends on its relationship to the other truths (James 1907), for example the emotional and rational spheres in the studied contexts (see on entrepreneurial context by Welter 2011).

Discussion and Conclusions

We have investigated how families and family firms cope with premature, unplanned succession caused by the sudden loss of a family member, a CEO and an owner. The study contributes to the family business succession literature, as unplanned successions due to sudden death are seldom studied empirically due to the sensitive nature of such an event. Previous family business succession literature focuses on proper and timely planning for succession in the presence of the predecessor but acknowledges that succession is both a family and a business matter. This requires that one manages to balance the rational and emotional embedded in both the business and family spheres. By focusing on family firms that had faced the sudden loss of a key person, we were able to investigate the subsequent coping processes in an unexpected situation. We consider this unique, as the firms and the families were unprepared and without the support of the predecessor needed to go through the succession unplanned. Furthermore, a sudden death stirs up emotions that shake up not only the family but also the family business.

First, our study provides new knowledge on the interconnectedness of families and their businesses and how this is interwoven with emotionality and rationality. Some studies have pointed out that it is not justified to consider that emotions only take place in the family sphere and rationality only occurs in the business sphere; rather, both penetrate both spheres (e.g. Berrone, Cruz, and Gomez-Mejia 2012; Carlock and Ward 2001). This is supported by our study. In addition, our study demonstrates how pragmatic decisions in the given circumstances may bridge emotional and rational coping. It is obvious that the sudden loss of the family member and CEO makes the family members and the family as a group feel grief. Our findings suggest that emotions, and particularly grieving, can also be a remarkable asset for the family business and can help the successor to keep the business alive. We argue that emotions are important in business life, although our cases might be extreme. In line with Brundin and Languilaire (2012) and Murray (2002), we suggest that emotions in family business studies should be studied in more detail, as we know too little about this phenomenon.

Shepherd (2009) has addressed the grief recovery process, although in a different setting, namely the loss of a family business. Inspired by his model on grief recovery, we suggest that it would be useful to explore grief recovery in a family business after a death of a family member and a CEO. Shepherd (2009) suggests that not only financial factors but also emotional factors are important in the business failure process to enable the entrepreneur's emotional recovery. This recovery process is likely to be applicable in the case of personal (e.g. father, husband) and business (e.g. CEO, owner) loss.

Second, building on our findings, we found that instead of thorough planning, the families, and in our cases the women, took immediate action to continue the business. They did not have a definite plan regarding the business succession but rather improvised based on their best knowledge and with the available resources. Our findings on the premature, unplanned succession in comparison to planned succession resonate with different decision making logics of effectuation and causation in entrepreneurial behaviour (see Sarasvathy 2001). We suggest that in an unexpected and uncertain situation, the successors had no time or possibility for a causal approach with pre-set goals for the succession but needed to rely on the means they possessed.

They reacted quickly to the changing situation, as suggested by the effectual approach. Although the women were not able to plan the succession in advance, as suggested by the causal approach (Sarasvathy 2001), it does not imply that their behaviour is not rational but that they faced the situation with limited decision-making capacity. Indeed, rational arguments such as taxation and securing the employees' jobs were used to justify their decisions not to sell. They continued the business by improvising and dealing with the hurdles day by day in a very pragmatic manner, taking into consideration both the rational and emotional aspects of coping (see on bounded emotionality in business transfers by Hytti, Stenholm, and Peura 2011).

Our findings suggest that applying effectuation theory, that is, "having no plan" and improvising in decision making regarding premature family business succession, might be useful to understand the decisions made during these succession processes. There is not always a chance to follow a predefined plan or path. Interestingly, Ahrens, Landmann, and Woywode (2015) find that in unplanned family business succession, the female succession rate is higher than in planned successions. Research shows that although not explicated the primogeniture norm is usually applied in succession processes. One could be tempted to suggest that when no other obvious options are available, women are more easily considered as successors. Although our study does not allow such comparisons, it highlights that daughters who were not considered as potential successors by their fathers ended up taking over the family business due to the lack of other options, again a very pragmatic choice in the given circumstances.

Finally, the premature death of a CEO and the subsequent succession are not rare phenomenon in real business life but are still surprisingly little studied. By focusing on such events, our study managed to tease out new insights regarding the interconnectedness of family and business systems and how emotionality and rationality penetrate both spheres, bridged by pragmatism. The main implication of our findings for family businesses is that it is fully possible to channel painful emotions, such as grief, for the benefit of the family firm and of the grieving individual herself. Therefore, there is no need to hide or isolate emotions from the business; rather, it can be beneficial to use them as drivers of future success.

References

Ahrens, J.-P., A. Landmann, and M. Woywode. 2015. "Gender Preferences in the CEO Successions of Family Firms: Family Characteristics and Human Capital of the Successor." *Journal of Family Business Strategy* 6 (2): 86–103.

Aldrich, H. E., and J. E. Cliff. 2003. "The Pervasive Effects of Family on Entrepreneurship: Toward a Family Embeddedness Perspective." *Journal of Business Venturing* 18 (5): 573–596.

Alsos, G. A., S. Carter, and E. Ljunggren. 2014. "Kinship and Business: How Entrepreneurial Households Facilitate Business Growth." *Entrepreneurship & Regional Development* 26 (1–2): 97–122.

Astrachan, J. H., and P. Jaskiewicz. 2008. "Emotional Returns and Emotional Costs in Privately Held Family Businesses: Advancing Traditional Business Valuation." *Family Business Review* 21 (2): 139–149.

Baron, R. A. 2008. "The Role of Affect in the Entrepreneurial Process." *Academy of Management Review* 33 (2): 328–340.

Basco, R. and M. J. Pérez Rodríguez. 2009. "Studying the Family Enterprise Holistically: Evidence for Integrated Family and Business Systems." *Family Business Review* 22 (1): 82–95.

Bennedsen, M., K. M. Nielsen, F. Pèrez-Gonzàlez, and D. Wolfenzon. 2007. "Inside the Family Firm: The Role of Families in Succession Decisions and Performance." *Quarterly Journal of Economics* 122 (2): 647–691.

Berrone, P., C. Cruz, and L. R. Gomez-Mejia. 2012. "Socioemotional Wealth in Family Firms: Theoretical Dimensions, Assessment Approaches, and Agenda for Future Research." *Family Business Review* 25 (3): 258–279.

Bloom, N., and J. van Reenen. 2007. "Measuring and Explaining Management Practices Across Firms and Countries." *The Quarterly Journal of Economics* 122 (4): 1351–1408.

Brundin, E., and J.-C. E. Languilaire. 2012. "Harmoni eller disharmoni? Känsloregler och gränsdragning." In *Familjeföretagande: affärer och känslor*, edited by E. Brundin, A. W. Johansson, B. Johannisson, L. Melin, and M. Nordquist, 276–293. Stockholm: SNS Förlag.

Carlock, R. S., and J. L. Ward. 2001. *Strategic Planning for the Family Business.* New York: Palgrave.

Chrisman, J. J., J. H. Chua, and P. Sharma. 1998. "Important Attributes of Successors in Family Businesses: An Exploratory Study." *Family Business Review* 11 (1): 19–34.

Daspit, J. J., D. T. Holt, J. J. Chrisman, and R. G. Long. 2016. "Examining Family Firm Succession from a Social Exchange Perspective: A Multiphase, Multistakeholder Review." *Family Business Review* 29 (1): 44–64.

De Massis, A., J. H. Chua, and J. J. Chrisman. 2008. "Factors Preventing Intra-Family Succession." *Family Business Review* 21 (2): 53–64.

Dyck, B., M. Mauws, F. A. Starke, and G. A. Mischke. 2002. "Passing the Baton: The Importance of Sequence, Timing, Technique and Communication in Executive Succession." *Journal of Business Venturing* 17 (2): 143–162.

Gilding, M., S. Gregory, and B. Cosson. 2013. "Motives and Outcomes in Family Business Succession Planing." *Entrepreneurship, Theory and Practice* 39 (2): 299–312.

Handler, W. C., and K. E. Kram. 2004. "Succession in Family Firms: The Problem of Resistance." *Family Business Review* 1 (4): 361–381.

Heinonen, J., and U. Hytti. 2012. "Gender in Family Business Research." Paper published in the *Conference Proceedings of the XXVI RENT Conference*, Lyon, France, November 22–23, 2012.

Helin, J., and M. Jabri. 2015. "Family Business Succession in Dialogue: The Case of Differing Backgrounds and Views." *International Small Business Journal* 34 (4): 487–505.

Hytti, U., G. A. Alsos, J. Heinonen, and E. Ljunggren. 2017. "Navigating the Family Business: A Gendered Analysis of Identity Construction of Daughters." *International Small Business Journal* 35 (6): 665–686.

Hytti, U., P. Stenholm, and K. Peura. 2011. "Transfer of Business Planning and Bounded Emotionality: A Follow-Up Study." *International Journal of Entrepreneurial Behaviour & Research* 17 (5): 561–580.

James, W. 1907. *Pragmatism: A New Name for Some Old Ways of Thinking*. New York: Longmans, Green and Co.

Keating, N. C., and H. M. Little. 1997. "Choosing the Successor in New Zealand Family Farms." *Family Business Review* 10 (2): 157–171.

Kuratko, D. F., J. S. Hornsby, and R. V. Montagno. 1993. "Family Business Succession in Korean and U.S. Firms." *Journal of Small Business Management* 31 (2): 132–136.

Lam, W. 2011. "Dancing to Two Tunes: Multi-Entity Roles in the Family Business Succession Process." *International Small Business Journal* 29 (5): 508–533.

Litz, R. A., A. W. Pearson, and S. Litchfield. 2012. "Charting the Future of Family Business Research: Perspectives from the Field." *Family Business Review* 25 (1): 16–32.

Murray, B. 2002. "Understanding the Emotional Dynamics of Family Enterprises." In *Understanding the Small Family Business*, edited by D. Fletcher, 75–93. London: Routledge.

Neergaard, H. 2007. "Sampling in Entrepreneurial Settings." In *Handbook of Qualitative Research Methods in Entrepreneurship*, edited by H. Neergaard and J. P. Ulhøi, 262–274. Cheltenham, UK: Edward Elgar Publishing Limited.

Patton, M. Q. 1990. *Qualitative Evaluation and Research Methods*. Newbury Park, CA: SAGE Publications, Inc.

Patton, M. Q. 2005. *Qualitative Research: Encyclopedia of Statistics in Behavioral Science*. Chichester: John Wiley & Sons, Ltd.

Salvato, C., and G. Corbetta. 2013. "Transitional Leadership of Advisors as a Facilitator of Successors' Leadership Construction." *Family Business Review* 26 (3): 235–255.

Sarasvathy, S. D. 2001. "Causation and Effectuation: Toward a Theoretical Shift from Economic Inevitability to Entrepreneurial Contingency." *Academy of Management Review* 26 (2): 243–263.

Schröder, E., E. Schmitt-Rodermund, and N. Arnaud. 2011. "Career Choice Intentions of Adolescents with a Family Business Background." *Family Business Review* 24 (4): 305–321.

Sharma, P., J. J. Chrisman, and J. H. Chua. 2003. "Predictors of Satisfaction with the Succession Process in Family Firms." *Journal of Business Venturing* 18 (5): 667–687.

Shepherd, D. A. 2009. "Grief Recovery from the Loss of a Family Business: A Multi- and Meso-Level Theory." *Journal of Business Venturing* 24 (1): 81–97.

Stafford, K., K. A. Duncan, S. M. Danes, and M. Winter. 1999. "A Research Model of Sustainable Family Business." *Family Business Review* 12 (3): 197–208.

Tagiuri, R., and J. Davis. 1996. "Bivalent Attributes of the Family Firm." *Family Business Review* 9 (2): 199–208.

Welter, F. 2011. "Contextualizing Entrepreneurship—Conceptual Challenges and Ways Forward." *Entrepreneurship, Theory and Practice* 35 (1): 165–184.

Zachary, R. K. 2011. "The Importance of the Family System in Family Business." *Journal of Family Business Management* 1 (1): 26–36.

Zahra, S. A., and P. Sharma. 2004. "Family Business Research: A Strategic Reflection." *Family Business Review* 17 (4): 331–346.

Appendix 2

Table 13.2 An overview of the studied cases

Case	*A: Engineering*	*B: Retail and wholesale*	*C: Conglomerate*
Industry	Engineering works	Retail and wholesale trade of machines	Wholesale trade, technical and construction services
Size	Small firm	From small to large firm (after rapid growth)	Large firm/ conglomerate
Founded	An older firm that was acquired in 2001	1925, but MBO for the family by the CEO 1987	1905
Current generation	2nd generation	3rd generation	4th generation
Important members and ownership	• Father, CEO (George)† • Mother (Mary), co-owner (50%), not working in the firm • Two daughters (Clare and Cecilia) in their 20s, co-owners (25% + 25%), working in the firm • An external CEO (Mark)	• Husband/son/ brother, CEO (Richard), died in an accident† • Widow (Laura), current Chair of the Board (owner with her children), a member of the board since 1987 • Mother of the deceased CEO (Rose), never worked in or owned the company • Brother of the deceased CEO (Robert), bought out in early phases, working as an employee	• Mother, owner, not working in the firm † • Father, not an owner but working in the firm† • Daughter, current CEO (Barbara) (70% ownership with her children, 80% of power) • Husband, currently working in the firm • Half-sister, owner but not working in the firm (30% ownership)

(Continued)

Table 13.2 (Continued)

Case	*A: Engineering*	*B: Retail and wholesale*	*C: Conglomerate*
Important event	After the unexpected death of the father, the mother and daughters continued the business. An external CEO was hired. The daughters plan to buy their mother out.	After the unexpected death of the CEO in an accident, the widow immediately continued the business with the help of subsidiary managers.	In the past, the firm was owned by the daughters and managed by their husbands. The current CEO took over after the father's and mother's deaths. Complicated family history with mother and half-sister.

Index

Note: Italicized page numbers indicate a figure on the corresponding page. Page numbers in bold indicate a table on the corresponding page.

Aberdeen Journal 113, 116, 119, 124, *124*
Åbo Akademi University Manuscript Collection 84
Adair, Issobell 76
adaptive family economy 204
AIkman, Katherine 67
AIkman, William 67
Aitkin, John 75
Anderson, Alistair R. 84
androcentric standpoint 180
apprenticeship 49, 116–130, **119**, *120*, *124*, **125**
Arthor, Elizabeth 78
Asplund, Johan 100–101
Augustin, Maria 135, 143–146
Augustin, Mathias 143–146
autonomy 17, 106, 169

Baer, Anna Elisabeth 143
Baloutzova, Svetlana 117
bankruptcy 52, 55, 158, 170, 205, 206, 225
Barclay, Kate 115
Barker, Hannah 112
Behind Closed Doors: At Home in Georgian England (Vickery) 87
Beverage, David 75
Billsten, Carl 56
Boswell, James 129
bourgeois *Gemeinschaft* 84
Boyd, John 210
Brok, Thomas 74
Brown, James 69
Burchett, Susanna 127
burgher profession 52–54, 86, 140–142
business economics 4, 15–17, 21–22
Business History Review journal 14

Cant, Barbara 76
capitalism 3–4, 7, 10, 17
Carlyle, Alexander 116, 129
Casson, Mark 84
Central Archives for Finnish Business Records 84
Chalmers, James 127–128
Chandlerian paradigm 17
Chell, Elizabeth 35, 36
Christieson, Katherine 76
Civil Code (1734) 138
civility 17
Clark, Alice 134
clear division of work 230–231
Cockburn, James 75
cohabitation by habit and repute 117
Colli, Andrea 84
communal cultural norms 89
conglomerate succession 227–229
consumption behavior 87–93
contingent burgher 145
"craft-based" skills 24
Craig, Beatrice 84
customable imports 69

daughters in family business:
  data analysis/collection 185;

family business (FB) succession 180–183; forced leadership profile 189–190; introduction to 179–180; invisible co-leader profile 191–192; leader-by-choice profile 185–189, **186–187**; manager-by-choice profile 190–191; methodology of 183–185, **184**; outcast profile 192–193; profiles of 185–193, **186–187**; summary of 193–196
decision-making power 154
Dee, Jane Fromond 22
Dee, John 22
Defoe, Daniel 211
demographic context of widowed businesswomen 202–203
Dick, Janet 73
Dingwall, Helen 70
distributor wives 75–77
Dodd, Sarah Drakopoulou 84
Dundas, Thomas 74

economic history and women 14–15
Edgar, John 76
egalitarianism 17
Ekman, Elias 55
Eleonora, Ulrika 139
embeddedness process in unplanned succession 219–221
emotional leadership of women 106–107, 155
emulation practices 89
endogamous marriage patterns 209
engineering succession 222–225
English common law 19
Enlightenment 17
entrepreneurial discourses 162, 169
entrepreneurial leadership 183
entrepreneurial personality 35, 42
entrepreneurial widows *see* widows as businesswomen; widows as heroic entrepreneurs
equal rights 17–20
Erickson, Amy 205, 207
Eriksson, Magnus, King 135–138, 140
European women 11
exporter wives 77–78

family business (FB): context discourses 162–163, **164–166**, 202–203; economic activities 10; gender inequality 155–156; interconnectedness of 219; introduction to 3–12, *11*, 15; women in family firms 84–87; *see also* daughters in family business; non-successor daughters in family business; Såger, Elin
family business (FB) succession *see* daughters in family business
father-daughter communication 182
female entrepreneurship: consumption choices of 87–91; exporters 70; introduction to 3–4, 11; management of Russian estates 86–87; printers 127–130, *128*; publicans 127–130; women in family firms 84–87; *see also* widows as businesswomen; widows as heroic entrepreneurs; women in family firms
feminist research interests 14
Finlaw, Susanna 76
Fleming, Agnus 213
Fleming, Janet 70, 75
Fleming, Mary 207
forced involvement in family succession 182
forced leadership profile 189–190
Frederick I, King 140
French, George 76
French Revolution 17
Fristo, William 74
Fyfe, Janet 211

Galbraith, John 207, 208
Gamber, Wendy 14
gambling behavior 90–91
Gardner, Elizabeth 206
gender inequality: career outcomes 8; equal rights and 17–20; in family business 155–156; introduction to 6, 14–17; merchant rights and 137–139; narratives of 20–23; relations in family firms 105; summary of 24–27; widowed businesswomen 201–202
Gibson, John 117
Glen, Alexander 76
Göransson, Anita 26, 49
Gordon, Eleanor 112
Grig, Grissell 73, 74
group identity 88–89, 92

guild system in Russia 86
Gustav III, King 145

Hackman, Marie (Hackman & Co.): case study of 85–87; consumption choices 87–93; introduction to 82–84; summary of 91–93; women in family firms 84–87
Hafter, Daryl 112
Hall, John 75
Hamilton, Christian 206
Hamilton, Eleanor 83, 200, 202
Hamilton, John 73
Hanawalt, Barbara 69
Hardwick, Julie 54
Harvie, Thomas 78
Hasselaer, Kenau 36, 39–44
Haverman, Helena 82
Henderson, Janet 206
Henry, Margaret 77
Henryson, Katherine 70, 73
heroic image of male entrepreneurs 3–6, 83
household-family, defined 203–204
housewifery 24–25
husbandry 24–25

import-export trades 68–73
individualism 7, 10, 17, 89, 202
inheritance issues 144–148
Innama, Henrik 37
Innama, Valborg 36–44
Innama trading house 37–39
intellectual cultural history 14
intra-family entrepreneurship 8, 154, 155–156, 170
inventories of testaments 71
invisibility of women *see* visibility and invisibility of women
invisible co-leader profile 191–192
iron works 52

Jack, Marjorie 75
Jackson, Elizabeth 73, 76
John III, King 38–39, 43

Kennedy, Margaret *see* Morice (John and Margaret) family case study
Kermode, Jennifer 69
Keskinen, Jarkko 17
Kinneir, Margaret 74
Kowaleski, Maryanne 72
Kushner, Nina 112

Lackington, Jack 113–114
Lane, Penelope 200
Laube, Johan Friedrich 82
Lauder, Margaret 73
Law, David 209
leader-by-choice profile 185–189, **186–187**
legal premises of family businesses 86
legal status of unmarried women 53
Lennox, James 76
Leyis, William 75
Lindström, Peter 142
Lothian, Thomas 78
Lutheran Church 57
Lyon, John 207
Lythe, S.G.E. 77

MacLeod, Catriona 23
Magnus Eriksson Town Law 135–138, 140
male entrepreneurs *see* heroic image of male entrepreneurs
manager-by-choice profile 190–191
marginalisation of women 202
marriage economy 19, 21, 23
marriage voluntariness 57
masculine economic agency 16
Masson, John 124
materialist feminism 21
McGhie, Margaret 111–115, 123, 127, 129
McGill, Laurence 76
McIntosh, Marjorie 72
McKenzie, Catherine 213
McMath, Alexander 77
McMorane, Katherine 77
Meikle, John 206
merchant daughters 68–69
merchant rights and gender 137–139
merchant trade by wives: as distributors 75–77; as exporters 77–78; as importers 71–73; introduction to 67; rights and roles of 68–71; as shipowners 73–75; summary of 78–79; *see also* Såger, Elin
Mill, John Stuart 17

Morice (John and Margaret) family case study 111–112, 116–130, **119**, *120*, *124*, **125**
Moring, Beatrice 200, 211
Muir, Barbara 74
Muir, David 207
Muir, William 78
Muirhead, William 76
Mulholland, Kate 83

Nisbet, Katherine 76
non-successor daughters in family business: business start-up 160–162; choice of 157–160; discussion over 167–170; family context and dominant discourses 162–163, **164–166**; intra-family entrepreneurship 154, 155–156, 170; introduction to 153–154; methodology 156–157; research on 154–155; study findings 157–160; summary of 170–171; theoretical grounding 154–157
Nottman, Catherine 206, 210–211

Ogilvie, Sheilagh 55
outcast profile 192–193

Park, Alexander 72
patriarchal system: boundaries on women's economic activities 17, 200; gender relations and 105, 154; legal status of unmarried women 53; primogeniture 8, 19, 154, 156, 179, 234; women as victims *vs*. victors of 170
petite bourgeoisie families 115
Phillips, Nicola 87, 88
planned succession 218–219
political culture and widow rights 139–143
postcolonialism 21
poverty concerns 200
pre-industrial period 15, 23
primogeniture 8, 19, 154, 156, 179, 234
printers, female proprietors 127–130, *128*
property rights of widows 26, 139–143
Protestant Reformation 53
Provand, John 70, 73
publicans, female proprietors 127–130
Pursell, Katherine 78
Purves, Hector 76
Pylkkänen, Anu 48

Quintin, Helen 73, 74

Rålamb, Claes 138
Ramsay, Cuthbert 70, 75
Reid, Marion 75
religious impact of visibility/invisibility of women 105–106
retail/wholesale succession 225–227
Richardson, Jonie 78
Richter, Helena Ottiliana 143
Ricoeur, Paul 23
right of wife 68
Riksdag 139–143
Robertson, Hannah 113
Robertson, Isabel 74
Rorke, Martin 69–70
Russell, Katherine 76

Såger, Elin: introduction to 47–48; scope of action 61–62; sons-in-law 57–61; Thorwöste family business 48–52, **50**; widowhood 52–56
Såger, Johan 49, 51, 55
Såger, Petter 51
Sandeman, Margaret 207
Scandinavian women's rights 19–20
Scheffer, Abraham Henrik 57–61
Schumpeter, Joseph 84
Schwartz Cowan, Ruth 24–25
science activities of women 22–23
Scott, Joan 14, 18, 21, 22, 26
Scottish cloth 71–72
Sealer, William 207
self-employment 15, 23
semantics of action 22
Semple, Lillias 212–213
Serlachius, Johan Danielsson 57–61
Seven Incorporated Trades 115
shared management roles 200
shipowner wives 73–75
Simiand, Francois 16
Simonton, Deborah 200, 206, 209
Simpson, Robina 207
Sjögren, Åsa Karlsson 55, 142
Smith, Jean 209, 212

Smith, Mary 207, 208
social exchange theory 201
socialisation 90, 100, 182, 195
social reproduction goal 85
social theory of responsivity 100–101
socio-symbolic norms/practices 21
Söderman, Hedvig 143
Sombart, Werner 84
special circumstances in family succession 182
Spence, Catherine 114
Stadin, Kekke 137
statutory invisibility of women: economic life and law 135–137; inheritance issues 144–148; introduction to 134–135; marriage and 143–144; merchant rights and gender 137–139; political culture and widow rights 139–143; summary of 148–149; *see also* visibility and invisibility of women
Stevenson, Elizabeth 72–73
Studieman, Christian 76
succession: family business (FB) succession 180–183; forced involvement in 182; process of 100; special circumstances in 182; widows as businesswomen 205–206, 211–214; *see also* daughters in family business; unplanned succession; women in family firms
sudden death *see* unplanned succession
superwoman discourses 163
Sustainable Family Business Theory 219
Svenonius, Enevaldus 47
Sweet, Rosemary 47
Symson, William 73, 74

Table of Duties *(Die Haustafel)* 53
Tadmor, Naomi 203
Tait, Issobell 73, 78
tar burning 51
tax burdens 141–142
Thorwöste, Petter 48, 49, 55–56
Thorwöste family business 48–52, **50**
Todd, Margaret 208
Toivo, Raisa Maria 48
Toropainen, Veli Pekka 137
Trail, Susan 111–112, 127–128, *128*
Trentmann, Frank 88
true burgher 141–143

unplanned succession: case studies 222–229; conglomerate succession 227–229; cross-case analysis 229–233, *232*; embeddedness process 219–221; engineering succession 222–225; introduction to 218–219; methodology 221–222, *222*; retail/wholesale succession 225–227; summary of 232–234

Vainio-Korhonen, Kirsi 17, 84
Veblen, Thorstein 87–88
Vera case study 102–108
verba de futuro marriage promise 117
verba de praesenti marriage consent 117
Vickery, Amanda 87
visibility and invisibility of women: case study 102–108; consciousness about 101–102; introduction to 3, 6–7, 99–100, 111–112; invisibility, defined 99, 112–115; moving between 104–108; summary of 108; theoretical development of 100–101; *see also* statutory invisibility of women
voting rights 141–143

Wall, Richard 204
Wallace, William 76
Wallis, Beatrice 75
Waugh, Miny 213–214
Western economic system 14
Wewitzer, Mårten 48–49
Whitson, Christian 210
Whittle, Jane 203
widows as businesswomen: family business and demographic context 202–203; gender inequality 201–202; historical context 203–205; as incumbents 210–211; introduction to 199–200; networks of 208–210; planning for succession 207–208; social exchange theory 201; succession and 205–206, 211–214; summary of 214
widows as heroic entrepreneurs: business opportunities of 41–44; household economic activities 23; Innama

trading house 37–39; introduction to 35–36; life courses of 37–40; property rights of widows 139–143; summary of 44; *see also* female entrepreneurship; Hackman, Marie; Såger, Elin
Wilkie, Isabel 73–74, 76
Wilson, Alison 213–214
wine trade 76
Wolle, Jacob 49, 52
women in family firms (succession) 84–87; commercial community 115–116; introduction to 3, 24, 111–112, 203; invisibility, defined 99, 112–115; Morice family case study 111–112, 116–130, **119**, *120*, *124*, **125**; summary of 130; *see also* non-successor daughters in family business; visibility and invisibility of women
Wood, Janet 75
Working Life of Women in the Seventeenth Century (Clark) 134
Wunder, Heide 68